Carl Maria von Weber and the Search for a German Opera

STEPHEN C. MEYER

Carl Maria von Weber and the Search for a German Opera

INDIANA
University Press

Bloomington & Indianapolis

This book is a publication of

Indiana University Press
601 North Morton Street
Bloomington, Indiana 47404-3797 USA
http://iupress.indiana.edu
Telephone orders 800-842-6796
Fax orders 812-855-7931
Orders by e-mail iuporder@indiana.edu

Library of Congress Cataloging-in-Publication Data
Meyer, Stephen C., date
Carl Maria von Weber and the search for a German opera / Stephen C. Meyer.
p. cm.
Includes bibliographical references (p.) and index.
ISBN 0-253-34185-X (alk. paper)
1. Opera—Germany—18th century. 2. Opera—Germany—19th century. 3. Weber, Carl Maria von, 1786–1826. Operas. I. Title.
ML1729 .M49 2003
782.1'0943'09033—dc21
2002006386

1 2 3 4 5 08 07 06 05 04 03

To my wife, Eileen, with love and gratitude

Contents

Acknowledgments

A Fulbright scholarship enabled me to complete the basic research for this book; subsequent research trips were funded by Syracuse University. Among the libraries that offered me hospitality and assistance are the University of California Music Library, Berkeley, California; the Musikwissenschaftliches Institut of the Freie Universität, Berlin; the Staatsbibliothek zu Berlin, Preußischer Kulturbesitz; the Indiana University Music Library, Bloomington, Indiana; the Sächsische Landesbibliothek, Dresden; the Stadt und Universitäts-Bibliothek Frankfurt am Main; the Leipziger Stadtbibliothek; the Bayerische Staatsbibliothek, Munich; the New York Public Library Performing Arts Division; the Music Library of SUNY Stony Brook, Stony Brook, New York; the Bird Library of Syracuse University; and the Library of Congress Performing Arts Division, Washington, D.C. The reproduction of paintings in this book has been made possible with the help of the Gustave Reese Publication Endowment Fund of the American Musicological Society. Many people read portions of this book in its preliminary stages, but I would especially like to thank Stefan Eckert, Aubrey Garlington, Joseph Kerman, Sarah Fuller, Richard Kramer, David Lawton, Jeffrey Magee, Donald Meyer, and Mary Ann Smart for their insightful comments and helpful suggestions. I would also like to acknowledge the kindness and support of my colleagues in the Department of Fine Arts, Syracuse University, as well as the assistance of Gayle Sherwood at Indiana University Press. Above all, I would like to thank my wife, Eileen Strempel, for her unfailing support and encouragement. Without her, this work would not be possible.

Carl Maria von Weber and the Search for a German Opera

Introduction: Inventing German Opera

Two Hunters' Choruses

By the end of act 3, scene 2, of Weber's opera *Euryanthe,* the fortunes of the heroine have reached their lowest ebb. Falsely accused of infidelity and banished by king and court, she has just been abandoned by her beloved Adolar deep in the forest, to perish of hunger or be devoured by wild beasts. In the scene and cavatina that forms the body of scene 2, Euryanthe prepares herself for this unjust death and calls on the fields, streams, and flowers to bear witness to her chastity and faithfulness. Death seems to settle around her, yet the orchestra is strangely turbulent. The upper strings pulsate while the cellos and basses play a fragmented melody in the new key of G minor. Suddenly we hear a horn, answered two measures later and then at more frequent intervals. The wandering tonalities of the end of the scene settle into a lusty E-flat major as the horns gather themselves together during an exciting accelerando, breaking out into a stirring call as the joyful hunters appear on the stage. The crisis has passed, for the hunters accompany a for-giving king who will soon put everything to rights. Euryanthe begins her path back toward exoneration and the loving arms of the tenor.

Weber was justifiably proud of the music of *Euryanthe,* for in passages such as these he seemed to realize some of his most deeply held critical and compositional ideals. Weber used transitions such as the one described above to smooth over and partially obscure the boundaries between the in-dividual pieces of the number opera and move toward a solution of what he saw as the essential problem of the genre, namely, to bring unity to an art form that was a "whole containing other wholes." Indeed, this passage is not only a kind of musical elision between two set pieces, but also a dra-matic transition from the feminine world of Euryanthe's spiritualized suf-fering, with its chromatic harmonies and irregular phrase structures, to the diatonic, masculine world of the hunters' chorus. Here Weber reconciles his goal of creating an organically unified opera with his self-imposed demand for music "full of situation and character"—through this transition these two strongly contrasting musico-dramatic environments are held in dynamic tension with one another. In this passage, it seems that chimerical "new German opera" moves from the pages of Weber's criticism onto the operatic stage.

Even before the premiere of *Euryanthe,* however, Weber was concerned that the extraordinary success of *Freischütz* would imperil his new *grosse romantsiche Oper.* That "cursed *Freischütz,*" he wrote to his friend Lichtenstein, "will make things difficult for his sister *Euryanthe,* and I sometimes get hot flashes when I consider the fact that the applause cannot really increase any more."[1] After the enthusiastic crowds that had applauded the Vienna premiere of *Euryanthe* failed to fill the opera house for subsequent performances, Weber also blamed *Der Freischütz.* "The expectations of the masses," he wrote to Franz Danzi, "have been puffed up to such an absurd and impossible pitch by the wonderful success of *Der Freischütz,* that now, when I lay before them a simple serious work, which only aims at truth of expression, passion, and characteristic delineation, without any of the exciting elements of its predecessor, what can I expect? Be it as God will!"[2] It was indeed *Freischütz* that in many ways became the German national opera, while the work that more closely reflected the critical goals of the "search for a German opera" quickly passed from the repertoire. *Euryanthe* was frequently admired but much less frequently heard, particularly after midcentury. The failure of *Euryanthe,* coming so closely after *Freischütz*'s phenomenal success, is even more striking in light of the many commonalities between the two works. In *Euryanthe* Weber is clearly moving beyond *Freischütz* into a different operatic genre; nevertheless, the two operas employ many of the same musico-dramatic tropes. If in his critical commentary Weber stressed the revolutionary elements in *Euryanthe,* he was also shrewd enough to recognize and "recycle" many of those elements that had made *Freischütz* so successful.

One of those elements was the hunters' chorus, part of the *volkstümlich* (folklike) musical environment that had proved so popular in *Der Freischütz.*[3] The similarities of musical style between "Was gleicht wohl auf Erden" and the chorus that follows Euryanthe's meditation on her own death, as we might expect, are quite striking. Both are highly rhythmic, homophonic numbers for four-part men's voices, with clear phrase structures in which tonic and dominant harmonies predominate.[4] In both choruses the men celebrate the joys of the hunt and imitate the horns that form such an important part of the orchestral texture. Moreover, the two pieces have a very similar function within *Freischütz* and *Euryanthe.* They appear at roughly the same point in the two operas—partway through the third act—where they function as part of the preparation for the finale. And the simple joys of nature evoked by the hunters' chorus serve in both operas as an important foil for the supernatural.

The transition into the hunters' chorus from *Euryanthe* that I described above, however, has no counterpart in *Freischütz*. In a through-composed opera such as *Euryanthe*, Weber was naturally more concerned with connecting the chorus to the music that precedes and follows it. What is more interesting is his effort to integrate the huntsmen into the drama of the opera. The hunters of *Freischütz* provide local color, but they do not take an active role in the drama. But in *Euryanthe* they actually discover the heroine —they are quickly convinced of her innocence and help bring about her reconciliation with her beloved. In both operas, as Warrack points out, the huntsmen "stand for the restoration of happy normality to a figure who has lost it" (Max and Euryanthe, respectively), yet in *Euryanthe* "they are the actual means of bringing this about and not merely a symbol."[5]

There are in fact many instances analogous to that of the two hunters' choruses, in which Weber transplants musico-dramatic elements from *Freischütz* to *Euryanthe*.[6] Kuno, for instance, bears much the same relationship to Max as the king in *Euryanthe* bears to the tenor hero, Adolar. More important are the similarities between Euryanthe and Agathe. Both sopranos are exemplars of chastity and virtue who, despite their central position, perform an essentially passive function in the plot. They sing of their constant love for the hero or the redemptive powers of Nature in music that is intensely lyrical and most often cast in a slow tempo. The happy peasants who bless the upcoming marriage of Max and Agathe with the tokens of spring (in the "Chorus of Bridesmaids," no. 14) also appear in the third act of *Euryanthe* (no. 21, "Der Mai bringt frische Rosen dar"), albeit with a different dramatic function. In some instances, such as the two hunters' choruses, Weber's self-borrowing is quite direct, while in others the relationship between corresponding musico-dramatic elements in *Freischütz* and *Euryanthe* is more complex. In all cases, however, the reconfiguration of these elements is conditioned by what was for Weber surely the most important distinction between the *Freischütz* and *Euryanthe*: that between a dialogue opera and a through-composed, organic work of art.

If *Euryanthe* is in some sense a recasting of *Freischütz* in the mold of a *grosse romantische Oper*, can we not then hold the ambitions of the search for a German opera responsible for its popular failure? Were the critical and compositional impulses articulated in essays such as "The Poet and the

Composer" or Weber's review of *Undine* merely the obsessions of a musical elite, serving only to stimulate a kind of operatic esotericism and the production of operas that had little or no popular appeal? Was Weber himself misled by unrealistic ambitions to abandon the musico-dramatic form (the dialogue opera) to which he was best suited? Much of the criticism surrounding *Euryanthe* strikes precisely this note.[7] And yet the relationship between the theory of German opera and its realization was not so simple. The search for a German opera may ultimately have failed to achieve all of its goals, yet its ideals were extraordinary stimulating, not only for Weber, but for a large group of composers in early-nineteenth-century Germany and beyond its borders.[8] The ideals that Weber tried to realize in *Freischütz* and *Euryanthe* had an important influence not only on the history of operatic style, but also on the history of opera reception, helping to change fundamental ideas about the connection between opera and society and the role of opera in the creation of national identity. The ambivalent and sometimes contradictory relationship between theory and practice was rarely straightforward, but it was always fertile. It is this relationship, manifested in Weber's *Freischütz* and *Euryanthe*, that forms the subject of this book.

Theoretical Contexts

"The great inspiration for this 'idea of the German opera,'" writes Wolfgang Becker in his book *Die deutsche Oper in Dresden unter der Leitung von Carl Maria von Weber*, "comes from the words of Herder: 'O eine neu zu schaffende Deutsche Oper! Auf Menschlichem Grund und Boden; mit Menschlicher Musik und Declamation und Verzierung, aber mit Empfindung; o großer Zweck, o großes Werk!'"[9] The quotation is an excellent example of Herder's breathless style. Reiterating the adjective "menschliche," Herder articulates one of the most important dichotomies of later operatic criticism, that between the stiff, artificial operas of the French and Italians and the natural, genuine, "humane" style of a yet-to-be-realized German opera. And yet these words had no direct influence on the search for a German opera, for they remained unpublished until 1846 and did not become widely available until after Suphan began his famous edition of Herder's works in 1877.[10] Despite Herder's interest in opera (he wrote two opera librettos during the 1770s), his main concern during the late 1760s and 1770s was with the origin and development of language. Although his ideas on this subject, contained in essays such as "Über den Fleiß in mehreren gelehrten Sprachen" (1764) and the "Abhandlung über den Ursprung der Sprache"

(1772), form an important part of the background to late-eighteenth- and early-nineteenth-century opera aesthetics, their influence on early-nineteenth-century composers was probably less direct than certain essays that Herder wrote late in his life, some of which may be found in his journal *Adrastea*. The fourth issue of this journal (1801) contains the last part of a loosely organized series of essays on "The Fruits of the So-Called Golden Age of the Eighteenth Century" ("Früchte aus den sogenannt-goldnen Zeiten des achtzehnten Jahrhunderts"). The ninth of these essays, entitled "Tanz, Melodram," begins with a brief account of the origins of dance but quickly moves on to a critique of contemporary opera. Although German critics interested in opera during the late eighteenth and early nineteenth centuries by no means spoke with one voice, Herder's essay serves as an excellent point of entry into the common elements of their ideology. It is well worth examining in some detail, for it contains *in nuce* many of the aesthetic and ideological assumptions that were to inform the search for a German opera during this period.[11]

The essay takes the form of what Nietzsche might call a "genealogy" of opera, beginning from a single observation:

> The most expressive allegory that we know is humankind itself. Powers, inclinations, thoughts, and the passions of the soul indicate themselves externally, on the body, only rarely, but rather present themselves in the mind. [Only while] resting do people show the visible expression of what the interior person is or may be. The inner workings of their character are revealed in those especially passionate and unexpected moments that are also so ephemeral. People are wandering portraits of themselves, in which their spiritual forms involuntarily appear.[12]

If the body is the mirror of "spiritual forms," then gesture is at once humankind's simplest and most powerful form of expression. Gesture, Herder continues, is naturally supported by music, for both are determined by measured movement.[13] Indeed, tones and gestures accompany each other in every human society. When tone and gesture are bound together with the word, "a new field of poetic art is opened up."[14]

Up to this point, Herder suffuses his essay with verbs expressing connection and interdependence: "unterstützen," "verbinden," "gesellen sich," and so forth. Herder's rhetorical strategy of developing his ideas out of a single observation (the way in which the body mirrors spiritual forms) reflects these concepts of connection and interdependence on the structural level of the essay. The essay is an eloquent argument for (I am tempted to write "performance of") the idea that opera develops organically from fundamental relationships between the body and the spirit. But when, in the next section of the essay, Herder begins to speak about contemporary realizations of this idea, his tone shifts abruptly. The vocabulary of unity is replaced by a rhetoric of dispersion. Opera's component arts—music, words, and decoration—are no longer united, but instead pursue their own, often contradictory ends:

> We know well where opera stands now; at the summit of compositional art and decoration, but with almost no attention given to the content and the story. Nowadays one hardly mentions the librettist. His words, which are seldom understood and even more rarely deserve our understanding, serve only to give the composer an opportunity for what he calls his musical thoughts, and to give the decorator and opportunity for his decorations.[15]

The poetic elegance with which Herder expresses these ideas is quite original, but the central idea of the essay is not. Complaints about the disharmony between libretto and music were a prominent part of Francesco Algarotti's widely read *Saggio sopra l'opera in musica* (1755), but the history of this critique stretches back further still, to the very beginnings of opera itself.[16] At the risk of generalization, I will call this argument the "holistic narrative."[17] Despite its many variants, this narrative revolves around the following ideas: (1) opera emerges from a unification of component arts (poetry, music, decoration, dance, etc.); (2) during some "golden age" in the past these arts were harmoniously and naturally combined to produce an art that was deeply, even supernaturally expressive; (3) this golden age stands in contrast to contemporary opera, in which the component arts work at cross-purposes to one another; (4) opera will be reformed by a recombination of its component arts that is at once a return to the organic unity of the golden age and a transfiguration of its fundamental principles. Needless to say, critics have articulated the details of this narrative in a bewildering variety of ways. Girolamo Mei and Friedrich Nietzsche located the "golden age" in ancient Greece, while Algarotti looked with favor on the Italian operas of the early to mid-seventeenth century. Others, such as Herder and A. B. Marx, found in the operas of Gluck an ideal unification of the arts.[18] What these critics share, of course, is the idea that the operatic art of their time is historically located "after the Fall." Opera, to extend the biblical metaphor, is "in need of redemption," and this need is all the more pressing because of the effects that the genre might have on the moral structure of society.

Herder explores this idea in a *Beilage* appended to his critique of opera in *Adrastea* that takes as its starting point a question that was to prove central to German opera aesthetics during the early nineteenth century: "Does music affect customs, manners, and modes of thought?" The question, as we might expect, is a rhetorical one. "The vigilance of the Greek lawgivers concerning music," writes Herder,

> is well-known. They forbade and punished the introduction of new, soft, and luxurious keys. Who does not know the complaints of the philosophers and statesmen when this vigilance was relaxed?
>
> To us this attitude towards a so-called beautiful and free art seems laughable, but upon what basis? Are not musical tunes [*Weisen*] (as the name says), ways [*Weisen*] and paths of sensibility; do they not, when they are connected with words, become genuine patterns of thought [*Denkweisen*]? The vocal melody steals into the heart and inclines it towards tones, wishes, towards striving in this [particular] melody, in this mode. . . . We cannot therefore be indifferent when thoughtless, flatteringly luxurious operatic songs or trivialities of the most general kind suppress every other type of song.[19]

If the holistic narrative of the birth, flowering, and degeneration of musico-dramatic art stretches back at least to the Renaissance, then Herder's warnings about the potentially corruptive power of music (particularly vocal music) go back of course much further (as Herder himself clearly states). In the context of the search for a German opera at the end of the eighteenth and beginning of the nineteenth centuries, these warnings take on a new urgency, but their fundamental outlines remain remarkably similar. Likewise, the technical prescriptions for the "new German opera" that suffuse the criticism of this time (concerning the proper relationship between text and music, the role of the recitative, the nature of the plot material, and other topics) have much in common with earlier criticism. The critical-compositional impulse toward a "new German opera" distinguished itself from other reform movements less by the nature of these technical prescriptions and moral critiques than by the ways in which these ethical and aesthetic concepts were combined with a new sense of German national identity. It is this constellation of new and old ideas that forms the essential background to the search for a German opera.

This search, then, was not merely an aesthetic movement, but also a po-litical and social critique. We may begin by positing three overlapping and interpenetrating impulses through which the search for a German opera op-erated: the search for a new, through-composed German operatic form; the effort to create a new audience and a new social position for German-language works; and finally the attempt to articulate a new national ide-ology through music and drama. It will be useful here to outline briefly each one of these impulses in turn.

Operatic Form

Critics who employed versions of the holistic narrative are often at pains to describe opera as a unification of all the arts, but it is of course the relationship between text and music that receives the most attention in their writings. For early-nineteenth-century German critics, the negative stage of the holistic narrative, in which music and text are working at cross-purposes to one another, is exemplified by contemporary Italian opera. In the opinion of these critics, Italian composers distorted and unbalanced the relationship between words and music through their inordinate love of "superficial vocalism": elaborate coloratura or "insinuating" lyricism that had no connection to the underlying text. The tone of this criticism is often highly satirical, as in the following quote from the *Berliner allgemeine mu-sikalische Zeitung*. Imagining the response of the "Italian faction" in Dres-den to a production of *Euryanthe,* the critic writes:

> "The music is beautiful," [say the Italians] "but the German singers do
> not know how to sing. They do not decorate the melody at all, they make
> no roulades etc. . . . Isn't that laughable?" It is those who really know
> *Euryanthe* who will do the laughing, those who understand the powerful
> difference between declamatory song and simple melody. The new Italian
> music has been stripped of all its harmonic beauties; it allows all possible
> ornamentation to the singer and treats the underlying text—words such
> as "giura quest'alma' ardita di vincere, o morir" etc.—as virtually mean-
> ingless.[20]

There are many critical strands woven into this passage. First the critic focuses on musical style, juxtaposing the "declamatory song" of German opera with the highly ornamented melodies of Italian music. Virtuosic vocal display was highly valued in the eighteenth century, when the ability to em-bellish and ornament was critical to a singer's mastery of style and tech-

nique. In terms of the eighteenth-century genre hierarchy, a skillfully ornamented melody was the mark of polish and an indicator of the "high" style.
Yet in this respect (as in so many others) the German critics of the early
nineteenth century inverted the values of the previous age. Ornamentation
and embellishment were now the signs of superficiality.[21]

Not all German critics, of course, were enemies of Italian music. Heine's
witty plea for the forgiveness of his anti-Italian compatriots, for instance, is
an eloquent defense of Rossini.[22] But a stereotype of the Italian composer
nevertheless emerges in the music criticism of early-nineteenth-century
Germany. Italian composers, according to this view, were so interested in the
superficial attractiveness of a beautiful or melody or virtuosic performance
that they paid scant attention to the meaning of the text. An extensive review of Rossini's *Elisabetta, Regina D'Inghilterra* by the Dresden correspondent for the *Allgemeine musikalische Zeitung* (most likely Carl Borromaeus
von Miltitz) may serve as an example of this type of criticism:

> One part of the local public finds the music beautiful and motives quite
> agreeable. We do not deny their judgment; but when we really consider
> the material, we find it more appropriate to a comic opera rather than a
> serious one. Many have remarked that the entire opera is nothing but a
> conglomeration of coloratura. . . . It is amazing that in Italy, where good
> singing has always been cultivated, and there are so many examples of art
> that obey the true rules (the first one is to be always simple and clear),
> how a song consisting of such a confused jumble of notes could have so
> much success. When listening to this music one believes that he is hear-
> ing an extended instrumental concert.[23]

In order to demonstrate Rossini's faults, the reviewer focuses on a passage
in the first finale. This music, he writes,

> is taken from the overture and comes at the precise moment when
> Elisabeth discovers that Mathilde is Leicester's wife. The queen's jeal-
> ousy is violently aroused by this discovery, and she places Leicester and
> Mathilde under arrest. They express their pain and sorrow over their
> impending separation with the cries "Sposo! Sposa!" that Rossini sets to
> a comic motive.[24]

The musical example that the reviewer includes at this point shows a restless
motive in the first violin, beginning with a three-note scalar ascent and
eventually noodling around a raised fourth scale degree. If the reviewer had
known that Rossini would use this same music in the overture to *Il Barbiere*

di Seviglia he might have been even more disdainful of the composer's lack of attention to the connection between text and music.

"Another, even more glaring offense against declamation, situation, and character," the review continues, "may be found in the duet from the second act, when Elisabeth forces Mathilde to forswear every claim on Leicester's heart. The queen exclaims:

> Pensa che sol per poco
> Sospendo l'ira mia
> Quando piu tarda fia,
> Più fiera soppierà."[25]

The reviewer appends yet another musical example to show how the two last lines "are expressed by a completely dance-like motive, more appropriate to wind instruments." "Does Herr Rossini, after all, follow the true knowledge of declamation?" he concludes. "We must answer no."[26]

By adhering to the closed musical forms of the Italian tradition, critics argued, composers (and librettists, for that matter) compromised their ability to respond to the nuances of the drama. Italian opera, they felt, used the drama merely as a vehicle for the music or, worse yet, merely as a vehicle for vapid and superficial vocalism. This relationship was completely wrong. In terms reminiscent of the Gluckian attack on *opera seria,* the early-nineteenth-century German critics called for an operatic music that would serve the demands of the drama. This "ideal type" would place more emphasis on the recitative. For in recitatives, as a critic for Friedrich Kind's journal *Die Muse* wrote in 1821:

> and particularly in those conspicuous places, where through quick rapidly changing words two passionately excited people are expressing their liveliest sentiments to each other, the music appears to be dramatic in and of itself, and expresses the complete individual: what one calls in the narrow sense "characteristic." This explains why the newer composers show a particular inclination for the so-called declamatory music.[27]

The music of the new Italian school represented, in the eyes of the pro-German critics, the triumph of the aria over the recitative. "With Rossini and his followers," wrote Theodor Mundt in his important article "Über Oper, Drama, und Melodrama in ihrem Verhältniß zu einander und zum Theater," "the recitative has almost completely receded. Its position has been overwhelmed by bubbling arias."[28] Mundt and other pro-German critics hoped that the new German opera would reverse this tendency and concentrate on the recitative, whose looser structure would allow for a more "characteristic" union of text and music.

Of course, recitative played only a very small role in the German operas of the first decades of the nineteenth century, or for that matter in the translated *opéras comiques* that were so important to companies such as Weber's. Even as late as the 1830s, the bulk of the native German repertoire consisted of dialogue operas similar to the early *Singspiel*, although they sometimes carried different names. For the most part, German critics had nothing but scorn for these *"Zwittergattung."* The idea that the absence of recitative was impeding progress toward a "genuinely dramatic German music" is clearly evident in Spohr's "Appeal to German Composers" (1823).[29] At the beginning of this essay Spohr somewhat optimistically heralds the decline in the popularity of both Rossini and French opera and calls on German composers to "take ownership of the opera repertoire."[30] Later he turns directly to the question of the recitative. "Another question," he writes, "is whether or not we Germans should finally elevate the opera into a thoroughly unified work of art by changing the dialogues of our operas into recitatives. When the aestheticians reject the idea of an opera as a work of art, and call it a monstrosity, it is principally the alternation between speech and song to which they object."[31] This continual alternation between speech and song made any type of larger dramatic unity impossible. Progress for the German opera, critics felt, was seriously impeded by its past. The bulk of our errors, wrote Heinrich Laube, "comes from the great number of these vapid operas, . . . the German 'hermaphrodite genre' in which the dialogue clatters in between the music pieces like the prosaic sounds of a mill, or like water mixed into wine. Our operas are for the most part merely agglomerations of music numbers."[32] Laube's complaint was of course not new. Both Weber, in his well-known review of Hoffmann's *Undine* (1817), and Hoffmann, in his equally famous dialogue from *Die Serapionsbrüder* known as "The Poet and the Composer," argued forcefully for a German opera in which the independent unity of the individual numbers would be completely subsumed into the organic unity of the whole.[33] Their attempts to "move beyond" the dialogue opera are a macrocosmic corollary of their call for a new type of "declamatory song" to replace the "bubbling arias" of Rossini. The closed musical forms of the "number opera" should be bound together into an indissoluble whole, just as text and music needed to be combined into a single dramatic impulse. The only true opera, Hoffmann felt, would be Romantic opera, one in which libretto and music would spring from the same creative source, uniting to transport the audience into that "mysterious spirit-realm" where souls could be awakened to a "higher, intenser awareness."[34]

German Opera and German Society

It was only natural, in the eyes of the pro-German critics, that the superficiality of Italian operatic music should be reflected in the behavior of its audience. In an article entitled "Ueber den heutigen Geschmack in der Musik," the new editor of the *Allgemeine musikalische Zeitung*, G. W. Fink, casts a disapproving eye at the Italian opera. Contemporary taste, he writes, falls into three factions: the supporters of the new Italian opera, the partisans of the old Italians, and what he calls the "new German school." "The first group," he continues,

> counts among its hangers-on the so-called refined and exclusive world . . .
> [the very same people] who come into the theater or concert-hall with an
> enormous amount of noise when the first act is already half over. While
> the music is playing they speak and laugh loudly, and leave again with the
> same amount of noise at the beginning of the Finale. To these people it
> doesn't matter how the music goes or who it is by, as long as the name
> sounds Italian. They are so crazed by Italian music, and so determined
> to be always up-to-date on the latest performances, that if Court X or Y
> were to establish a Lappish theater tomorrow, they would be just as ex-
> cited over the song "ierda moke angekoke" as they are today about "tanti
> palpiti."[35]

Fink is leveling his attack at the "courtly, aristocratic" world, a world that he associates closely with the "Italian school." The new German school represents not only new compositional techniques, but also a new attitude toward music and art, located not in the "so-called refined and exclusive world" but in the solidly middle-class readership of the *Allgemeine musikalische Zeitung*. The tone of Fink's article may be flippant, but its underlying ideology was central to the search for a German opera at the beginning of the nineteenth century. This ideology involved the revaluation of what we might call the "genre hierarchy" of the eighteenth century and the social hierarchy with which it was closely allied.

The extent to which distinctions of musical form and language reflected the economic and social divisions of the ancien régime hardly needs to be emphasized. In the early eighteenth century, these distinctions were often

enforced by laws that excluded the lower classes from *opera seria* performances.[36] Although these types of restrictions had been largely eliminated
by 1800, their echo was still strongly felt. In Dresden this division can be
seen in the contrasting repertoires of the centrally located Morettische Haus
and the suburban Linkesche Bad Theater, but this type of genre specializa-
tion was by no means unique to the city. Powerful traditions associated individual opera companies with particular types of opera, not only in Dresden, but also across Europe. In Paris, for instance, these traditions were
reinforced by laws which prohibited the Opéra Comique from producing
operas with recitative, an institutional division that was reproduced in less
formal ways in many European cities.[37] The Viennese counterpart to the
Morettische Haus during this period was the Kärtnerthortheater Theater,
which often housed an Italian opera company and used the best singers and
the most skillful painters and mechanics.[38] Members of the aristocracy and
the royal (or ducal) family attended performances and sometimes even rehearsals. German-language dialogue opera was more often performed at the
Leopoldstadt and Josefstadt Theaters, as well as the Theater an der Wien. In
Munich this same type of genre distinction is embodied in the contrasting
repertoires of the Hof-und National Theater and the Isarthortheater.[39] In
Dresden the distinction between the downtown and suburban theaters was
accentuated by their contrasting performance seasons. The Linkesche Bad
Theater was only open during the summer months (usually from the end
of May to mid-September), and its repertoire consisted primarily of vernacular dialogue opera. Foreign-language operas were also performed at the
"Bad," but they were almost always comic or partly comic works such as
Fioravanti's *Le cantatrici villane*. Serious opera in Dresden was largely con-
fined to the fall-spring season at the Morettische Haus.[40] In Vienna, Dresden,
and Munich, vernacular opera was thus quite often literally marginalized,
exiled to suburban venues such as the Linkesche Bad or the Josefstadt Theater. Until German-language opera could find a permanent home within the
city walls it would remain culturally, as well as geographically, peripheral.

The location of operatic theaters corresponded closely to the social geography of European cities. In the late eighteenth and early nineteenth centuries, the central city was the indisputable seat of political and economic
power, and the poor were often concentrated in suburbs.[41] Up until the early
nineteenth century the distinction between "center" and "periphery" was
reinforced by the presence of massive fortifications, which the historian
Günther Jäckel describes in an article concerning the cultural history of
Dresden. "Around 1800," Jäckel writes, "Dresden was still a fortress, with

seven bastions in the Altstadt and six in the Neustadt, with three gates, mighty walls and moats, palisades, lunettes, and often insufficiently guarded buildings, behind which, in the Residenz, the dukes and duchesses carried on an urbane existence of the first rank."[42] These mighty bulwarks embodied the social divisions that separated the working class suburbs from the city's central core.

That German cities shared a similar social and cultural geography should not lead us to overexaggerate their similarities. The social and economic conditions of Germany in the late eighteenth and nineteenth centuries were of course quite diverse. There were tremendous differences between the well-developed, partially urbanized arias in the Rhineland and the semi-feudal estates of the north and east. Furthermore, Germany was subjected to a wide variety of different foreign influences during this period. Most of the Palatinate was under direct French rule for more than twenty years during the Napoleonic period, while in other sections of Germany the effects of the French invasion were much less pronounced. Parts of Mecklenburg and Pomerania, on the other hand, were still ruled by Sweden in the late eighteenth century. Austria and southern Germany remained open to Italian influences, particularly in music and art. There was also a tremendous difference between large cities, such as Vienna, Dresden, Munich, and Berlin, and the smaller courts. In cities such as Frankfurt and Hamburg, which retained their status as Free Cities, the nature of the social and economic hierarchy was obviously different than it was in the *Residenzstädte.*

In Dresden the traditional constellations of genre, language, and class remained rooted in the ancien régime. But in other parts of Germany, particularly in the more cosmopolitan centers of Berlin and Vienna, there were signs that these constellations were beginning to fall apart. Surprisingly, the most direct challenge to the genre hierarchy came from the monarchs themselves, who were in many ways trying to disassociate themselves from the traditional aristocracy. "Reforming" monarchs in Austria and Prussia often saw the entrenched power of the noble classes as an impediment to the political and economic changes that their countries so desperately needed. Attempting to ally royal power with the new forces of liberalism and nationalism, they brought vernacular opera into the city centers and provided it with state support. Joseph II of Austria, for instance, dismissed his Italian troupe in 1776 and brought German drama into the centrally located Burgtheater, as well as opening up the Kärntnerthor theater to German-language *Singspiel.*[43] Elector Carl Theodor, the famous patron of the Mannheim orchestra, was also interested in German art. In the 1770s he sponsored a German National Theater at his court, where the young Mozart heard the original German opera *Günther von Schwarzburg* (1777). Friedrich Wilhelm of Prussia, who inherited the throne from his father Frederick the Great in 1786, was also an enthusiastic supporter of German-language opera. And in Munich, an important center for the *opera seria,* Italian opera was even outlawed for a period during the late eighteenth and early nineteenth centuries.

Monarchs such as Joseph II and Friedrich Wilhelm were not alone in wishing to harness German opera to serve a particular political agenda. Although German intellectuals seldom clearly defined the role that German-language opera could play in the creation of a German nation, many of them felt that opera was an essential part of the nationalist enterprise. The yearning for a new German nation was most deeply rooted in the upper bourgeoisie, the narrow stratum of highly educated men and women that German scholars have called the *Bildungsbürgertum,* and although there is no doubt that the experience of defeat and liberation in the Napoleonic Wars is the most dramatic event during the early nineteenth century, for our purposes the most salient development in German political and social history during this period is the transfer of power from the old courtly, aristocratic elite to a new group.[44]

German Opera and National Identity

If the revolutions of 1830–31 and 1848–49 mark episodes in the German bourgeoisie's attempt to attain political power, their efforts to attain cultural hegemony can be read, among other places, in the music criticism of the early nineteenth century. For the first time in Germany, the number of musically literate people had expanded enough to support a diverse musical press, and this new market made possible what many have regarded as a "golden age" of criticism.[45] Many new periodicals devoted wholly or in part to music were established during this period, including the *Allgemeine musikalische Zeitung,* the *Dresden Abend-Zeitung,* the *Berliner allgemeine musikalische Zeitung,* and the journal *Cäcilia.*[46] These journals, with their predominantly bourgeois readership, helped place discourse about music firmly in the public sphere. Music critics themselves were often deeply engaged in public life as active musicians. Weber, Hoffmann, Spohr, Schumann, and Wagner were only the most well known of a host of "critic-composers," and other music critics, such as Friedrich Kind or J. P. Lyser, were also opera librettists or song lyricists. At no other time and in no other place were the creators of opera so involved with its critical and philosophical interpretation. Through their work the struggle between native and foreign opera was integrated into a broader effort to define and articulate national identity.

The connection between "nationalist" music criticism and the liberal nationalism of the early nineteenth century is hardly surprising, for the critics and composers who were most deeply concerned with operatic reform, people such as Weber, Hoffmann, Spazier, Laube, Rellstab, and so forth, came from the same class of people, the *Bildungsbürgertum*, that was working for political reform. The political ideology of the *Bildungsbürgertum* was predominantly liberal—indeed, the term itself first acquired something like its modern political meaning during this period.[47] "What is called liberalism," wrote W. T. Krug in one of the first histories of the movement, published in 1823, emerged from the struggle between the defenders of the status quo and "the evolutionary drive in humanity, which is only the struggle for liberation from limitations of time and place."[48] Yet the struggle for "liberation" was not only political. It was also played out in social, cultural, and even emotional terms as a struggle for a new personal and national identity. The fight for political liberalization was an important component of this struggle, but it was only part of a broader process of transformation through which a new personal and social ideology emerged. Through this ideology, early-nineteenth-century Germans articulated new attitudes toward their community and their nation and new concepts about culture and history.

In their quest for political power and influence, the men and women of the *Bildungsbürgertum* employed the idea of a *Mittlelstand* or *Mittelklasse* lying between the aristocracy and the working classes, a group that in their view constituted the "real *Volk*."[49] The *Mittelstand* was not based on wealth or ancestry, but, as James Sheehan puts it, was rather "a social and a moral category."[50] It depended less on objective criteria than on the existence of shared moral virtues." For German liberals, the "evolutionary drive in society" would be furthered not merely by a redistribution of political and economic power, but also by a transformation and deepening of an entire nation's emotional life. Cultural institutions were important to German liberals at least in part because they could be the vehicles for this articulation.[51] Through culture, Germans hoped to find a transformative unity that did not yet seem possible in the political sphere, a "fatherland of the soul" that could compensate for the lack of political unity and could also help to bring that unity about. For this "fatherland of the soul" was above all an interior world, determined by "structures of feeling" rather than a particular political agenda. Indeed, it was the apolitical or transcendent nature of German culture that was taken to be its most defining characteristic. German philosophers, historians, and critics from the early nineteenth century differentiated the deep, spiritual, and inward nature of their national culture from what they viewed as the superficial culture of France and Italy, driven by fashion (*Mode*) and vanity. German cultural identity was increasingly bound up with the inward gaze.

The *Mittelstand* used their "shared moral virtues" to differentiate themselves not only from other European cultures, but also from the aristocracy, a process that began as early as the 1760s. In his book *Male Fantasies,* Klaus Theweleit describes this development:

> In Germany, as elsewhere, the bourgeoisie became more powerful and self-assured. Out of the aristocratic-bourgeois public, there evolved a new bourgeois public sphere which, though opposed to the courts, lacked the power to attack them in an fundamental way. What then happened was typical of power constellations of this kind. Attacks against the absolutist nobility began to center on its *immorality,* rather than its political hegemony.[52]

This moral attack on the aristocracy was easily combined with German nationalism, for the aristocracy had most conspicuously adopted foreign tastes in dress, language, behavior, and artistic preferences. To many German nationalists during this period, it seemed that the nobles and princes, jealously guarding their provincial powers, were the primary impediments to national unity. The "old order" meant a fragmented Germany, politically repressive and economically backward, dominated by petty princes and locked forever in the past. The search for a German opera could not be separated from the search for a new German national identity, an identity that was articulated against both the ancien régime and the cultural influences from beyond Germany's somewhat nebulous borders.

The task of creating a new German opera and the struggle for a new liberal political structure were ultimately part of a larger search for a new collective identity, and in both the political and the aesthetic sphere the task of forming this identity was one of deciding what belonged and what did not belong, of what was inside and what was outside. The nation's character, in other words, was constructed through discrimination. The amount of ink spilled by nineteenth-century Germans in classifications and categorizations is a measure of the difficulty that this task of identity formation posed for them. Nationalists even had trouble defining the borders of an ideal Germany, a difficulty that would prove to be a major stumbling block to the

Frankfurt Parliament in 1848. Did Germany include all of Prussia and Austria, even their non-German lands? Was Alsace a part of France or Germany? From reading the pages of the *Allgemeine musikalische Zeitung* or the *Tagebuch der deutschen Bühnen,* one has the impression that many Eastern European cities, such as Riga, Prague, or even St. Petersburg, were a part of the German cultural sphere, even though they were surrounded by non-German populations.[53] The effort to define a specifically German opera was an aesthetic corollary to this political border anxiety. Like the German nation itself, the character of German opera had to be located on a kind of "mental map," in this case a mental map of musical genre. Terms had to be defined and borders erected. Just as the *Mittelstand* carved out a place for itself between the aristocracy and the lower classes, just as liberal politicians decided on the borders of a hypothetical national state, so critics struggled to identify a specifically German operatic genre from a plethora of different styles and traditions. The German opera of the critical imagination, emerging from an inner, organic, unifying "character," can be read as a kind of metaphor for both the individual and the national soul.

Just as critical efforts to define a new German operatic form often began with an attack on the disunity of text and music in Italian opera, so too did attempts to articulate the social ideology of the new German opera frequently incorporate a moral critique of transalpine music. Indeed, the technical prescriptions of early-nineteenth-century German criticism are in many ways less interesting than the moral critique of Italian opera, with which it was often supplemented and combined. One of the most common rhetorical strategies of this moral critique was to compare Italian opera to a disease that had "infected" Germany from the south. The popularity of foreign works was undeniable, but their aesthetic and moral wholesomeness was called into question. Rossini was of course the most dangerous of all composers, and German critics often likened the progress of his operas through the various German theaters to the spread of an epidemic. The casual manner in which Weber mentions this "disease" in a letter to his friend G. F. Treitschke shows how commonplace references to the "Rossini fever" had become:

> On the 26th of May I brought Meyerbeer's *Emma di Resburgo* onto the stage. We gave the opera in Italian, and it was an extraordinary success. Almost every number was applauded, something that happens only rarely with our frosty public. But they have the Rossini-fever now, and Meyer-

beer has followed the dictates of this fashionable ignorance almost to the point of impropriety.[54]

Although Weber's words seem to imply a moral critique of Rossini and Meyerbeer's operas, it is also clear from his writings that he found much to admire in the Italian style. The metaphor of Italian music as a disease appears much more clearly in the work of R. O. Spazier, a novelist, historian, and the Dresden correspondent for A. B. Marx's *Berliner allgemeine musikalische Zeitung*. In a half-ironic book entitled *Scherz und Ernst über Ernst Scherzlieb's Dresden wie es durch eine Goldbrille ist; nebst Bemerkungen über Nationalität in der dramatischen Musik,* Spazier writes:

> Already, two years ago I remarked in passing in the *Münchner Musikzeitung* what a sickness [the Italian opera] has brought into our native house. Already at that time I made it clear that the Italian opera in Munich should be answerable for the great confusion of musical perception and opinion which the imitators of Rossini have brought into our native land. From beyond the Alps they came first to Munich, and implanted themselves there. Dresden became their second indestructible nest, and Vienna followed soon afterward.[55]

For the most part, even the most virulent critics of Italian music, such as Spazier, did not deny its attractiveness. Indeed, in their writings the "insinuating beauty" of Italian opera appears as its most dangerous characteristic, for its very beauty threatens to seduce the listener away from the true music of his or her homeland and the spiritual truths that music represents. It is the duty of every German to further the development of a genuine dramatic music and to defend the homeland against the "deadly sexuality" of the Italian opera:

> The genuine German prince, living only in wisdom and carrying the welfare of his people in his heart, already recognizes the necessity to create a German national dramatic music, in the highest and most well-cultivated sense. This music alone will resonate in the innermost spiritual fibers of the people, it alone will stimulate with mighty power the ideas and emotions of composers, and enable them to create great works and bring them to completion. The true prince recognizes that Italian music from Italian throats seduces the sensibilities of the people and spoils their native worth. True consciousness is buried, as in the ancient German popular legends of the dangerous magic ring, or the Maget or Venusberg,

whose irresistible attraction leads thousands to a shameful, inglorious grave.[56]

That the Venusberg and the magic ring would find their way into later nineteenth-century opera plots points to an inner correspondence between the moral defense of German opera and the musico-dramatic structure of the operas themselves, a correspondence that was probably the strongest connection between music criticism and opera performance in early-nineteenth-century Germany. For the bifurcated view of the operatic world shared by many critics, in which aesthetic and moral issues were framed as a complex of dichotomies, corresponded in many ways to the dualistic moral universe of the German Romantic opera. The same tensions and polarities that inform the critical writings of this period—between vice and virtue, the inner and the outer, authenticity and falsehood, and the native and the foreign—also find their way into the musical and dramatic structures of the operas themselves. Ultimately the search for a new German operatic form cannot be separated from the effort to articulate a new social and national ideology.

In stressing the connections between national ideology and the history of musical style, however, we must be careful not to reduce the critical and compositional impulse toward a "new German opera" to a single voice. Carl Maria von Weber (as this book will argue) may have been the most influential composer behind this impulse, but he was certainly not the only one. Louis Spohr, Johann Nepomuk von Poissl, E. T. A. Hoffmann, Franz Schubert, and other composers made important contributions to German opera during this period, and their works by no means always manifested the same aesthetic principles. Of this group of Weber's contemporaries and near-contemporaries, the most important (at least for the history of German opera) was Louis Spohr. Spohr's most important period of operatic composition coincided nearly exactly with Weber's, and there are many points of intersection between the two men's careers. Weber conducted the Prague premiere of Spohr's *Faust* on 1 September 1816, and after Spohr moved to Dresden in October of 1821 the two composers had frequent occasion to hear each other's works and to share musical ideas. Although Spohr did not think very highly of *Der Freischütz*, it is clear that he and Weber shared many of the same artistic goals.[57] There is a particularly close parallel between *Euryanthe* and Spohr's *Jessonda*, which premiered only a few months before Weber's opera. Spohr published his "Appeal to German Composers" (from which I quoted above) in conjunction with the premiere of

Jessonda, and he clearly intended his opera to be interpreted as a manifestation of the aesthetic principles that he articulated in this essay. With its unusual orchestration, expressive chromaticism, and tonal symbolism, *Jessonda* shows many affinities with *Euryanthe.* Weber and Spohr were clearly working along the same lines.[58]

Spohr's *Jessonda,* as Clive Brown points out, was more successful than *Euryanthe* and held an important place in the repertoire of German theaters for half a century. But despite *Jessonda*'s historical significance, it is Weber's works, rather than Spohr's, which provide the most logical point of entry for a consideration of the search for a German opera. Weber's central place in this search is due first of all to the extraordinary success of *Der Freischütz,* which transformed the composer from a provincial *Kapellmeister* into a national hero virtually overnight. Weber also participated in the peculiar cross-fertilization of literary prose and music that was such an important feature of German Romantic aesthetics. To a far greater degree than Spohr, Weber was interested in using music criticism to shape the attitudes of his audience. Finally, Weber's work as the head of the German opera company in Dresden (1817–26) made him a central figure in the institutional history of the genre. Weber's position frequently put him into direct conflict with the preexisting Italian opera company, headed by Francesco Morlacchi. Both Weber's contemporaries and subsequent historians often interpreted the situation of opera in Dresden as a microcosm of its position in Germany as a whole, elevating petty local squabbles into aesthetic conflicts between national schools. But even if critics and historians misinterpreted Weber's administrative position, his efforts toward institutional reform are an important part of the search for a new German opera and manifest much of the same social and national ideology that informs his compositions.

Creation of the German Opera

Dresden, as John Warrack points out in his biography of Weber, did not provide a favorable environment for the cultivation of a new national opera. "With a backward economy and lack of external trade," Warrack writes, "the life of the country was inward-turning by comparison with the rest of Germany; and in the conservative atmosphere people were accustomed to look to the king as an example and a leader."[59] As in virtually every other German city, the upheaval of the Napoleonic Wars severely disrupted the musical life of Dresden.[60] Although operatic performances continued (even while the city was under siege during part of 1813), the genre divisions that had been such a part of late-eighteenth-century opera in the city were deeply undermined. Joseph Seconda, who earlier in 1813 had hired E. T. A. Hoffmann as his conductor, was suddenly given permission to produce operas in the court theater, something, as Hoffmann wrote in a letter to his friend Speyer in July of 1813, "which is something quite unheard of and possible only since the time when the King of Saxony began to wear a hat with plume and chin strap" (that is, only in times of war).[61] Herr Seconda, he continues, "now has not only the Court Theater but also free use of the back drops, props, and royal wardrobe, so you can imagine, dear doctor, that our performances are not lacking in outward splendor. So far we have staged *Don Giovanni, The Water Carrier, Iphigenia in Tauris, The Abduction from the Seraglio, Cendrillon, Joseph,* and *Helena,* both by Méhul, and *Sargino.*"[62]

Operatic performances came to a temporary halt after the Battle of Leipzig, when the allies reoccupied Dresden and began to reform the Saxon court. Under the Russian governor Prince Repnin-Volkonsky, the various theatrical and musical groups of the city were consolidated into a single *Staatskapelle.* This reorganization continued the dismantling of the genre hierarchy that had begun during the war, for it put the German theater and the Italian opera on equal footing, at least in terms of their stature within the government bureaucracy.[63] When the king returned to his capital in 1815, the *Staatskapelle* was disbanded, but the unified direction of the theaters was to some extent retained. The king appointed Count Heinrich Vitzthum the first *Generaldirektor* of the *Königliche Kapelle* and court theater. Vitzthum was a strong supporter of German opera, and it was he who originally had the idea to establish a special state-supported opera company in Dresden for the performance of vernacular works. Since the late eighteenth century the court had intermittently given subsidies to itinerant companies such as Seconda's, but Vitzthum envisioned a permanent company that would be a separate division of the court theater.

In order to garner support for his idea from the king and court, Vitzthum does not seem to have employed the nationalistic aesthetic and artistic arguments that were to become so strident in the next decade, but focused instead on the economic benefits that the new institution could bring. The king had taken over the Leipzig opera administration from the Seconda brothers on the first of April, 1816, inheriting a substantial deficit. Vitzthum apparently presented the idea of a German opera to the king as a way of making up some of this loss. From the success of Seconda's company, it was clear that German *Singspiel* could draw large audiences. "It is completely certain," Vitzthum wrote:

that the local public, as in other great cities, greets the performance of German *Singspiel* with great applause, and on the average attends them more often than the performances of the reciting drama. All of the larger stages and most of the smaller ones [in Germany] have acceded to the wishes of the public and combined the drama with a German opera. The Dresden public has already enjoyed this pleasure in a small way through the opera performances of Joseph Seconda's drama company at the Linkesche Bad. That these *Singspiele* drew great crowds of people, despite their defective nature, clearly shows the great popularity of this type of performance.[64]

The order from the king came on 18 April 1816:

> In consideration of the rise of the deficit, we consider the suggestions that you have made in reference to combining the reciting drama with a good German opera to be quite suitable, and we await your next suggestions concerning how the preparation and performances of such an opera might take place.[65]

Weber was invited to head the company and, later in 1816, he accepted. His first performance as head of the German opera in Dresden, Méhul's *Joseph*, took place on 30 January 1817.[66]

Weber's subsequent importance for the development of German opera makes it difficult not to overestimate the significance of this event. It is good to remember that German vernacular opera had been performed in Dresden since the 1770s, and that Weber's company, like many other German opera companies of the period, was very dependent on foreign works. Vitzthum's invitation to Weber was less of an ideological statement than an effort to shore up the shaky economic foundations of the *Hoftheater*. It is important to remember that the very term "German opera company" is more of a convenient abbreviation than an accurate description of the men and women that Weber led in Dresden. Weber did not develop a completely independent organization, in opposition to the existing Italian opera. Contemporaries spoke not of a "German opera company" but of a "German department" or a "German institution." The *Tagebuch des Königl. Sächs. Hoftheaters,* printed in 1818 for the new year 1819, begins with a list of personnel that makes the sometimes confusing organizational structure of the *Hoftheater* more clear.[67] The Italian and German "companies," as well as the *Schauspiel,* are considered as part of one organization, under the direction of Count Carl von Vitzthum. As the senior *Kapellmeister,* Morlacchi is mentioned next, followed by Weber as *Kapellmeister des deutschen Theaters*. The *Tagebuch* next mentions Franz Anton Schubert, *Kirchenkompositeur*, indicating the continued importance of music for the *Katholische Hofkirche*. Although the position of *Musikdirektor* was vacant in 1818, it existed theoretically as a kind of "assistant *Kapellmeister*." The king first hired Weber as *Musikdirektor* (see below), and this was the position that Heinrich Marschner held during the period from late 1823 until 1826.[68] The list of personnel in the *Tagebuch* continues with Friedrich Hellwig, as regisseur of both the German opera and the German *Schauspiel*, followed by Luigi Bassi as regisseur of the Italian opera (Bassi was also one of Morlacchi's more important singers). Winkler appears here as *Theater-Sekretär* for both theaters. The register includes prompters, court painters, and so forth and is completed by a list of the singers and actors.

The position of men such as Winkler and Hellwig, holding posts in two or more "departments" of the *Hoftheater*, hints at the large amount of cross-fertilization between the Italians and the Germans, an aspect of Dresden operatic history that was often obscured by late-nineteenth- and early-twentieth-century scholars intent on developing the idea of national conflict (see below).[69] Weber was often compelled to direct rehearsals or performances of the "rival" company, and many of the most important singers at the German opera, such as Friedericke Funk and Charlotte Veltheim, also sang successfully with the Italian troupe. Fewer Italian singers performed at the German opera, but the practice was not unknown. The court also demanded a large amount of "festival music" for the Saxon court—a cantata for the marriage of a Saxon princess or special music for the fiftieth jubilee of King Friedrich Augustus—for which the resources of both companies were used.

But despite the fact that both companies were ultimately dependent on the same government support, Weber and Morlacchi jealously guarded their own prerogatives and often competed fiercely with each other. The first of many struggles between the two men broke out soon after Weber arrived in the city. Weber was at first unaware that his title of *Musikdirektor* ranked below Morlacchi's position as *Königliche Kapellmeister*. Warrack describes Weber's response when he discovered his lower status:

> from him [the bass Luigi Bassi] Weber learned, on 16th January, the truth about his appointment. Vitzthum confirmed the situation, whereupon Weber presented his resignation on the point of principle that a German appointment should not rank as inferior. Vitzthum took the matter to the

King, and, to Morlacchi's chagrin, was after the success of *Joseph* able to achieve equal status as *Königlich Kapellmeister* for his protégé.[70]

The triviality of this squabble masks the deeper significance of the conflict between the two companies, for Weber's and Vitzthum's successful efforts to establish German opera in the middle of the city on an equal footing with Morlacchi's company were revolutionary in terms of the eighteenth- and early-nineteenth-century genre hierarchy. A conflict over theater space reveals how closely the struggle between the two companies was rooted in the ancien régime. Morlacchi, it appears, was reluctant to accept the German opera as a coequal company and hoped that the German opera would perform only at the Linkesche Bad Theater. The centrally located Morettische Haus could then be reserved for the Italian opera, thus preserving the social and geographical distinctions of the eighteenth century. Weber's company would be little more than the successor to Seconda's troupe. That Morlacchi's attempt to exile Weber's company to the suburbs failed shows that the eighteenth-century constellation of genre, language, and social class was beginning to come unraveled.

Morlacchi's repertoire shows that the Italian opera in Dresden was by no means "*exclusiv-höfisch*," but it is nevertheless clear that his company remained firmly rooted in the operatic traditions of the eighteenth century.[71] The *Kapellmeister* did little to temper the exclusively Italian nature of his troupe. Throughout his tenure in Dresden, Morlacchi took frequent trips to Italy in order to conduct his operas and to absorb the latest musical styles of his native land. Morlacchi was slow to learn German (in 1813 Hoffmann described him as "knowing as much German as I know Chinese"), if indeed he ever mastered the language at all. Italian remained not only the performance language of the Italian opera, but also its daily language of social intercourse. When one of Morlacchi's principal singers, Madame Sandrini, was asked to sing a role in Weber's company, it was discovered that she did not know any German, even though she had been working in German theaters for nine years. Madame Sandrini was compelled to sing her part in Italian.[72] For Morlacchi and his company, Italy remained the homeland of music, just as it had been in the eighteenth century. When the German soprano Friedericke Funk was hired to sing at the Italian opera, she was sent to Italy (at the expense of the government!) to learn Italian diction and vocal technique.[73] The genre of Italian opera remained quite popular in Dresden, but the language and traditions of Morlacchi's company tended to isolate it from a local society that was becoming increasingly conscious of its national identity. Morlacchi seems to have been either unable or unwilling to foster contacts among the local cultural elite, and in the competition for financial and artistic resources he was almost completely dependent on a few connections at court. Morlacchi's isolation became more pronounced during the 1820s, but it was already apparent in the immediate postwar years.

Weber's position in Dresden was of course quite different. The personal contacts that he cultivated amongst the *Bildungsbürgertum* of the city helped to ensure support for his work in the local press and in wider cultural establishment. Weber's visibility and influence also grew tremendously after the wildly successful Berlin premiere of *Der Freischütz* in 1821. But Weber's personal popularity was ultimately less important for the success of his company than the ideological affinity between the new German opera and the emerging *Mittelstände*. Weber appealed to this group by undermining the genre hierarchy that had exiled them to the fringes of operatic culture during the eighteenth century. He brought bourgeois opera into the center of the city at the same time as the *Mittelstände* were asserting themselves as the center of a new community. Politics and aesthetics commingled, and the opera became a many-faceted stage upon which the social transformation from a courtly, aristocratic culture to an aristocratic, bourgeois culture was played out.

Of course, the traditions of the eighteenth century did not suddenly disappear. Weber's German opera occupied a strangely transitional situation: the voice of the *Bildungsbürgertum,* still dependent on the court society centered around a king, struggling to present a new type of national opera without being able to clearly articulate what that opera should be. Indeed, Weber's choice of repertoire during his first years as head of the new German opera company in Dresden seems determined at least as much by practical considerations as by ideology—the abilities of his singers and the meagerness of the resources dedicated to his company largely restricted him to simple, easily produced works. Weber's repertoire during this period falls almost exclusively into two broad categories. First, as we might expect, Weber performed operas by German composers, particularly works such as Weigl's *Die Schweizerfamilie,* Peter von Winter's *Das unterbrochene Opferfest,* and Mozart's *Zauberflöte* that in some ways approached the more "elevated" musical style of the *opera seria*. But another group of operas formed, at least at the beginning of Weber's tenure in Dresden, an even more significant part of the repertoire: translated *opéra comique*. Each of these two types of operas satisfied some of the ideological demands of the search for a German opera in different ways and left others unfulfilled. In the following pages I will use two operas, *Das unterbrochene Opferfest* and Etienne Méhul's *Joseph,* as representative examples of these two fundamental elements of Weber's early repertoire. They served, I will maintain, as incomplete models for the new German operatic genre that Weber attempted to create, first in *Freischütz* and then in *Euryanthe.*

2 The Native and the Foreign: Models for the German Opera

Defining German Opera

Late-nineteenth- and early-twentieth-century historians of German opera often characterize Weber's move to Dresden as a turning point in the history of the genre, but in 1817 it was not entirely clear what "German opera" meant. Was it simply that operas in Weber's new company would be performed in German, or did the idea of a German opera imply some qualitative distinction from the predominantly Italian repertoire of Morlacchi's company? Would the new company specialize in some particular type of opera, or would it present a broad variety of works? Long before *Freischütz* and *Euryanthe*, Weber was faced by the problem of defining a German operatic genre, and if these two operas represent his compositional responses to this problem, they are rooted in the repertoire choices that Weber was making in his role as a Dresden *Kapellmeister*. Naturally, these choices were conditioned by all sorts of factors outside of Weber's control. Nevertheless, the operas that he conducted during this period served as important models of what a German opera should (and should not) be.

I have chosen *Das unterbrochene Opferfest* and *Joseph* as "model" works for the German opera first because of the way that they represent the two types of opera that made up the overwhelming bulk of Weber's repertoire in Dresden: German-language dialogue operas and translated *opéra comique*. Second, despite his preference for "authenticity," Weber presented *Das unterbrochene Opferfest* and *Joseph* in versions that differed in significant ways from the original scores of Winter and Méhul. By looking more closely at these changes we gain insight into what "German opera" meant to critics, composers, and audiences of the early nineteenth century. Third, I have chosen these works for the ways in which they illuminate two topics central to early-nineteenth-century understanding of operatic genre: first, the topic of performance language and second, the issue of subject matter or dramatic content.

That Weber's company should perform its repertoire in German was self-evident; less clear were the social and musical relationships that the vernacular implied. The relatively strong associations between performance language and operatic genre that had characterized most eighteenth-century works were now being broken down. In many German cities, operas were performed in both Italian and German, but some theaters, particularly in the north and west, also put on French-language performances. The *Allgemeine musikalische Zeitung*, for instance, reports French opera performances in Schwerin (Mecklenburg) in 1800 and devotes a short article to the French opera in Braunschweig.[1] French-language opera performances also took place in Hamburg and Bern.[2] As we might expect, French was more prevalent as a performance language in those parts of Germany that were under the control of Napoleon. There was, for instance, a French opera-ballet in Dresden during part of the time the city was under direct Napoleonic occupation (Hoffmann mentions this company in some of his letters from 1813).[3] But despite these French influences, Italian must have remained for many Germans of this period a badge of urbane sophistication, the language of art and culture. The language associations of the high baroque were particularly strong in cities such as Dresden that had had flourishing traditions of Italian opera. By continuing a tradition of operatic performances in Italian, Dresdeners could reaffirm their connection to the splendor and glory of the mid-eighteenth-century *opera seria*.

Performance language also implied certain ideas about the relationship between text and music: Italian operas, of course, employed recitatives, whereas German operatic forms used dialogue.[4] For many late-eighteenth- and early-nineteenth-century writers, the divisions between Italian and German musico-dramatic forms were far more important than the divisions between German types such as *Schauspiel* and *Singspiel*. Many German plays from this period called for songs, marches, or other incidental music; often these were substantial enough to make them in some sense "music dramas." On the other hand dialogues in "German opera" during this period were sometimes quite extensive. When critics wrote about these operas they tended to refer to them as a spoken drama with added music. The librettist was almost always mentioned first, even as late as the 1820s and 1830s. In their discussion of Italian opera, by contrast, the composer assumes priority. A report on operatic performances in Dresden from the *Allgemeine musikalische Zeitung*, dated 31 March 1823, may serve as a typical example:

> During the period from January until April the following new operas
> were given: *Jery und Bäthely* (3 times), an opera in one act by Goethe,

with music by Reichardt . . . *Die Bürgschaft* (2 times), a drama in two
acts, after Schiller's Ballade, put to music by Herr Mayer . . . [and] *Abu
Hassan* (2 times)[,] an opera in one act by Hiemer, with music by Herr
Kapellmeister von Weber. . . . At the Italian opera only [the following]
were new: the long-promised opera by Herr Rastrelli, *Welleda* (4 times);
the text from Kotzebue's play *Die Kluge Frau im Walde.*[5]

This emphasis on the operatic text makes perfect sense when we remember the extent to which early-nineteenth-century writers defined "Germany" as a *Sprachraum* (language space) rather than as a political or cultural entity.

The existence of many bilingual librettos for Italian operas, with the
original Italian text and a German translation on facing pages, seems to imply that a large proportion of early-nineteenth-century opera audiences had
difficulty understanding Italian. In these circumstances, it makes sense that
their attention would be drawn to the music of the opera rather than its
libretto, and that Rastrelli should be seen as the primary creator of *Welleda*
and not Kotzebue (or the unnamed writer who adapted Kotzebue's original
play into an opera libretto). Yet this relatively simple distinction in the way
in which critics referred to Italian and German works also intersected with
one of their principal complaints against Italian opera: its inattention to the
dramatic meaning of the text.

If the traditional connections between performance language and operatic form were being contested in early-nineteenth-century Germany, the
associations between performance language and subject matter or dramatic
content were even more tenuous.[6] The plots of late-eighteenth-century German *Singspiele* and related forms of music drama come from a large variety
of different sources. Fantastic or magical plot devices were popular (during the late 1790s librettos developed from Shakespeare's *The Tempest* were
particularly in vogue), but many *Singspiele* used domestic plots similar to
eighteenth-century *opera buffa.*[7] *Große Oper* (which before the advent of
French *grand opéra* we may roughly translate as "serious opera") was theoretically characterized by more exalted plot subjects. The dramatic material
of this more serious genre was discussed by an anonymous critic in 1800, in
an article for the *Allgemeine musikalische Zeitung* entitled "Welches Stoff ist
der beste Stoff zu einer großen Oper?":

> Because of its elevated musical declamation, the *große Oper* is a drama
> that is completely separated from our everyday surroundings. Its dra-
> matic material must therefore not lie too near to us, so that the contrast

between this thoroughly poetic world and our prosaic existence is not diminished. . . . The dramatic material of a *große Oper* is customarily taken from ancient or modern history.[8]

During the first decades of the nineteenth century, these customary associations between operatic genre and dramatic material became increasingly out of date. "Vernacular" genres such as the *Singspiel* or the *opéra comique* began to the same kind of "grand" historical material that had once been the exclusive purview of *opera seria*. The dramatic material of both *Das unterbrochene Opferfest* and *Joseph,* for instance, is "taken from ancient or modern history" and has little to do with the bourgeois, domestic world of the eighteenth-century *opera buffa*. In sum, we may say that all the criteria through which music drama was traditionally classified—performance language, the relationship between text and music, dramatic material, and so forth—were becoming less clear as the dramaturgy and musical styles of "high" and "low" forms increasingly penetrated each other.

In an article entitled "Übersicht der verscheidenen wesentlichen Gattungen des musikalischen Drama" (*Berliner allgemeine musikalische Zeitung* 5) the early-nineteenth-century critic and theorist A. B. Marx attempted to summarize this critical discourse and to create a more universal system of genre classification.[9] His work may be seen, at least in part, as a way to preserve the traditional genre classifications and adapt them to the new conditions of early-nineteenth-century opera. Marx makes distinctions between the various forms of music and drama along a variety of axes, using criteria such as musical form, text, language, and subject matter. His scheme is complex, but it tends to group operatic forms into a "genre continuum" stretching from what we might call "high art" to "popular art" (these are my terms, not Marx's). At one end of the spectrum is "serious opera": Italian *opera seria* and later French *grand opéra*. *Opera semiseria,* with its mixing of musical styles and tragic and comic characters, occupies an intermediate position, as would the more complex *Singspiel* and *opéra comique*. At the "lowest" end of the spectrum are simpler *Singspiel* and vaudevilles, together with the *Zauberspiel* and *Liederposse*.

In the first installment of his article, Marx classifies operatic music according to its dramatic function. Music, Marx writes, can have two purposes in drama, serving the actors as "actual speech" (as in the recitatives of serious opera) or appearing as it does in life ("wirkliche Lebenserscheinung"), in the form of dances, marches, songs, and so forth.[10] Using this distinction Marx classifies musico-dramatic genres into many types:

1. Opera
2. Dramas with occasional music (such as in Shakespeare or in *Jungfrau von Orleans*)
3. "Older melodramas" (such as Benda's *Medea*)
4. Dramas with choruses
5. Dramas with choruses and occasional music
6. "Newer melodramas"[11]

Here Marx is principally concerned with the function that music has within a drama. In his scheme there is no absolute division between opera and spoken drama; there are only various theatrical forms that use music in different ways.

The second installment of Marx's article focuses on opera, beginning with a brief review of Algarotti's distinctions between the different operatic genres.[12] Algarotti, Marx writes, essentially divided opera into tragic and comic genres, a distinction that Marx feels is not satisfactory. Marx substitutes a more nuanced scheme, which classifies opera (1) according to the *Fabel* (i.e., the subject matter, mythological, historical, etc.), (2) according to the comportment of the characters (i.e., heroic, idyllic, etc.), and (3) according to the dramatic content of the work (i.e., heroic-comic, comic-romantic, heroic, tragic, etc.). Marx does not think very highly of all the mixed appellations that are applied to opera and hopes that in the future opera will free itself from this deforming mixing of different genres, modeling itself instead on the work of Shakespeare or Goethe. But for the present, Marx continues, musical drama is divided into many genres, which he places along a continuum stretching from more "elevated" forms of opera to more "popular" types of musico-dramatic entertainment. Simplifying Marx's argument, I have summarized the opposing terms of his genre classification in table 2.1.[13]

Genre in Operatic Practice

Of course, Marx's discussion is an abstraction: the divisions between various musico-dramatic forms were in reality far less clear. Indeed, the prominence of genre in the critical discourse of the late eighteenth and early nineteenth centuries may itself be read as evidence that traditional classifications and relationships were breaking down. The need to clarify genre divisions becomes most pressing, it may be argued, precisely when these divisions are being challenged and disturbed. One of the most interesting de-

Table 2.1   Opposing Terms in A. B. Marx's Genre Classification

Elevated	Popular
Serious	Comic
Music very important	Music less important
Complex musical forms	Simple musical forms
Recitative	Spoken dialogue
Classical subject matter	Folklike subject matter
Singers	Actors
Present-day Italian opera	Present-day German opera
The German opera of the future	

velopments during this period is the increasing popularity of those types of works that incorporated elements from *both* the "high" and "low" ends of the genre continuum: more sophisticated *Singspiele* such as *Die Zauberflöte* as well as the *opere semiserie* of composers such as Paer and Mayr. Late-eighteenth- and early-nineteenth-century composers tended to work all along the continuum of language and genre, writing in Italian or German and changing their musical style to suit the demands of the work with which they were engaged.[14] Weber himself, despite his reputation as an opponent of Italian music, composed music to Italian texts, including the cantata *L'accoglienza* (*Die Begrüßung*), written for the marriage of Princess Marianne of Saxony in the fall of 1817. Carl Reissiger, who succeeded Weber as the head of the German opera in 1828, had even more striking connections to the musical traditions of the eighteenth century: he wrote a *Didone abbandonata* to a Metastasio text which was performed at the German opera early in 1824.[15]

Kapellmeisters and opera directors also felt free to alter particular works in order to make them appropriate to new genre spaces. Mozart's *Don Giovanni*, for instance, was translated into German soon after its premiere, and during the early years of the nineteenth century Hoffmann and other music critics claimed it as a central part of the German heritage. The opera was an important part of the repertoire at many German opera companies, including the German opera in Dresden. But when it was translated into German, its musical form was altered as well as its language, for the recitatives were given as spoken dialogue. *Don Juan* retained the musico-dramatic form of the *Singspiel* until the 1840s, when its recitatives were finally translated into German.[16] The eighteenth-century custom of performance flexibility whereby operas and dramas were cut, new arias or scenes were inserted, and dialogue was eliminated, revised, or translated persisted well into the nineteenth century. Indeed, for many of the music dramas of this period, particularly at the more "popular" end of the genre continuum, the performance version of a particular piece had less to do with the composer and librettist's original conception of the work and far more to do with the particular circumstances in which it was performed.

The alterations that changed *Don Giovanni* into a *Singspiel* may have been motivated primarily by the desire to make the work more accessible to a German-speaking audience. But the same process of translation and transformation sometimes worked in the opposite direction, "elevating" dialogue operas into recitative operas and translating their German text into Italian. In the late eighteenth and early nineteenth centuries, for instance, the Italian opera in Dresden adopted popular German-language works such as Weigl's *Die Schweizerfamilie* into its repertoire, but translated the operas into Italian and added recitatives to replace the German prose dialogue sections so that they took on the form of more "serious" or "elevated" works. The language of the work and its musical form were transformed to make it appropriate to its new position on the genre continuum.[17]

The curious phenomenon of German operas being reworked into Italian operas and performed for a German-speaking audience symbolizes the transitional nature of early-nineteenth-century operatic life. German opera companies during this period were forced to rely on translations of foreign works in part simply because there were so few German-language operas, but Italian opera companies obviously did not have this problem. That works such as *Die Schweizerfamilie* could find a place in their repertoire testifies to the increasing popularity and significance of German opera during this period. The translation and transformation of these operas into Italian, on the other hand, embodies the persistence of the ancien régime. The operatic traditions of the eighteenth century—the use of the Italian language, the patterns of recitative and aria, and so forth—had powerful momentum, and Italian companies such as the one in Dresden headed by Weber's rival, Morlacchi, no doubt found it easier to perform Weigl's opera as *La famiglia svizzera* then as *Die Schweizerfamilie*. But the patterns of the Italian opera also fulfilled the expectations German audiences, particularly in *Residenzstädte* such as Dresden. In these cities the language and structure of *Singspiel* or even of the more ambitious *heroisch-komische* operas still exiled them to the suburbs, despite their growing popularity.[18]

Operatic Style in Winter's *Das unterbrochene Opferfest*

One of the best examples of this type of genre transformation is Peter von Winter's *heroisch-komische Oper Das unterbrochene Opferfest,* one of the most popular works in Germany during the early part of the nineteenth century. The opera had its premiere at Vienna's Kärntnertortheater on 14 June 1796 and traveled quickly to most of the major German-language opera houses, including Berlin (1 March 1797), Munich (19 August 1797), and Hamburg (1 September 1797), where it was performed in a four-act version with a libretto revised by C. A. Vulpius.[19] In 1798 *Das unterbrochene Opferfest* premiered in Dresden. But here the opera was translated and transformed into Italian as *Il sacrificio interotto.* Recitatives were added to replace the dialogues, certain musical numbers were cut and others were added, while still others were revised and transformed. The Dresden performance appears to have been the premiere of this Italian version of the opera, which also found its way to other cities, including Florence (1818).[20] Roughly a decade after its premiere (perhaps in 1811), the opera was again produced in Dresden in its original language, but in a revised version, purged of its comic characters. It is this *heroisch-tragische* version of the opera that Weber used in his performances of *Das unterbrochene Opferfest* during his tenure in Dresden.[21] Winter's original score was thus molded into two strikingly different versions, one resembling the *opere semiserie* that were popular with contemporary Italian composers such as Paer and Mayr, and the other adumbrating, in many ways, the "new German opera" that composers such as Weber hoped to create.

As with many other operas, the plot material of *Das unterbrochene Opferfest* has a long prehistory. It is set in sixteenth-century Peru, during the Spanish conquest of the Incan Empire. The original source for the story, surprisingly enough, may be found in the writings of the Jesuit reformer Las Casas. Las Casas's criticism of the conquistadors found new life in Jean François Marmontel's novel *Les Incas* (1778). Las Casas himself actually appears as a character in the book, which is an attack on the fanaticism, avarice, and intolerance that supposedly motivated Pizarro and his followers.[22] Immensely popular in Germany, Marmontel's work inspired a host of plays and *Singspiele,* including a *Cora,* a *Singspiel* by Naumann (Leipzig, 1781), and *Kora und Alonzo* by von Babe, a "Drama mit Musik vermischt" (Regensburg, 1781).[23] The most influential adaptation of Marmontel's novel was probably the play *Die Sonnenjungfrau* by the prolific August von Kotzebue (Reval,

1789).[24] It was Kotzebue's play that served as the immediate source for the libretto of *Das unterbrochene Opferfest*, which is by the playwright and novelist Franz Xaver Huber.[25] A fuller discussion of the plot, which takes place in ancient Peru, may be found in appendix 1.[26] For the purposes of the following discussion, it will be enough to divide the characters into three types —virtuous, evil, and comic—and outline their relationships to each other.

Winter differentiates the various categories of characters from each other not only by what Marx might call their dramatic comportment, but also by musical style, a practice that closely resembles that which Mozart employs in *Die Zauberflöte* and *Die Entführung aus dem Serail*. The comic characters sing in what we might loosely call a *buffa* style. For their arias and duets Winter uses a variety of different formal patterns, most of which involve a modulation to the dominant and the short, contrasting sections in more distantly related keys. All of the comic numbers are in major keys and most of them use fast tempos. The syllabic text declamation, short phrases, and relatively limited vocal range of this music is well adapted to the singer-actors who populated the *Singspiel* stages of the late eighteenth and early nineteenth centuries. The most important of the comic characters, and the center of the comic subplot, is Murney's servant Pedrillo. Pedrillo is closely related to many other similar figures in eighteenth-century opera (Huber may have even taken his name from the Pedrillo in *Die Entführung aus dem Serail*). Like Leporello, he often mocks the aristocratic values of the *seria* characters, and like Papageno, he incarnates the base desires that stand in opposition to those of his betters. Pedrillo's first-act aria "Man rückt in grösser Eile," the first music that he sings in the opera, provides a good example of Winter's comic style. The aria comes immediately after the first tableau, in which the *seria* characters and the chorus give their reactions to the hero's great victory over the enemies of the Inca. The second tableau is quite literally a different world: the ceremonial palace of the Inca is replaced by a "meadow with a view." Pedrillo enters and in his aria (no. 5) gives his own far more colorful version of the battle, telling us how he saved his life by fleeing the field.

Within the context of this opera, the music for the evil characters stands at the opposite end of the spectrum from the cheerful arias and duets of the comic characters. Their idiom is far more dramatic, with rapid changes in volume and shifts in range. Often their arias are quite complex, with subsections in contrasting tempos and keys. Mafferu's C-minor aria (no. 8) "Allmächt'ge Sonne, höre der Rache grössten Eid!" is a good example of this type of number. In contrast to Pedrillo's aria, "Allmächt'ge Sonne, höre der

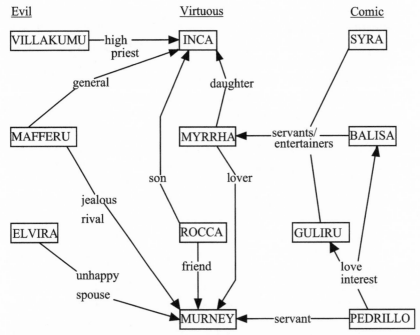

Evil   Virtuous   Comic

Note: For the sake of clarity I have adopted the most common German spellings of the characters in *Das unterbrochene Opferfest* (i.e., "Myrrha" instead of "Mirha," "Mira," or "Mirrha," and "Elvira" instead of "Elwira"). I have also chosen a single spelling of the Italian title of the work, which by no means corresponds to all of the Italian language scores. The numberings of the individual pieces are also those of the early German sources.

    Villakumu does not fit easily into any of the categories I have proposed. His music is primarily ceremonial, rather than the *kraftvolle* or *laüfige* styles of Mafferu and Elvira.

Figure 2.1   **Characters in *Das unterbrochene Opferfest***

Rache grössten Eid!" is "active" rather than narrative—Mafferu is not describing events but rather experiencing them. These events are internal rather than external—driven by jealousy, Mafferu seeks and eventually finds a way to revenge himself on Murney. Winter depicts this process of discovery in a musical style that is far more complex than that which he uses for the comic characters. The arias of Mafferu and Pedrillo thus represent the opposing poles of Winter's operatic practice. If in the music for the comic characters motivic and harmonic relationships tend to play an external and descriptive role, in the arias of the evil characters they work to intensify internal, psychological meanings of the text. The contrast between the vocal style of the evil and the comic characters is even more striking. Pedrillo and his cohorts combine square-cut *Volkstümlichkeit* with the *zärtliche* ("tender") style, whereas the idiom of the evil characters is the exact opposite, a combination of what German critics might call the *läufige* and *kraftvolle* styles, characterized by large leaps and spectacular scalar passages.[27] Mafferu's mighty leaps and coloratura descent from a high F to a low F-sharp near the end of his aria, for instance, have no counterpart in the music of the comic characters. Only Elvira, the jealous rival for the hero's love, partakes of this highly dramatic musical style. It was no doubt the flamboyant "rage coloratura" of Elvira's first-act aria "Süss sind der Rache Freuden" that prompted Winton Dean to characterize Winter's sopranos as "embryo Queens of the Night with a tendency to fire rockets into the stratosphere on the slightest provocation."[28]

The musical style of the virtuous characters, by contrast, employs the complete stylistic vocabulary of late-eighteenth-century opera. On one hand, Murney and Myrrha often sing like *opera seria* characters, dominating the stage with vocal pyrotechnics. In the finale to the first act, for instance, Myrrha soars above the chorus and the other principals with coloratura which approaches Elvira's displays earlier in the act. The coloratura of these types of passages obviously has different connotations from that of Elvira's rage aria—here coloratura is the ornament of the prima donna rather than a symbol of anger. Myrrha sings the highest, most ornamented part because she, rather than Elvira, is the center of dramatic attention. Murney's part is not so richly endowed with coloratura, but it shows a level of musical complexity that goes far beyond that of the other characters in the opera. The showpiece of the role, and the longest aria in the opera, takes place in the second act as Murney is languishing in prison, awaiting his death. Although it is somewhat longer than Mafferu's "Allmächt'ge Sonne, höre," Murney's aria ("Mir graut vor dem Tode nicht") follows essentially the same form, a structure that is closely related to Mozart's two-part *rondòs* and similar to some of the large-scale arias in *Freischütz* and *Euryanthe*. The dramatic situation—a tenor in prison anticipating death—also finds direct parallels in operas such as Le Sueur's *Ossian* or the "conjugal love" operas such as *Fidelio* or Mayr's *L'amor coniugale*.

But if "Mir graut vor dem Tode nicht" links Murney with serious characters both within *Das unterbrochene Opferfest* and in other late-eighteenth- and early-nineteenth-century operas, both he and Myrrha also sing in a more *volkstümlich* style, similar in many ways to that of the comic characters. The direct, square-cut idiom of these numbers is reminiscent of the duet between Pamina and Papageno in *Die Zauberflöte*, or of the strophic lieder of Reichardt and Zelter. This musical style is most clearly seen in

Myrrha's first-act aria (no. 9), "Ich war, wenn ich erwachte." Here Myrrha contrasts her present emotional state, disturbed by her awakening love for Murney, with her daily life before she met the hero. The simple arpeggiated accompaniment, syllabic text setting, regular phrase structure, and predominantly tonic and dominant harmonies reflect Myrrha's lost innocence. The *Volkstümlichkeit* of the aria is further heightened by its placement in the score: right after the rage aria of Mafferu and shortly before Elvira's "Süss sind der Rache Freuden." But just as in the contrasting coloratura passages of Myrrha and Elvira, the dramatic implications of this musical style are different here. The *Volkstümlichkeit* of the hero and heroine is not comic but "sentimental" in the Schillerian sense of the term, recalling simplicity rather than enacting it, and the "purity" of their musical style signifies virtue rather than naïveté.

From *Das unterbrochene Opferfest* to *Il sacrifizio interotto*

Apart from its implications for the drama, the music for Murney and Myrrha, with connections to the style of both the comic and evil characters, reflects the diverse heritage of turn-of-the-century German opera. This heterogeneity of musical styles is certainly not unique to *Das unterbrochene Opferfest*—it is a defining characteristic of late-eighteenth- and early-nineteenth-century German opera.[29] This diversity also reflects the institutional position of German opera companies during this period, which had to be "fluent" in a wide variety of musical idioms. Weber's letter of 22 May 1817 to the intendant Count Vitzthum, "An attempt to express in tabular form the organization of a German opera company in Dresden," is quite interesting in this regard. Pleading for more substantial funding, Weber wrote: "Both Italian and French opera have their recognized vocal types and dramatic figures, in *opera seria* and *opera buffa*. When it comes to a German opera company, however, these different types have to be combined, seeing that Italian and French opera are given in translation, and the singers for the characters proper to German opera have also to be found."[30]

An opera such as *Das unterbrochene Opferfest* would require each of the "recognized vocal types and dramatic figures" all by itself. And yet the strategy of combining different musical idioms within one opera was not exclusively German. It may also be found in abundance in the *opere semiserie* of Paer, Simone Mayr, and other turn-of-the-century composers of Italian opera. The transformation of the *heroisch-komische Oper Das unterbrochene Opferfest* into the *opera semiseria Il sacrifizio interotto* thus seems in many ways a natural development. But this transformation actually involved many important changes, which include but are certainly not limited to the translation of the libretto.[31] The changes to the score may be divided into three categories: (1) genre modifications: the translation of aria and ensemble texts and the substitution of recitatives for German dialogue sections, (2) the structural modification of individual numbers, namely Murney's second-act aria, and (3) other cuts and additions.

Genre Modifications

Although the translation of the opera from German into Italian is the most obvious modification of *Das unterbrochene Opferfest*, it is in many ways least disruptive of the musical fabric. Many of the German texts were written in iambic trimeter, a metric pattern that was easily Italianized into the common *verso settenario* used in many Italian librettos from this period. A comparison between the German and Italian versions of the first stanza of Villakumu's aria (no. 2) shows how this "metrical transfer" might take place:

Wenn Sieges Lieder tönen	Negl'Inni trionfali
den Sieger Palmen krönen	del popolo festoso
nennt man auch Murneys Namen	il nome del tuo sposo
in unsrer Helden Zahl.[32]	a celebrar s'udrà.[33]

As a direct translation of the meaning of the German text, this Italian version is obviously a failure. In the German original Villakumu directs his remarks to a general audience, whereas in the Italian he is speaking specifically to Elvira. But the translation perfectly preserves the pattern of stressed and unstressed syllables, making the text underlay of the Italian version appear completely natural.[34] The Italian version of the libretto is thus less of a translation than a "naturalization" of the text into conventional Italian metric patterns, a process made easier by the form of Huber's libretto.[35] The similarity of German verse forms to Italian models is obviously no accident. Huber was almost certainly quite familiar with Italian opera librettos, and it is probable that he based his metrical forms on Italian models. The translation of *Das unterbrochene Opferfest* into *Il sacrifizio interotto* could therefore almost be seen as a "retranslation" of a model back into the original. In any case, the priorities of the translator conform to the aesthetics of the *opera seria*, in which the meaning of the libretto is conveyed in the recitative and the euphony of the aria texts is more important than the precise meanings of individual words.

Structural Modifications to Murney's Aria

Although some of the revisions serve simply to clarify the plot, many more seem motivated by the desire to move Winter's score toward the conventional forms and musical idioms of Italian opera. These kinds of modifications may readily be seen in the Italian version of Murney's second act aria "Mir graut vor dem Tode nicht." The changes that the Italian composer-arranger of *Il sacrifizio interotto* made to this number merit particularly close scrutiny, for they form in many ways a microcosm of the entire German-to-Italian adaptation process. As we would expect, the entire scene is lengthened in the Italian version by the addition of a recitative, but for the most part the "Italianized" aria follows the same musical form as its German model. Indeed, for the first three sections of the aria the Italian and the German music is virtually the same, with only minor differences to facilitate the text declamation. It is in the final part of the aria (the C-major allegro agitato) that the two versions diverge most significantly. Here the Italian composer-arranger has modified certain details of texture, orchestration, and melody to make the formal divisions between the various subsections of the allegro (one could now almost call it a *cabaletta*) stand out more clearly. But the most striking difference between the final sections of the Italian and German versions of the aria lies in the character of the vocal line itself. This difference is the most significant in the section in which the "German" Murney sings "Der Geist zum sitz der Freuden." Here the Italian composer-arranger replaces the harmonic interest of the secondary dominant (V6/vi) in measure 99, as well as the striking leaps on the word "Unsterblichkeit," with a longer and more florid melody. The melismatic triplets and appoggiaturas leading up to the cadence in measure 104 of the Italian score form a particularly strong contrast with the more declamatory German vocal line. The strength of this tonic cadence in the Italian version (the corresponding cadence in the German version is on the dominant) helps make the next subsection sound more like a new beginning. The violin flourish in measure 104, repeated in measure 106, also helps give this subsection a separate character that is less marked in the German score. While "Mi tolga pur la vita" and "quel Popol ch'ho diffeso" (measures 105 through 108) are clearly related to "lass Peru mich verdammen" (measures 105 and

Example 2.1   German version of "Der Geist zum sitz der Freuden" from Murney's 2nd-act aria

106), the approach to the dramatic half-cadence on the dominant (measure 108 in the German and measure 110 in the Italian) is quite different in the two versions. Again, the German score is characterized by declamatory leaps, while the Italian version, doubling the continuo line, uses stepwise motion.

Throughout the allegro agitato, the Italian composer replaces many of the large leaps, which are so much a part of Winter's original idiom for the aria, with scalar passages. The declamatory, primarily syllabic text setting of the German becomes much more melismatic and florid in the Italian. The tessitura of the aria is also clearly higher in the Italian version. This upward shift is most conspicuous during the final cadential section of the aria, but

Example 2.2   Italian version of "Der Geist zum sitz der Freuden" from Murney's 2nd-act aria

the changes at the low end of the range are probably more significant. Only briefly does the vocal line of the Italian score dip below a G. The Italian composer-arranger modifies descending lines such as "lass Peru *mich verdammen*" so that they end on higher notes, and the entire section has a more ornate, virtuosic character.

One is tempted to see in these differences an early manifestation of those binary oppositions between the native and the foreign that were to preoccupy early-nineteenth-century critics and composers: between "organic unity" and sectionalization, between dramatic declamation of the text and "superficial, pleasing melody." But it is almost certain that the changes to the allegro agitato were driven far more by practical considerations than by ideology. The tenor who sang Murney in *Il sacrificio interotto*, for instance, may have found the big leaps in the German version (which probably required an awkward shift from the chest voice to the head voice and then back again) difficult to negotiate, or his low range may have been particularly weak. It is also clear that a practical and prolific *Kapellmeister* such as Winter would not have written the aria in such a dramatic and declamatory style unless he had a particular vocal style in his ear, or perhaps even a particular tenor voice. The changes to this aria remind us that movement along the genre continuum never took place in a vacuum, but rather was highly conditioned by local conditions and needs. The ideological distinctions between German and Italian that were to be so important in the search for a German opera developed in conjunction with differences in vocal style and probably differences in vocal training as well.[36] German and Italian singers sang in different ways; musical styles, and the ideologies that supported and defended these styles, emerged to a large degree out of the environment of practical music making.

Other Cuts and Additions

The changes to the second part of Murney's "Mir graut vor dem Tode nicht" provide a fascinating insight into stylistic differences between German and Italian opera, but the most striking additions to the original German score involve the insertion of two big arias for Myrrha, one in each act. The first of these, "Quelle pupille tenere," is a replacement for Myrrha's *volkstümlich* aria "Ich war, wenn ich erwachte." The aria is essentially a recomposed mélange of "Ich war, wenn ich erwachte," a shortened version of which forms the middle section of the aria, and the two outer sections of another "Quelle pupille tenere" from the *opera seria Gli Orazi e i Curiazi*

(1796) by Domenico Cimarosa.[37] That "Quelle pupille tenere" was exported from *Gli Orazi e i Curiazi* is hardly surprising—substitution and insertion of arias had been a part of *opera seria* performance tradition for a century or more. What makes the recomposed "Quelle pupille tenere" interesting is the way that it borrows music from both the *opera seria* and the *Singspiel*. The increasing fluidity of genre boundaries that characterizes operatic performance and composition around the turn of the century is here incorporated into a single work.

Myrrha's part is further enlarged by the addition of another aria in the second act, "Io sento già che l'alma." The aria appears immediately after Murney's "Mir graut vor dem Tode nicht," to which it forms a close counterpart. Myrrha visits Murney in his prison cell, and although the hero's fortitude and nobility prohibit him from trying to escape from his impending death, Myrrha knows that he can be saved. The vocal writing in this aria resembles that of Cimarosa's "Quelle pupille." Indeed, it seems likely that "Io sento già" is also largely borrowed from another late-eighteenth-century *opera seria*, although I have not yet been able to discover a source. Just as in the first-act aria, the vocal writing here is florid and melismatic, and the aria includes long cadenzas that are perhaps even more dazzling. Indeed, the thematic and harmonic content of the main body of the aria is so simple that the "center of gravity" is completely shifted to these long coloratura passages. These passages are particularly important in the second part of the aria, where they constitute nearly half of the music (forty-one out of ninety-nine measures). One fourteen-measure melisma in the middle part of the aria employs a range of more than two octaves, from a low G to a high B, and the penultimate cadenza is still more impressive. This long passage contains the most striking harmonic and melodic moment of the aria. This gesture begins with a florid chromatic ascent in triplets up to a high Bb, which is harmonized as part of a B VI chord. The voice line then leaps almost two octaves down to C-sharp, which forms part of an Italian augmented sixth chord, eventually resolving to I⁶⁄₄. The composer of "Io sento già" emphasizes this gesture through repetition, creating an effect that in certain performances must have bordered on the comic.

Like the outer sections of "Quelle pupille," "Io sento già che l'alma" employs what seems almost a parody of late-eighteenth-century Italian vocal style: florid, highly melismatic, and organized around an extremely straightforward harmonic structure. The Italian composer-arranger was not interested in integrating "Quelle pupille" and "Io sento già che l'alma" into the original characterization of Myrrha. Myrrha's *Volkstumlichkeit*, the childlike purity and innocence that are so important to her character in Winter's original score, are here overbalanced and enveloped by a completely different idiom. The "new" Myrrha takes on the lineaments of a true prima donna, an Italianate sister, perhaps, of Mozart's Queen of the Night. The virtuosic vocal lines and formal conventions of these two arias place them firmly in the *opera seria* tradition of the late eighteenth century, a tradition to which the original score of *Das unterbrochene Opferfest* bears only a tangential relationship.

The revisions to *Das unterbrochene Opferfest* not only transform Myrrha's role, but also radically alter the relationship between the various characters of the opera. In the German version Myrrha and Elvira have roughly the same amount of music to sing. Each has one aria, and if Myrrha also has a duet with Murney (no. 7), this is balanced by the extended solo passage for Elvira in the introduction. Furthermore, Elvira's solo aria is far longer and more vocally demanding than Myrrha's. Myrrha is the heroine, but it is not certain that she is the prima donna. One of the clearest effects of the Italian revisions to the score is to change this balance between the two sopranos, not only by adding an aria for Myrrha and by expanding her relatively unassuming "Ich war, wenn ich erwachte" into a grand aria, but by eliminating Elvira's showpiece in the first act. Without "Süss sind der Rache Freuden" Elvira is reduced to a supporting character, and "Io sento già che l'alma" is left as the real coloratura showpiece. Of course, Elvira's aria may have been eliminated for completely practical reasons—it was unlikely that the Italian opera in Dresden possessed two sopranos capable of the vocal pyrotechnics that this aria and the inserted arias for Myrrha demanded. Nevertheless, the hierarchy of prima donna and seconda donna is far more secure in the Italian version of the opera than in the German original. In *Il sacrifizio interotto*, Myrrha's position thus approaches that of an *opera seria* heroine or, better, of a *seria* character in the *opera semiseria* that *Das unterbrochene Opferfest* had now become. Although the revised opera does not perfectly conform to the conventions of *opera semiseria*, the modifications to the parts of Murney and Myrrha effectively change the character of the entire opera.

Das unterbrochene Opferfest as *heroisch-tragische Oper*

That the most extensive changes concern the parts of the hero and heroine is not surprising, for of all the characters in the opera, their musical identity is the most fluid. Encompassing both the *Volkstümlichkeit* of the

Liederspiel and the grandiose forms and musical gestures of the *opera seria*, their status in many ways parallels the condition of the early nineteenth-century audience, which partook of the old aristocratic world as well as the emerging bourgeois order. Without translation and revision, *Das unterbrochene Opferfest* was unsuitable to the courtly, aristocratic world of the Dresden Italian opera. But Winter's original score, curiously enough, also fit only uncomfortably with the emerging bourgeois aesthetic of new German-language opera companies. German conductors and impresarios subjected the opera to cuts and additions that were in many ways more drastic than those imposed by the Italians. These changes may be clearly seen in a series of librettos from Berlin that chronicles the evolution of performances in that city.[38] The earliest libretto, from 1805, presents a version of the opera virtually identical with the earliest printed scores. The first number appears divided as number 1 and number 2, and Myrrha's part includes an additional recitative and aria in the second act: "Daß er mich täglich liebt, von ihm zu hören / Ha! durch mich droht seinem Leben."[39] But by 1825 (probably before), another version of the opera was in use, in which the role of Pedrillo, together with his duets with the other comic characters, is completely excised. Weber's 1811 review of a Munich performance of the work shows that the similar versions (without some or all of the comic characters) were common in other German cities as well: "That the work was given as a completely serious opera, and the role of Pedrillo etc. completely eliminated was very agreeable to this reviewer, for although one lost a few very cute little pieces, the entire opera gained considerably in plot and unity."[40] Weber's comments are echoed by some remarks of E. T. A. Hoffmann regarding a 9 September 1815 performance of *Das unterbrochene Opferfest:* "It is well to mention first of all that the entire part of Pedrillo was cut out. This jokester runs panting alongside the entire opera without a single time being able to get into it. Many charming pieces that we sorely miss were eliminated along with him, but we rejoice over the increased roundness of the whole."[41] Performance materials bearing the date 24 September 1811 show that this *heroisch-tragische* version of *Das unterbrochene Opferfest* was also in use in Dresden during this period (for a comparison between this version and both the Italian and the earliest printed versions of the opera, see appendix 2, "Comparative Table").[42] Although the elimination of Pedrillo seems at first to be somewhat drastic gesture (after all, he sings two arias and two duets), a glance at Winter's score shows that this was actually a fairly easy cut to make. In the original version the comic and tragic characters inhabit different worlds and only rarely appear on the stage at the same time. Pedrillo's skirt chasing is in every sense a subplot and is absolutely unnecessary to the development of the main drama. In the original score of the opera there is only one short scene, immediately before Pedrillo's last aria in the second act, in which he appears on stage with any of the serious characters. Neither Pedrillo nor any of the comic characters play any part in the two finales. It would be hard, if not impossible, to imagine a *heroisch-tragische* version of *Die Zauberflöte,* stripped of its comic characters. If Papageno's yearning for Papagena is a subplot, it is also completely integrated into the drama of trial and initiation. The entertainment that Pedrillo gives, on the other hand, may provide necessary comic relief, but it plays no role in the development of the plot.

The transformation of *Das unterbrochene Opferfest* from a *heroisch-komische* into a *heroisch-tragische* opera represents a different type of elevation of the work than in the Italian sources, and in this guise *Das unterbrochene Opferfest* approximates German Romantic dialogue operas from the 1820s and 1830s such as *Der Freischütz* or *Der Templer und die Jüdin.* But although the comic numbers of *Das unterbrochene Opferfest* seem to have been largely eliminated from German productions of the work, they were by no means forgotten. Not only are they present in the numerous piano-vocal scores of the opera printed during the early and mid-century, but they also find their way into many of the piano-vocal or guitar-vocal songbooks that were such a large part of German musical life during this period.[43] The comic music of the opera was thus relegated to a different genre space, appropriate to the bourgeois home but no longer to the opera house. The reception of *Das unterbrochene Opferfest* in Germany thus curiously parallels the Zeno and Metastasio reforms of seventeenth-century Italian opera. Like these earlier reforms, it was a way to deal with the complicated heterogeneity of the musical work and separate the tragic and comic into different spheres. The exile of the comic characters from the opera stage to the *Musikzimmer* clearly makes *Das unterbrochene Opferfest* more stylistically homogeneous, and thus reflects the efforts of Hoffmann, Weber, Poissl, Spohr, and others to create a unified operatic style.

If the stylistic changes accomplished by the elimination of the comic characters brought the opera more into line with the bourgeois aesthetic of early-nineteenth-century German composers and critics, they also transformed the opera's ideological balance. In the *opere semiserie* of Paer and Mayr, as well as *Il sacrifizio interotto,* the central duality is that between tragic and comic characters. The operas themselves embody the polarity of *seria* and *buffa* that typified the genre hierarchy of the eighteenth century (see Marx's criticism of Algarotti, above). In Mozart's operas the class associations of this polarity become more pronounced: it has become a commonplace of *Don Giovanni* criticism to speak of Donna Anna, Donna Elvira, and Zerlina as representatives of the aristocracy, bourgeoisie, and peasantry, respectively. The German revision of *Das unterbrochene Opferfest* eliminates not only the comic characters but also the class differences that are so much a part of operas such as *Le nozze di Figaro* and *Die Zauberflöte* (and, we might add, *Il sacrifizio interotto*). In Winter's original version of the opera, as well as in the Italian revision, musical simplicity can signify both rustic naïveté, as in the arias of Pedrillo, or sentimental virtue, as in Myrrha's "Ich war, wenn ich erwachte." By eliminating the comic characters, *Volkstümlichkeit* becomes more clearly a symbol of goodness. The old contrasts between tragic and comic or between aristocrat and peasant begin to be replaced by a new duality between good and evil characters, a duality that looks forward to the world of *Der Freischütz* and *Euryanthe*. Eliminating comic characters from *Das unterbrochene Opferfest* thus clothed the opera in the ideological as well as the stylistic garments of the new German Romantic opera.

But despite these transformations, *Das unterbrochene Opferfest* could not be completely purged of its stylistic and ideological connections to an earlier age. The old implications of musical style were too firmly imbedded in the score. If, as I have argued, musical simplicity becomes the signifier of virtue in the revised *Opferfest*, then a certain musico-dramatic logic would imply coloratura as the symbol of evil. Up through the middle of the first act these dichotomies map onto each other quite well: the musical contrast between "Ich war, wenn ich erwachte" and "Süss sind der Rache Freuden" seems to embody the dramatic conflict of the opera. But in the first-act finale and many other ensembles, Myrrha and Elvira sing music that is often virtually identical. In these numbers Myrrha seems, if anything, even more addicted to coloratura than her evil counterpart. These stylistic gestures make sense within the dichotomy of *seria* and *buffa,* for both Elvira and Myrrha are aristocrats (therefore *seria* characters), but they transgress the moral dualities of the new bourgeois aesthetics.

Dresden Performance History

The use of the revised version of the opera in Dresden meant that for a short period audiences in the city could see two different versions of the opera: the *opera semiseria Il sacrifizio interotto* and the *heroisch-tragische* opera *Das unterbrochene Opferfest,* neither of which corresponded to Winter's original score. Some of the surviving instrumental parts in Dresden also suggest that other performances, combining elements from both the Italian and the German versions, also took place.[44]

Unfortunately there are no dates in these performing materials, but given Weber's preference for the *heroisch-tragische* version of the opera, we can put together a tentative performance history for *Das unterbrochene Opferfest* in Dresden. We know (from contemporary reports in the *Allgemeine musikalische Zeitung*) that the premiere of the opera in 1798 was in Italian, and that it was almost certainly the version of the opera preserved in the score I have labeled "Dresden Italian" in appendix 2. But German-language performances of the opera certainly took place soon thereafter, at the latest by 1811 (probably by Seconda's company). Many different versions of the opera were probably used, but it seems that performance practice moved gradually in the direction of the German-language materials described above. It seems almost certain that German-language performances were produced using the "Italian parts," until at some point all the cuts, the additions, the pasteovers, and the fold-downs simply became too complicated, and a new set of parts had to be written out, this time without any of the Italian modifications. Weber first produced *Das unterbrochene Opferfest* in Dresden, 25 November 1819, and the opera seems to have passed completely into the repertoire of the German opera after that date.[45] It could be that the conductor's score I describe as "Dresden German" was actually prepared for Weber's company. In any case, Weber's preference for the *heroisch-tragische* version of the score makes it likely that Pedrillo and his cohorts never found their way onto the stage of the new Dresden German opera.

Das unterbrochene Opferfest was an important part of the repertoire of the German opera during the early 1820s, but after Weber's death productions became less frequent. By this time the opera was a generation old, and in an age that placed such a high value on "organic unity," the heterogeneous, occasionally Italianate musical style and dialogue-opera structure of *Das unterbrochene Opferfest* played an ever-dwindling role in the repertoire. The opera enjoyed a brief return to the stage from 1844 to 1849, most likely due to the historicizing influence of Wagner. But ultimately *Das unterbrochene Opferfest* proved unsuited for revival. Gluck's and Mozart's works could claim a place in the new historicized repertoire of the mid-nineteenth century, for these composers were increasingly seen as the "heroes of German music," paving the way for the "triumphs of German art." Peter von Winter was for the most part excised from this illustrious genealogy, despite his popularity during the early decades of the century. His heterogeneous, occasionally awkward musical style may have been far more normative than inspired works such as *Die Zauberflöte* or *Fidelio*, but for this very reason he had to be left out of later histories of German opera.

Resistance and Emulation

If the stylistic heterogeneity of works such as *Das unterbrochene Opferfest* tended to undermine the sense of a particular musical identity for German opera in the late eighteenth and early nineteenth centuries, we can nevertheless speak about a group of tendencies or practices, characteristics of vocal style and musical form, that distinguished German operas from contemporary Italian and French works. German opera did have a distinct voice, despite its dependence on foreign models. Yet this relationship to the other became increasingly problematic during the first decades of the nineteenth century. On one hand Napoleon's conquest of Germany made the nation even more receptive to cultural influences from the west, and French opera became enormously popular. Numerous works were translated and adapted for German stages, and German opera composers adopted many aspects of French operatic style. But on the other hand, the War of Liberation and the national aspirations that it evoked aroused cultural opposition to the French and reanimated the search for a new, more genuinely German operatic style. The combination of resistance and emulation, so central to the relationship between German and foreign opera, became ever more volatile in the first decades of the nineteenth century, as nationalist critics and the new bourgeois opera audience of the post-Napoleonic period began to interpret the various distinctions of style and performance practice that we have examined in the previous chapter in light of their hopes for a new German nation. Yet ironically, it was precisely these hopes for a transformed and united Germany that found expression in the music of the former enemy, the French *opéra comique Joseph.*

It was in fact *Joseph*, rather than a "native" opera such as *Das unterbrochene Opferfest* or *Die Zauberflöte*, that Weber chose for his first production at the new German opera in Dresden. Weber's decision to mount a production of *Joseph* was largely dictated by practical considerations, some of which I will briefly touch upon below. But the opera achieved its great success, I will argue, because its music and drama so deeply resonated with the emotional needs of its audience, in particular, the yearning for a new national community, transformed and united by the bonds of love. The "shared moral virtues" of the *Mittelstand* found its voice in operas such as *Joseph*, through which the very idea of the nation could be re-envisioned. For these men and women, the opera could provide an idealized script for the moral regeneration of a community, a regeneration they hoped would be actualized in post-Napoleonic Germany. For despite the physical destruction wrought by the opposing armies, many intellectuals in Saxony and throughout Germany saw this period as a time of national renewal. The Napoleonic Wars were for them a kind of national purging, a clearing away the fractured vestiges of the old Germany so that a new Germany might emerge. The fall of the Holy Roman Empire and the physical devastation of city and countryside created the environment in which the very idea of the nation could be reinvented.

German Nationalism and Ernst Moritz Arndt

Nowhere is the call for a national renewal more clear than in the voluminous writings of Ernst Moritz Arndt, a clergyman, poet, and pamphleteer born in the same year (1769) as his inveterate enemy Napoleon.[46] An ardent patriot, Arndt believed that spiritual morality, not politics or economics, was the guiding force in history. According to Arndt, the Germans' defeat in the early Napoleonic Wars was merely an outward symptom of an inner process of moral decay. Victory would come only when the Germans reversed this process and rediscovered their heroic past.

Arndt's personal contribution to the war effort was the *Kurzer Katechismus für deutsche Soldaten*, which appeared in 1812, just before Germans were to begin their War of Liberation against the "French tyrant."[47] It is doubtful that this work ever circulated among the various armies that opposed Napoleon at the Battle of Leipzig; it is far more likely that it found an audience among the civilian patriots who were seeking to redefine the nation in cultural terms.[48] Like so many other nationalistic writers during this period, Arndt is attempting to describe those characteristics which make the Germans a unique nation, to establish the emotional borders of his homeland. In the *Katechismus*, Arndt defines nationality in moral rather than in political terms, and the book often takes the form of a catalog of German virtues. In terms reminiscent of the "moral attack on the aristocracy" described by Theweleit, Arndt contrasts the simple honesty of the Germans with the over-refined and decadent French. Throughout the *Katechismus*, Arndt uses a self-consciously simple and straightforward style, a style that is very much a part of the content of the work. Faith in God is interwoven with faith in the nation, so that the *Katechismus* occasionally adopts the tone of a children's sermon. Indeed, it is the innocent faith and love of the child that truly locates the Fatherland. For the Fatherland, as Arndt writes, is not "where [the soldier] can live carefree in luxury and opulence, but where he spent the innocent years of childhood, the happy years of youth, where he first heard the sweet tones of friendship and love, where the first star shone above him and the first spring bloomed before him."[49]

This German Fatherland, Arndt writes, was once rich and noble, stretching from the Baltic to the Adriatic, from the North Sea and the Alps all the way to the Vistula, "called with a great and holy name: Kaiser und Reich." Arndt is of course referring to the Holy Roman Empire. Like many other nineteenth-century German nationalists, Arndt idealizes the Middle Ages and devalues the early-modern period that succeeded it.[50] In Arndt's work the Middle Ages emerges as a kind of national childhood, when simplicity, honesty, and faith united the German people. Innocent virtue made the community whole.

The complicated political struggles that led to the disintegration of the medieval German kingdom are far beyond the scope of the *Katechismus*. Arndt is concerned not with relating specific historical events, but rather with presenting a moral fable, a narrative template of innocence, sin, and redemption that he maps onto the German past. For like Adam and Eve, the Germans were thrown out of their medieval paradise, or, rather, saw it crumble around them because of their own sins. This "fall from grace" was precipitated by the kings and princes who, dissatisfied with their position, began to cater to foreign powers. Foolishly they adopted the language, the manners, and even the morality of the outsider, until like senseless animals they turned their armies against their own nation.[51]

Arndt sounds this theme of betrayal as early as the introduction to the *Katechismus* where, in a single long sentence, he summarizes the history of Germany. It is a good thing for the German soldier to be educated, he writes, and to learn the truth about his national heritage: "how in the Middle Ages, which the misinformed often call the time of barbarity and brute force, the German people excelled all others in power, dominion, freedom, art, and science; how when the time of duplicity and lies and betrayal came, which set one against the other; when the German princes had already frequently begun to depend on foreigners."[52] This sentence provides only a brief glimpse of Arndt's interpretation of German history. He gives a more fully developed account of the past in his *Geist der Zeit* (1805), among other places. That work opens with an attack on the Enlightenment. "The era that appeared to be so youthful when I was a boy," Arndt says, speaking of the late eighteenth century, "now resembles a decrepit old man." Although many "enlightened" and intellectual people persisted in describing the late eighteenth century as a progressive and rational era, says Arndt, it was just in this period that eighteenth-century rationalism culminated in the "most grotesque and tragic distortions."[53] Only by returning to the simple virtues of the Middle Ages, Arndt writes, can we reclaim the Fatherland: "And if you feel this love truly and inwardly, then harmony and faith in God and the Fatherland will bring back our lost freedom, and your children and children's children will bless you, that you have done the right and honest thing."[54] The call of the *Katechismus* is thus essentially a call of return. And although Arndt's goal is national revitalization, this call is directed at the individual soul. The lost community will be restored, but only when the narrative of innocence, betrayal, and redemption is enacted within each German heart.

In Arndt's reconstruction of German history, France, more than any other nation, plays the role of the serpent in the garden, corrupting the German spirit and thus enslaving the holy *Reich*. The extremely anti-French rhetoric of Arndt's work was shared by many other German authors of the time. In the *Vorrede* to his *Historische Entwickelung des Einflusses Frankreichs und der Franzosen auf Deutschland und die Deutschen*, for example, Friedrich Rühs writes: "One would not be wrong if one were to describe all of modern history as a chain of confusion, unrest, and wars, that has come to pass merely because a single people, the French, through their overwhelming power have been able to gratify their rough arrogance and insatiable greed as often as they wanted."[55] And yet the same narrative of innocence, betrayal, and redemption that was so important to Arndt and other German nationalists was also a central part of French national mythology, particularly during the late eighteenth and early nineteenth centuries. For, like Arndt, the French revolutionaries were concerned with articulating a new moral world in which the nation was defined no longer by class and tradition but by shared emotions and moral virtues.

This new moral world was to have an important influence on Germany. For although most Germans did not ultimately adopt the political goals of the French Revolution, they were deeply influenced, even overawed, by the French idea of nationhood. In an essay of 1797, for example, the Prussian military analyst Scharnhorst tries to explain how the poorly equipped volunteer armies of the Revolution could defeat the well-trained professional forces of Prussia and Austria. The French victories, Scharnhorst felt, were due to the political and psychological advantages of the revolutionary armies.[56] During the period after its disastrous defeat at Jena in 1806, the Prussian government attempted to gain some of these psychological advantages for itself. It embarked on a comprehensive plan to reform the state, incorporating many of the cultural and educational reforms of revolutionary and Napoleonic France. "What the French have done from below," remarked one of the Prussian ministers to his king, "we must do from above."[57] By adopting some of the educational and bureaucratic reforms of the French Revolution, the Prussians hoped to instill in German citizens that quality that seemed to make the French armies so invincible: devotion to a nation bound together by ties of love. The French were enemies, but they were also exemplars, for they had in a certain sense already realized the goal so passionately articulated by Arndt's *Katechismus:* a national community renewed and restored by an inward transformation of each of its members.

The *opéra comique*

This same mixture of resistance and emulation also characterizes the German response to what we may call the French "operatic invasion" during and immediately after the Napoleonic Wars. This was the time when the "quest for a German Romantic opera" reached its peak—when composers and critics such as Hoffmann, Spohr, and Weber were trying to develop a new German operatic style, free from foreign influences. Yet during the first decades of the nineteenth century French *opéra comique* was perhaps the most popular type of opera in Germany. This apparent paradox makes more sense when we consider the *opéra comique* in the context of the native German repertoire typified by *Das unterbrochene Opferfest*. Like the *Singspiele* of the last decade of the eighteenth century, the *opéra comique* was a mixed genre that could employ a variety of musical dialects, stretching from the folklike idiom to the more complicated and serious music of the tragic opera. Once translated into German, the music and drama of the *opéra comique* would thus be quite similar to "native" opera. Translated into German, the *opéras comiques* of composers such as Grétry, Dalayrac, Méhul, Isouard, Boieldieu, and Cherubini would have easily corresponded to the "genre expectations" of German audiences.

A more important reason for the rapid "naturalization" of French operas in Germany has to do with what we might call a "consonance" between the aesthetics of the *opéra comique* and those of the opera-going (and opera-producing) *Bildungsbürgertum*. As Wolfgang Wagner points out in his book

Carl Maria von Weber und die deutsche Nationaloper, German critics, composers, and audiences looked upon French opera much more favorably than operas from the Italian school. "On the basis of its emphasis on the element of the sentimental, its foregrounding of songlike elements and its delight in the continual representation of a *couleur locale,"* Wagner writes, "the *opéra comique* was universally prized, precisely because it fulfilled the demands that were being valorized in connection with the German comic opera."[58] If Arndt's description of the "new Germany" ironically parallels much of the French revolutionary rhetoric concerning *la patrie,* so too does German opera criticism resonate with the artistic goals of the *opéra comique.* The notion of *Charakter* that I will explore in more detail in the following chapter, for instance, overlaps to a considerable extent with the idea of *couleur locale* that was so central to opera aesthetics in late-eighteenth- and early-nineteenth-century France.[59] The "nationalist" opera criticism of the early nineteenth century, in short, probably facilitated rather than hindered the easy passage of *opéra comique* onto the German stage.

If critics and aestheticians had little objection to the "foreignness" of the *opéra comique,* so too could performers and producers easily adapt its dramaturgy and musical structure to the physical limitations of German opera companies. The same quality of "earnest simplicity" which helped make *Joseph* so appealing to German audiences (to take just one example) also made it a logical choice for *Kapellmeisters* dependent on small and undependable subsidies. Provincial theaters such as the German opera in Dresden, for instance, often had to work with severely limited resources, and the relatively simple sets and costumes of Méhul's opera made it well suited to German theaters. The limited finances available to Weber also compelled him to staff his new German opera primarily with young, inexperienced singers, for whom the ornate vocal writing of the Italian and French serious operas, or for that matter in the parts of Myrrha and Elvira, was far too difficult. Some of these singers would develop into accomplished performers, but Weber realized that in early 1817 his choice of repertoire would be largely determined by the capabilities of his personnel. The relatively simple music of *Joseph* was well adapted to these capabilities. Extended dialogue sections were easier to learn than recitatives, especially for the "actor-singers" that filled the ranks of Weber's company.[60] The formula of alternating prose dialogue with simple musical numbers also made *Joseph,* as well as other *opéras comiques,* relatively easy to translate and adapt for German audiences. Because translators did not have to fit the prose sections of librettos to the musical accents of the recitatives, they were more free to naturalize the opera into their own tongue. To the target audience of the German opera—the German-speaking upper bourgeoisie—the texts that they produced were clear and easy to understand. The accessible musical language and emotional weight of these French operas found a receptive audience in Germany, and up until the premiere of *Der Freischütz* in 1821, translated *opéra comique* often had more success at the box office than German attempts at serious opera.

The popularity of French opera was obviously an extremely important factor in Weber's choice of repertoire for his early years in Dresden. Translated *opéra comique* had been popular throughout Germany for at least two decades. Works such as Méhul's *Joseph*, Boieldieu's *Jean de Paris*, and Isouard's *Cendrillon* had already found a large audience in Munich and Vienna, and they were likely to fill up the theater in Dresden as well. Weber had made translated *opéra comique* an integral part of the repertoire during his years as the director of the German opera in Prague (1813–16), and it is not surprising that he continued producing French operas in Dresden.[61] In this context, Weber turned to translated French *opéra comique* for the bulk of his repertoire in the early part of his tenure at the German opera company. During his first year at the German opera, for example, Weber presented *Joseph* six times, more than any other opera. Other *opéras comiques*, such as Grétry's *Raoul Barbe-bleu* (in German as *Blaubart*), Boieldieu's *Jean de Paris* (*Johann von Paris*), and Isouard's *Cendrillon* (*Aschenbrödel*), were also very important at the German opera from 1817 to 1821.

Weber's choice of *opéra comique* was popular and financially profitable, but it was also part of a plan for the stylistic evolution of his company. Ironically, it was to be through these performances of foreign operas that Weber was able to firmly establish his new institution, preparing the way, he hoped, for a truly national operatic genre. Although Weber did not speak of *opéra comique* in precisely these terms, it is clear from an analysis of his repertoire that the realistic drama of the French operas made them a natural "stepping stone" between the *Singspiel* and the "new German opera."[62] A few decades later Wagner would express the same idea of the *opéra comique* as a transition to the mature German style (exemplified, of course, by Wagner's own works). In a letter of 22 May 1851 to Liszt he writes:

> Before all, accustom your singers to looking upon their work in the first
> instance as a dramatic task; the acceptance of their lyrical task will after
> that be an easy matter. Works of the earlier French school are most
> adapted to the purpose because in them a natural dramatic intention is

most perceptible. Singers who cannot execute well and effectively the *Water Carrier* by Cherubini or *Joseph* by Méhul—how are they to be able to master the enormous difficulties of, for example, one of my operas?[63]

This idea of the French *opéra comique* as a stage on the way to German Romantic opera originated in the early nineteenth century, and it has remained a key part of our interpretation of opera history to the present day. Edward J. Dent's *The Rise of Romantic Opera* is perhaps the most famous work to trace the genealogy of German Romantic opera back through *Fidelio* to the *opéra comique*.[64] Many scholars whose interests are more narrowly focused on Weber have followed in the wake of this classic book, uncovering examples of musical and dramatic ideas in Weber's operas that seem to be directly borrowed from French operas. In his chapter on French opera in volume 8 of the *Oxford History of Music,* for example, Winton Dean notes many significant examples, such as the close similarity of plot between Méhul's *Ariodant* (1799) and *Euryanthe,* between the opening gestures of Méhul's *Melidore et Phrosine* and *Der Freischütz,* and between the allegretto of Amazily's air in Spontini's *La vestale* and Max's cantabile "Durch die Wälder."[65] In his article "Französische Elemente in Webers Opern," John Warrack analyzes more general aspects of Weber's style that seem derived from specific operas of Grétry, Dalayrac, and Méhul.[66] The "prehistory" of the leitmotiv and its origins in turn-of-the-century French opera are an important subject of Robert Tallant Laudon's *Sources of the Wagnerian Synthesis: A Study of the Franco-German Tradition in Nineteenth-Century Opera.* My concern here, however, is less with these issues in the history of musical style than with the emotional and ideological legacy of the *opéra comique.* For *opéra comique* was able to express and stimulate certain emotional patterns whose influence would be felt not only in the German Romantic operas of composers such as Weber, Spohr, and Marschner, but also in the Wagnerian operas that would dominate the German stage during the latter part of the nineteenth century. It is to these patterns, expressed in the music and drama of *Joseph,* that we now turn.

Joseph

Méhul's opera received its Parisian premiere in 1807, just as the French were celebrating their victories over the Prussians. The libretto of the opera, by Alexander Duval, is based on the biblical story but focuses on the final part of the narrative when Joseph is already the chief minister of pharaoh (for a synopsis of the opera's plot, see appendix 3). Beginning shortly before Joseph's father and brothers arrive in Egypt, the opera ends with the final reconciliation of the Hebrew people. *Joseph* capitalized, as Elizabeth Bartlet has noted, both on an Egyptian craze, stimulated in part by Napoleon's campaign there (1798–99) and by "a marked religious revival, partly in reaction to the anti-clericalism of the Revolution."[67] Despite the convulsions of war, *Joseph* traveled quickly to Germany, and the first German-language performance was given in Munich in 1809.[68] The opera was very successful and quickly spread to most of important opera houses in Germany. Many different translations were in use, and the opera was known under variety of titles (*Jacob und seine Söhne, Joseph und seine Brüder, Joseph in Aegypten,* etc.). Weber seems to have heard the opera first in a translation by Matthias Lambrecht, but a different translation by Hassourek was being used in Vienna around 1810.[69] Performers or conductors also felt free to mix the various translations. Librettos from this period often contain extensive annotations that usually concern revisions to the set pieces: the two romances, the "Morning Prayer of the Hebrews," and the "Chorus of the Young Maidens of Memphis."[70] Often the translator (or adapter) is not credited. During the late 1810s and 1820s, however, performances of the opera, at least in northern Germany, tended to employ a version by the Berlin translator Carl August Herklots. Weber seems to have used the Herklots translation for his 1817 production of the work.

The various layers of annotations in the well-thumbed German performance materials of *Joseph* may make it sometimes difficult to determine which version of the opera was performed at what time, but they do make it clear that the opera was an important part of the German repertoire during the first third of the nineteenth century. The popularity of *Joseph* is in many ways surprising, for the work lacks several of the characteristics that tend to typify popular operas. Many of the most dramatic parts of the Joseph story are left out of the plot, to be told only through narrative recollection. There are no principal female characters (although the role of Benjamin is a pants role), no villains, no romantic interest, and very little action in the conventional sense of the term. The opera resembles a series of tableaux in which emotional states are presented statically rather than dramatized. Its focus remains securely on the inner emotional life of the characters and on the religious devotion of the community.[71]

But despite these potential drawbacks, the plot of the opera resonated strongly with the emotional tenor of post-Napoleonic German nationalism. Like Arndt's *Katechismus, Joseph* tells a story of innocence, betrayal, and redemption, a pattern that is played out on both the individual and the national level. Joseph has attained great wealth and status in Egypt, but they count for nothing in his eyes. His greatest desire is to be reunited with his father and reintegrated into the community of faith, and until these goals are accomplished he can never be truly happy. By the grace of God Joseph is given a chance to realize his most cherished hopes when his father and brothers arrive in Egypt, searching for relief from the famine. But Joseph can only be reconciled with the community when Simeon and the other brothers own up to their sins. They must show true remorse for their actions: the outward manifestation of an inward transformation. Only by admitting their guilt can they be forgiven, and only through deep remorse can their sin of betrayal be erased. This inward transformation will allow Joseph and his brothers to restore the past, to return to the time when the community was still a group of children ruled by a loving father. The opera is suffused with nostalgia for this long-ago time, a nostalgia so deep that it almost amounts to a rejection of the adult world.

The correspondence between inner transformation and the renewal of community and nation is an integral part of what we may call the ideological substratum of *Joseph*, and helps to account for the extraordinary popularity of the opera, not only in Napoleonic France, but also in post-Napoleonic Germany. For the opera captures what was for Germans the most important lesson of the French Revolution: that national strength is founded ultimately on the inward transformation of each individual. The grand tableau at the end of the opera, in which Joseph embraces his brothers surrounded by the community of faith, enacts an ideal of nationhood essentially the same as Arndt's vision of the purified and united Germany he hoped would arise from the ashes of the Napoleonic Wars.

For the music of *Joseph*, Méhul used a self-consciously austere style, the musical counterpart of the pure and noble faith of the ancient Hebrews. His depiction of earnest piety seems to have been deeply moving to contemporaries. In his introduction to the Dresden performance of the opera, for example, Weber wrote:

> A truly patriarchal atmosphere and way of life are here combined with a childlike purity of religious devotion. Strong characterization and a passionate sincerity of expression are unmistakable in the overall mastery, the theatrical experience and the clear grasp of what a work demands. The composer here disdains all tinsel and tawdry; truth of expression is his endeavour, and beautiful, moving melody guides his genius.[72]

The "childlike purity of religious devotion" that is so important to the plot of the opera is also a touchstone for its musical color. Indeed, *Joseph* is a good example of the stylistic unity that typified *opéra comique*.

If the characters in *Das unterbrochene Opferfest* belong to different types, each associated with a particular musical idiom, the characters of *Joseph* all inhabit the same musico-dramatic world. Everyone is "virtuous," and everyone employs the same rather limited range of musical styles. This range is determined not by the contrast between the *seria* and *buffa* characters, but rather by the various roles that the music plays within the drama. Three different types of musical numbers may be distinguished.

(1) At one end of the spectrum are the musical numbers that appear as what A. B. Marx would call "wirkliche Lebenserscheinung": the "Morning Prayer of the Hebrews" (no. 6) and the "Chorus of the Young Maidens of Memphis" (no. 11). The texts for these numbers are "ceremonial" and have no direct connection to the plot of the opera. They articulate values and religious ideals that stand outside and above the opera, and their static dramatic function is reinforced by their strophic musical structure.

(2) The two romances of Joseph (no. 2) and Benjamin (no. 7) form the next category. The nature of this music is well described by the words from the definition of "Romanze" in J. G. Sulzer's *Allgemeine Theorie der schönen Künste* (1787):

> one gives the name of a Romance to small narrative songs, in the highly naive and somewhat old-fashioned tone of the old rhymed Romances. Because the Romance is made to be sung, the verses are lyric, but extremely simple, as they have been in all times—comprising short lines of equal numbers of syllables. . . . In order for Romances to please persons of good taste, they must have so much excellence that more than common taste is required for their production. They must place us into those times when people overall had fewer concepts about the general order of things, when [people] lacked scientific or exact and convincing knowledge, and yet were by no means ignorant or barbaric; into those times when superstitious, gullibility, and lack of knowledge had nothing offensive about them, because they belonged to the customs and character of the times.[73]

Like the musical numbers listed in the first category, Méhul's romances are strophic, but their texts are narrative rather than ceremonial and give the audience information that is important to the plot.

(3) In the next group of musical numbers are Joseph's aria (no. 1), the brothers' ensemble (no. 3), and the second-act trio featuring Jacob, Joseph, and Benjamin (no. 9). In these numbers, to use Marx's distinctions, "music functions as actual speech." Their through-composed musical structure corresponds to their "kinetic" dramatic texts. The three finales are also largely kinetic but contain important ceremonial elements as well.

Méhul employs three distinct musical styles largely in order to articulate contrasting emotional states. The simple music of the two romances evokes the innocence of a lost childhood, just as the ceremonial music of numbers such as the "Morning Prayer of the Hebrews" embodies the stability of the redeemed community. The dynamic music of the third category dramatizes the emotional torment that is the result of sin. And although there is no direct connection between Méhul's opera and Arndt's *Kurzer Katechismus*, these three different types of music can be seen to correspond to the three different stages in Arndt's mythologized narrative of innocence, sin, and redemption. That is not to say that *Joseph* presents a chronological analog to German history. On the contrary: in each of the three acts there is a rough balance between these three different types of music, contributing to the overall sense of proportion in the opera. The promise of the transformed community is present from almost the beginning of the opera, just as the sin of betrayal is not redeemed until the penultimate number.

Musical Style in *Joseph*

Joseph's romance, in which he tells his trusted advisor Utobal the story of his early life, may stand as an example for the narrative music of the opera (category 2). Like the *Katechismus*, the romance is written in a self-consciously simple style that becomes the emblem of an innocent past, an innocence that is shattered by the events that it narrates. The Canaan of Joseph's childhood, when he was folded in the loving arms of the father, plays the same role in Méhul's opera as the Middle Ages plays in Arndt's *Katechismus*. In the first verse of the romance, that innocence is undisturbed. Surrounded by his father's love, Joseph is at one with nature, the choicest lamb, we might say, in his father's herds. The second verse tells of the brothers' betrayal. Duval expands the sparse biblical narrative, so that Joseph is attacked by the brothers as he is in prayer. They throw him into a dark and cold pit. In the third verse the slave traders arrive and rescue Joseph, only to sell him into slavery. These are the events that motivate the rest of the opera, whose evil must be expiated before all of the characters may be reunited. But Méhul does not contrast these verses musically; even the accompaniment remains the same for all three verses. We may speak of a "dissonance" between text and music whereby Joseph's melody, the innocent song of his childlike love, endures "underneath" the narrative of betrayal. The words speak of the grim reality, but the music continues to sing of an idealized past.

The dissonance between the text and music of Joseph's romance thus embodies the tension between innocence and betrayal that is so central to the plot of the opera. This tension forms the subject for the kinetic music of the opera (category 3). These musical numbers correspond to the "time of duplicity and lies" in Arndt's narrative, "which set one against the other; when the German princes had already frequently begun to depend on foreigners." Arndt's words well describe the spiritual condition of Simeon and the other brothers, a spiritual condition that is explored in the third musical number of the opera, the brothers' ensemble. This is not a set piece like the romance, but a complex *scena* with a great deal of dramatic action. Its music and drama move us from the static reflective world of the past into the dynamic world of the present, made almost unendurable by remorse.

Throughout the preceding dialogue the brothers have been trying to console Simeon and control his volatile emotions, but in the first section of the ensemble Simeon categorically rejects their efforts. God, Simeon tells us, is already punishing him for his misdeeds, and this punishment will doubtless go on forever. It takes an interesting form. Simeon is not plagued by boils or cancers; rather, he is to be banished into a kind of "internal exile," alienated from his family, from the community, and from God himself. This punishment is thus a mirror image of Simeon's crime against Joseph and his father. By selling Joseph to the Egyptians Simeon and his brothers cut him off from the father's love. Simeon's punishment, therefore, is to be cut off himself, banished from the "natural community" of the family. In the first four lines of his opening solo passage, Simeon dismisses any hope of forgiveness. In contrast to the long, arching melodies of the romance, this section, like the entire ensemble, is built up largely from a group of small, condensed motives. The most important of these is the rising chromatic motive with which the number opens, a clear musical picture of Simeon's inner torment. The surging, reckless quality of this motive is accentuated by the dynamic markings, which call for rapid crescendos and decrescendos. The obsessive, repetitive use of this motive seems to be a musical portrait of Simeon's inner life.

Simeon begins the next large section of the ensemble by asking how he

Example 2.3 The Brothers' ensemble (beginning)

may give a child (namely, Joseph) back to his father. Memories of the father
lead Simeon into thoughts of his own children, and as he imagines the punishment of God the rising chromatic motive returns. But when Simeon sings
of his children's innocence, this obsessive motive dies away into a unison
A-flat, which Méhul reharmonizes to lead us toward a local tonic of E major.
We are as far as possible from the F-minor tonic of the ensemble, a trans-

Example 2.3 (*continued*)

formation that Méhul underscores with a shift in dynamics from forte to piano as well as a textural shift to a chordal wind accompaniment. Simeon is imagining the lost childhood purity of Joseph's romance, and as he does so, his melody takes on some of the graceful, arching quality of Joseph's music. But for Simeon, this world is only an eight-measure dream. Using the chromatic motive in sequence, Méhul moves away from the half-cadence on

Example 2.4   The Brothers' ensemble (middle section)

a B-major chord (measure 97) back toward F minor, and from pianissimo
to forte once more. As in Simeon's first solo passage, his melody is overwhelmed by orchestral chromaticism and disintegrates into a cry. Through
his sin Simeon has condemned not only himself, but his innocent children
as well.

The contrast between this brief subsection and the music that surrounds
it is thus a microcosm of the contrast between the romance and the rest of
the ensemble, a contrast that informs the entire opera. These two musical
numbers set up a polarity between purity and sin, between innocence and
betrayal, even between the past and the present. Simeon's music embodies

Example 2.4 (*continued*)

these tensions, but in the imagined drama of his punishment these tensions are also folded into another dichotomy, the dichotomy between alienation and integration. Both Simeon and Joseph long for the past, but they also hope for a future in which they may be reabsorbed into the community of love.

The striking textural shifts, unusual harmonic gestures, and more complex musical form of this ensemble make it the most dynamic and imaginative number in the opera. It is remarkable that Méhul should employ his most dramatic musical language for an ensemble in which nothing really "happens." But just as in the rest of the opera, the real drama of this ensemble is interior. Simeon can be released from his punishment only by moral transformation, and the ensemble serves to make this moral transformation imperative—to bring Simeon's anguish to the point where it is unendurable.

Simeon's remorse is of course intimately bound with the longing to be folded again in the loving arms of both the earthly and spiritual fathers and to be reabsorbed into the community of love. The combined voices of the brothers within this ensemble represent but a pale reflection of this community. In their unsuccessful attempts to calm Simeon, they can offer him sympathy but not the moral transformation that he so desperately needs, for they share Simeon's spiritual dilemma. The ideal community of love is larger and more diverse than the band of brothers, and it is represented in this opera by the mixed chorus.[74] As we might expect in an early-nineteenth-century opera, the chorus appears prominently in the finales of each of the three acts. But in *Joseph* the chorus also appears at the beginnings of acts 2 and 3, in the "Morning Prayer of the Hebrews" and in the "Chorus of the Young Maidens of Memphis." For these large ensembles Méhul writes steadfast and simple homophony, music that contrasts sharply with the music for the smaller "Chorus of the Brothers." It resembles nothing so much as a classicized hymn.

The music and drama of these choruses affirm a central supposition of the opera: the intimate connection between religious faith and communal feeling. For although the principal characters often refer to the God of their fathers, they do not describe their faith. The mixed chorus, and in particular the voices of the women, appear instead as the carriers of the creed. Apart from the chorus that ends the finale of the second act, in which the men and women of Memphis praise Joseph's wisdom and foresight, the mixed chorus sings nothing but religious music. The position of the mixed chorus at the beginning and end of the second and third acts allows it to function as a musical and dramatic bookend, framing the more complex and emotionally tormented solos and ensembles which fill the inner parts of each act. Just as in Arndt's mythologized history of Germany, the narrative begins and ends with the image of the united community.

The symmetrical phrase structures, moderate tempi, and straightforward harmonies help to link the music of the mixed chorus to the first act "music of innocence" in the two romances and in Simeon's vision of his children. Yet unlike these earlier numbers, the scenes for mixed chorus are not nostalgic, but rather look forward to a future of reintegration and reunification.

Example 2.5   The Morning Prayer of the Hebrews (beginning)

Not until the final number of the opera do Simeon and the other brothers announce their redemption in musical terms, by being reabsorbed into the hymnlike voice of the community.

This final chorus, as I mentioned above, seems to be the only part of the opera that was substantially revised for German performances. The ending number in Méhul's original score was only thirty-nine measures long and all in a single tempo; this ending was too simple and brief, German audiences seemed to feel, for an operatic finale. A piano-vocal score from 1810 preserves a replacement finale by Joseph Seyfried that seems to have been used for some Vienna performances of the opera.[75] This version of the finale is slightly longer (forty-four measures) and uses a text that does not seem to be derived from Duval's original. The music is predominantly homophonic, but Jacob, Simeon, Benjamin, and Joseph are foregrounded with brief solo and trio passages. Although the style of Seyfried's new finale is quite similar to Méhul's original, his version contains a short introductory section, marked lento e religioso, that contrasts with the following allegro. Seyfried's finale, however, does not seem to have been used widely outside of Vienna. Other German opera companies usually replaced Méhul's final chorus with a much more extensive version by Ferdinand Fränzl.[76] It seems likely that Fränzl composed this new finale for the first Munich performances, for the revised text is printed in a Munich libretto from 1808 (the text for Méhul's original version appears handwritten on the next page).[77] A comparison of the two versions may be found in appendix 4.

Although Fränzl makes free use of Méhul's original music, the bulk of the new finale is his own work. Perhaps the most conspicuous change that Fränzl made concerns the beginning of the number. Méhul's version opens directly with the "Brothers' Chorus," which Fränzl displaces to the end of the finale. His new version starts instead with a long solo section for Joseph. In Méhul's original, Joseph sings only a brief phrase: "My father forgives his sons." But in Fränzl's version Joseph speaks directly to Simeon and personally assures him of their father's forgiveness. Simeon and Joseph embrace each other, and their reconciliation leads directly into the next section of the finale, which celebrates the larger reconciliation of the community of brothers. The final section of the number, augmented in Fränzl's version by a "Chorus of the People," expands and universalizes the spirit of forgiveness and joy.

The overall effect of these changes is to restructure the finale so that it follows a progression from the private drama of sin and forgiveness to the national drama of reintegration. The personal and the political emerge as but two facets of the same process of transformation and redemption, a relationship that is reinforced by the explicit stage directions. I quote from the score of Fränzl's revised version of the finale:

> Joseph stands in Jacob's arms, reaching his left hand to Benjamin. Simeon kneels before Joseph and kisses his cloak. Jacob lays his left hand with forgiveness on Simeon's head. The brothers are grouped to the right and left, and gaze upon Joseph with joy. The nobles and the Egyptians fill the middle ground, with the slaves, carrying gifts, behind them. The bodyguard stands in the back.[78]

Reunification and reconciliation ripple out from the central group in concentric rings of joy.

Die Geschichte Josephs

In 1817, just as Weber was directing the premiere of *Joseph* in Dresden, a group of German painters was creating its own version of the Joseph story. Led by Johann Friedrich Overbeck (1789–1869), the *Lukasbund* (better known as the Nazarene brotherhood) was active in Rome during the first decades of the nineteenth century. Its members were deeply affected by the religious revival of Romanticism and lived together like monks in a deconsecrated monastery. In 1816–17 they chose *Die Geschichte Josephs* as the theme for a large cooperative fresco to decorate the Casa Bartholdy in Rome,

"Joseph gibt sich seinen Brüdern zu erkennen" by Peter Cornelius

one of only two such works that they completed.[79] The scenes from the fresco are unusually evocative of Méhul's music. Both share a neoclassic nobility of sentiment, in which early-nineteenth-century Germans could perhaps see and hear an idealized version of their own history. The final scene in the fresco series, "Joseph gibt sich seinen Brüdern zu erkennen" (Joseph reveals his identity to his brothers) by Peter Cornelius, is remarkably similar to the final tableau of Méhul's opera.

Joseph embraces the boyish Benjamin with his left hand while Simeon, kneeling, bathes his right hand in tears. Joseph's Egyptian advisor (the Utobal figure) stands in the middle ground, and through the arches in the back we can glimpse the luxurious gardens of Joseph's palace. Like Méhul's music, the architecture of the colonnaded portico in the background, as well as the details of the palace itself, evokes not so much ancient Egypt as a generalized classicism (a tower in the left background actually seems to belong in Renaissance Italy). Joseph himself wears a suitably Oriental turban, but some of the brothers' clothes would seem to be more at home in medieval Europe. In another fresco from the series (also by Cornelius), in which Joseph interprets the dream of pharoah, pharoah himself appears in a flowing robe and pseudo-medieval regalia—he seems more like Charlemagne than Ramses II. Cornelius is motivated, we sense, not so much by historical realism (at least how we would understand that term today) as by the desire to express the "childlike simplicity of religious devotion" embodied by the clear, simple lines of the inner court and the background buildings.

If the fresco paintings share some aesthetic principles with Méhul's music, so too does the ideology surrounding *Die Geschichte Josephs* resonate with early-nineteenth-century German music criticism. As Keith Andrews makes clear in his discussion of *Die Geschichte Josephs,* fresco painting had particular significance for Cornelius: "Cornelius realized that if they were to make their impact on a larger public, if their works were to be part of a national artistic regeneration, then they must make their mark by means of a new monumental art that would proclaim itself from the walls and façades of churches and monasteries, municipal buildings and private houses."[80] Andrews continues by quoting directly from a letter that Cornelius wrote at the end of 1814: "At last I come to what according to my innermost conviction would, I feel, be the most powerful, I would say the infallible, means of giving German art a new direction compatible with the great era of the nation and with its spirit: this would be nothing less than the revival of Fresco-Painting as it was practised from the great Giotto to the divine Raphael."[81]

That the theme of Joseph and his brothers should figure so prominently in Cornelius's plans for national artistic regeneration is surely no accident. Like Méhul's opera, his "Joseph gibt sich seinen Brüdern zu erkennen" depends for its effect upon the amalgamation of the personal and the political —the same ideology that informs Arndt's *Katechismus.* As Terry Eagleton points out in *The Ideology of the Aesthetic,* the new bourgeois state of the late eighteenth and early nineteenth century created new methods of social cohesion and social coercion, based on inner subjectivity. "Such organic liaisons," he continues, "are surely a more trustworthy form of political rule that the inorganic, oppressive structures of absolutism. . . . It is for this reason that the early bourgeoisie is so preoccupied with *virtue*—with the lived habit of moral propriety, rather than a laborious adherence to some external norm."[82]

Joseph too is preoccupied with virtue, a characteristic that is shared by many German operas of the late eighteenth and early nineteenth centuries, not least *Der Freischütz* and *Euryanthe.* The plot of *Joseph* must surely have appealed to Weber, but the musical influence of Méhul's opera is less clear.

Although he praises the "strong characterization and a passionate sincerity of expression" in *Joseph*, Weber does not single out any number for particular praise. If we may judge from the printed sources that survive from the early nineteenth century, *Joseph*'s first-act romance appears to have been the most popular number in the opera, for it appears in many different arrangements for various combinations of instruments, as well as in numerous operatic collections from the period. But it was the kinetic music of the brothers' ensemble, I believe, that had the most important influence on Weber's operatic style. Here Weber found a model for the intense interior drama that would be such a prominent feature of his later works. Méhul's dramatic use of orchestral motives in the brothers' ensemble foreshadows similar techniques in Weber's operas, and the richer harmonic palette and looser, more through-composed formal structure of the number clearly point toward *Freischütz* and *Euryanthe*.

Joseph in Performance

Although the specific nature of *Joseph*'s influence on Weber must be left largely to conjecture, it is clear that Weber thought very highly of the opera. His high regard for Méhul's craftsmanship made him somewhat uneasy about using the Fränzl version of the finale, even though in Germany this revised version seems to have been almost universally seen as an improvement to the original. In an introduction to the opera he wrote shortly before its Dresden performance, Weber defended his decision to use Fränzl's music. "The present writer," Weber wrote,

> is the declared enemy of all such additions, cuts, and other mutilations of an original work. . . . If he shows himself tolerant in the present instance, it is owing to a feature common to all French operas, namely the almost complete triviality of the final chorus. This can be explained by the fact that after the final dénouement of the drama the lively French intelligence tends to lose interest in a work and lets it play itself out without paying any attention. The German listener enjoys savoring the dramatic situation, and his sympathies are still engaged by the emotions of the stage characters who have won his affection.[83]

Given Weber's attitude to "all such additions, cuts, and other mutilations of an original work," it seems likely that in Dresden *Joseph* was performed in its entirety, at least during Weber's lifetime. But performance materials from later in the century indicate that this changed drastically during the

Table 2.2   Comparison between Méhul's Original Score of Joseph and Later Dresden Performing Version

Original Score	Performing Version
Act 1 Overture 1. Recitative and Aria (Joseph)	—
2. Romance (Joseph)	1. Romance (Joseph)
3. Ensemble (the brothers)	2. Ensemble (with an expanded first section, but without the final section of the original score
4. Finale (Joseph, Utobal, and the brothers, later chorus of the people)	3. Ensemble (the original finale to act 1, present as a loose sheet, not bound with the other materials)
Act 2 5. Entr'acte	—
6. "Morning Prayer" ("Chorus of the Hebrews")	4. "Morning Prayer of the Hebrews"
7. Romance (Benjamin)	—
8. Trio (Benjamin, Joseph, Jacob)	—
9. Finale (Jacob, Joseph, Benjamin, later a chorus of the people)	5. The original finale to act 2 appears here as the finale to act 1
Act 3 10. Entr'acte	*Act 2* 6. Entr'acte
11. "Chorus of the Young Maidens of Memphis"	7. "Cantique" ("Chorus of the Young Maidens of Memphis")
12. Duet (Jacob, Benjamin)	—
13. Ensemble (Jacob, Benjamin, Simeon, the brothers, later Joseph)	—
14. Final chorus	8. Final chorus (Fränzl version)

1830s and 1840s. A prompter's score from this period is particularly interesting, for it contains only eight musical numbers organized into two acts.[84] Librettos from this period show that not only the music, but also the interleaved dialogues were dramatically cut. Table 2.2 compares this version with the original score.

The fate of *Joseph*, we might say, was exactly the opposite of the fate of *Das unterbrochene Opferfest*. Both the Italian translation-adaptation *Il sacrifizio interotto* and the German *heroisch-tragische* version of *Das unterbrochene Opferfest* are "elevations" of the original score, moving the opera up the genre hierarchy. These cuts to *Joseph* had the opposite effect. By the 1830s and 1840s *Joseph* was primarily a "summer opera" in Dresden, more suitable to the Linkesche Bad than to the Morettische Haus, much less to the grand new Semper Oper that opened in 1841. During this later period a truncated *Joseph* was occasionally performed as the first opera in a double bill. The opera was never very dramatic, and shorn of most of its dialogue it must have seemed more like a series of set pieces than an opera. One suspects that the finales were saved from the blue pencil mainly because they provided an opportunity to display the Egyptian sets and costumes.

The performance history of *Joseph* typifies many trends of the 1820s and 1830s, not only in the repertoire of the Dresden opera, but throughout Germany. Critics and composers of this period were increasingly interested in discovering, or creating, a national German operatic style, an enterprise in which translated operas usually played only a negative role. A distinct "nationalization" of the repertoire in Dresden is evident as early as 1820 and 1821. Within a few years of his appointment to the German opera, Weber was already performing fewer translated *opéras comiques* and more Mozart operas, particularly *Die Zauberflöte, Die Entführung aus dem Serail,* and *Don Giovanni* (in German as *Don Juan*).[85] With the Dresden premiere of *Der Freischütz* on 6 January 1822, Weber began to add his own operas to the repertoire of his German opera company.[86] As the German opera developed and became more self-assured, it was no longer necessary to restrict the repertoire to *opéra comique* and other similar genres. Even by the early 1820s the company was performing more complex operas by Spontini, and in 1824 Weber's own *Euryanthe*. Weber's new prestige combined with his position as the head of the German opera in Dresden afforded him the opportunity to articulate a positive image of a new type of native German opera, one that would both reflect and serve to develop the character of the nation.

3   *Der Freischütz* and the Character of the Nation

Charakter

The mid-nineteenth-century German dictionary of Daniel Sanders defines *Charakter* as

> 1) originally an impressed or engraved sign, a particular sign for an object or a concept, for example, an astronomical, algebraic . . . etc. character.
> 2) The label or emblem that differentiates and distinguishes a being and marks its particular properties; its essence or distinctiveness; by extension also a person with particularly strong, sharply defined qualities. Every being that feels itself to be a unity wants to retain its indivisible and unalterable essence—this is an eternal and necessary gift of nature. . . . But the word "character" is usually used in a higher sense, namely, when a person abides by his or her own distinguishing particularities and can in no way be estranged from them. . . . [In this sense] there are strong, consistent, thick, elastic, flexible, malleable etc. characters.[1]

That this word should have such strong positive connotations in nineteenth-century Germany is no surprise, for in many ways the idea of a distinguishing mark or emblem articulated the yearning for national unity that was so important to the cultural and political zeitgeist. Arndt's mythologized history can easily be read through the context of these words, as the story of how the Germans were estranged from this "eternal and necessary gift," and of how they might rediscover their own character. "Every *nation*," we might paraphrase the words of the definition, "wants to retain its indivisible and unalterable essence—this is an eternal and necessary gift of nature."

The term *Charakter* also found its way into the numerous musical lexica and "conversation books" of early-nineteenth-century Germany. But in these works the emphasis often falls on diversity rather than on unity. In his *Musikalisches Lexicon* of 1802, for instance, H. C. Koch defined *Charakter* in the following manner:

When one speaks of musical pieces one understands character as those
properties and signs through which one piece is distinguished from
another. Meter, tempo, rhythm, the type of melodic figures and how
they are used, the form, the accompaniment, modulation, style, the basic
feeling and the particular way in which it is expressed, all of these things
contribute now more and now less to the particular character of a musical piece.[2]

For Koch *Charakter* is above all composite—it emerges from a dynamic
interplay of many different features. It should therefore not be surprising
that the term should play such a large part in the criticism surrounding the
search for a German opera, for it embodied the concept of creating unity
out of diversity that was so central to the enterprise. Here, as in other instances, criticism often played a compensatory role: the idea of "character"
took on such importance for early-nineteenth-century critics in part because the ideal of a *charaktervoll* opera, in which the different elements of
the artwork would be informed by a single distinctive and unifying spirit,
seemed so distant. The problem of how to find that unifying spirit forms
the keynote of I. F. Mosel's *Versuch einer Aesthetik des dramatischen Tonsatzes*
(1813).[3] Although Mosel's work contains a historical section, it is primarily a
guide to composition, related in style and structure to the works of Riepel,
Koch, and Mattheson.[4] Mosel devotes almost a third of his book to a discussion of character, which operates on three distinct levels.

(1) Character in the Opera as a Whole

"Above all," Mosel writes, "the composer should attempt to penetrate into the spirit of the poetry that he must then clothe with music":

He contemplates exactly the type, the progress, and the goal of the plot
that is placed before him, and then determines the *general character* of his
musical composition. In tragic opera this character should be great and
deeply moving, in heroic opera brilliant and worthy, in romantic *Singspiel*
tender and touching, and in comic *Singspiel* charming and cheerful.[5]

(2) Character within the Individual Musical Numbers

For Mosel, just as for Koch, the composer must create character
within the individual musical numbers by skillfully manipulating many
different parameters:

Der Freischütz *and the Character of the Nation*   77

In addition to this general character, every piece of music (following the content of the text) also demands a certain key, movement, rhythm, intervals and accompaniment; everything is important, and everything makes its own essential contribution to the true expression [of the whole]. In the determination of keys every composer may be led by Schubart's *Charakteristik der Töne* (if he does not already have his own proper feelings for a leader), but for the choice of movement [meter], rhythm, appropriate intervals, accompanying instruments the composer must be led by his own feelings, for the use [of these musical elements] is as various as the sensations that can be expressed through the poetry.[6]

(3) Character of the Individual "handelnde Personen"

Each of the characters on the stage, whom Mosel calls *handelnde Personen,* must also have their distinct quality or essence, which must combine with and function within the demands for "character" both in the individual musical numbers and in the opera as a whole. In order to avoid confusion with "character" used in the aesthetic sense, I have translated *handelnde Personen* as *dramatis personae:*

> The physical, moral, and conventional character of the individual
> *dramatis personae* must be just as carefully observed by the composer
> of dramatic music as the spirit of the plot and the text of the individual
> music pieces. In general the man should express himself more powerfully
> and the woman more tenderly. The hero, who makes the nations tremble,
> should not lisp and gurgle like a tame bird, the song of the king should
> be noble and majestic, that of the peasant light and naïve, without being
> common, for "the nature of music is to beautify everything that it imi-
> tates." It is impossible to discuss all the various characters which may
> occur in opera in this short space; it seems sufficient to remark that the
> individuality of the singers, in all the expressions of their feelings and
> passions, must be communicated not only through their song but also
> through its accompaniment.[7]

Mosel does not discuss specific situations in which the character of the entire work, of the individual musical numbers, and of the *handelnde Personen*
might put contradictory demands upon the musical text. He speaks instead
in general terms about attention to the "true spirit of the poetry," which
will overcome or sublimate the diversity inherent in opera.

Mosel's idea of "character" as a unifying inner essence stands in marked contrast to the use of the term in the early and mid-eighteenth century. In the baroque period "character" found its place in the aesthetics of imitation: raindrops or birdsongs were mimicked in countless *pièces caracteristiques*. But as Carl Dahlhaus makes clear in his essay "Die Kategorie des Charakteristischen in der Ästhetik des 19. Jahrhunderts," the term began to take on exactly contrary meanings toward the end of the eighteenth century:

> In the article "On the Representation of Character in Music" which appeared in Schiller's newspaper *Die Horen* [The Hours] in 1795, Christian Gottfried Körner understood character as ethos, the opposite and counterpart to affect, or pathos. If affect, that breaks over the soul as "storm of passion," is just as powerful as it is temporary, then character by contrast appears as the steady and fixed. The expression of an interior essence, through which characteristic beauty differentiates itself from empty or formal beauty must (as Wilhelm von Humboldt formulated . . .) "be lifted up from the temporary image of an affect to the image of the enduring character, a character that is created not merely from one side, but is rather formed from a harmonious blending of all its parts." Affect, which was celebrated by baroque aesthetics, appears as the "self-foreign" a power enforced from the outside, while character, as understood by the classical, anti-baroque aesthetic, works from the inside out.[8]

For Wilhelm von Humboldt the idea of a unifying, organic power working from the inside out had a social as well as a merely aesthetic function. In his 1795 review of *Hermann und Dorothea* Humboldt praises Goethe's concentration on the private sphere. "It has never been more necessary to shape [*bilden*] and consolidate the inner form of character than now," Humboldt concludes, "when external circumstances and habits are threatened by the terrible power of universal upheaval."[9] This "terrible power" was made tangible in the form of the revolutionary armies that threatened Germany in the late eighteenth century, and Humboldt's words remind us of Arndt's response to the French armies at the end of the Napoleonic period. Humboldt's argument is more sophisticated than Arndt's, but for both men the development of the nation is dependent on a moral transformation, the consolidation of an inner essence. The opposition between "universal upheaval" and the "consolidation of the inner form of character," of course, has deep roots in German history. We may read it in Luther's vicious condemnation of the 1525 Peasants' War, when German peasants confused the "priesthood of all believers" with political and economic self-determination. We find it in the Pietist movement of the seventeenth and eighteenth centuries, and it is not surprising that the opposition should surface again a century later. Despite their complexity, the arguments of Humboldt, Körner, and others can be seen as an extension of this old moral and political polarity between the inner and the outer, or better, between that which works from the "inside out" and that which works from the "outside in." The aesthetics of character and the "politics of character" mirrored each other.

Indeed, we might extend Mosel's threefold classification of "character" to postulate a fourth level upon which the idea operates: the political and aesthetic level of operatic genre. The hopes of the search for a German opera were of course not merely toward a single work of art, but for a new operatic style that would both reflect and help to form the character of the nation. But if the "nature and inner constitution of opera—as a whole containing other wholes" (see Weber's famous review of *Undine* quoted below) made it difficult to achieve a unified character within a single opera, the lack of a strong, specifically German operatic tradition made a new national operatic genre seem even more remote. As we have seen, late-eighteenth- and early-nineteenth-century German operas such as *Das unterbrochene Opferfest* were typified precisely by their *lack* of a unified musical or dramatic character. This lack of unified character was reflected on the level of operatic genre as well—despite hopes for a national operatic style, German operas of this period display a bewildering variety of different musical and dramatic forms. *Euryanthe* was certainly not the only attempt at a through-composed opera, and the demands for a more organic or natural relationship between text and music can be seen in many operas that retain the dialogue-opera form of the *Singspiel*.[10] But these works also contain many musical and dramatic patterns adopted from foreign opera or carried over from older traditions. The German operas of composers such as Weber, Spohr, Marschner, Lindpaintner, and Kreuzer did not form a genre in the same way as the *opere serie* of the early and mid-eighteenth century, because these German works did not share anything which might correspond to well-established musico-dramatic conventions, such as the *da capo* exit aria and the *lieto fine*. What they did share was a particular ideology, built up out of certain plot tropes that occurred with great regularity. This ideology was typified by an extraordinarily strong contrast between good and evil—only in the early-seventeenth-century operas of Monteverdi and his contemporaries, perhaps, did opera so strongly take on the outlines of a morality play. It is in the character of this dichotomy, not in any particular musico-dramatic form or gesture, that the German Romantic opera found its distinctive voice.

In the context of these dualisms, the concept of *Charakter* thus pulled German opera in contradictory directions. On one hand, critics wanted the opera to be "characteristic" in the sense of Mosel's "general character": unified by a single poetic idea. But the plot structures of German Romantic opera, with their interplay between cosmic forces of good and evil, seemed to require an even stronger delineation of musico-dramatic character on the level of the individual musical numbers and of the *handelnde Personen*. The need for unity of the whole, in other words, often conflicted with the need for unity of the parts. That Weber himself was very aware of these contradictions is apparent from his famous review of Hoffmann's *Undine*: "The very nature and inner constitution of opera—as a whole containing other wholes—has this essential drawback, which only a few heroes of the art have managed to surmount. Every musical number has its own proper architecture, which makes it an independent and organic unity; yet this should be absorbed in any study of the work as a whole."[11] *Das unterbrochene Opferfest* and the hundreds of other operas of its type may have been in Weber's mind as negative examples. The individual musical numbers of the opera have a clear "inner organic unity," but not even in its revised, *heroisch-tragische* version could *Das unterbrochene Opferfest* claim to have a distinct character that informed the entire work. In this respect Méhul's *Joseph* stands at the opposite extreme. Even though the music is interrupted by dialogues, Weber admired the work precisely for its unified musical and dramatic character (see Weber's quotation in chapter 2, p. 60).[12] But *Joseph* is able to articulate a "genuine patriarchal character" in part because its characters do not display what we might call the moral diversity of characters in operas such as *Das unterbrochene Opferfest*. There are no villains in *Joseph*, only the individual brothers struggling with varying degrees of guilt and longing. The cosmic forces of good and evil at work in *Der Freischütz* (and also in *Euryanthe*) and the moral diversity that was so essential to the character of German opera play no role in *Joseph*. The search for a German opera can be seen as an effort to chart a middle ground between these two demands, to find a musical style that would be "characteristic" both on the level of the individual numbers and of the entire work.

The Character of *Freischütz*

The problem of "character," understood in this multilayered sense, is one of the central topics in Johann Christian Lobe's "Gespräche mit Carl Maria von Weber." The "Gespräche" are supposedly Lobe's recollections of two meetings that he had with the composer, probably in 1825. The authenticity of Lobe's account has been called into question, in part because Lobe recorded his "conversations" three decades after they took place. At best, Lobe's work is an imaginative reconstruction of an actual conversation— most likely, it occupies a gray area between journalism and historical fiction.[13] Yet even if Lobe's account can give us only dubious evidence about Weber's composition of *Der Freischütz,* it is nevertheless an important document in the reception history of the opera. The comments with which Lobe began his purported conversation with Weber touch directly on the themes of character and unity that were so central to the concept of a new German opera:

> What astounds me so much in *Frieschütz* [Lobe supposedly said to Weber] . . . is first of all the totality of the style, of the tone, or whatever you may call it. It seems to me as if every melody and every sound in this opera could appear only in *Freischütz* and would be completely out of place in any other work. I hear in these tones not merely the expression of a particular feeling, but the expression of the feelings of a certain person—I can even hear the particular time in which the opera takes place and the particular place in which the plot unfolds.[14]

Weber brushes off Lobe's compliments with becoming modesty—one may see the same sort of thing, he says, in *Don Giovanni,* in *Die Zauberflöte,* or even more in Méhul's *Joseph.* The conversation turns to the methods whereby the composer may imbue his work with this "totality of style." Instead of "totality" or "totality of tone," Weber says, we may speak of "character" or "characteristic tone." A brief discussion of "character" ensues, in which Weber defines the concept in words that sound suspiciously like Koch's definition quoted above. Pressed by Lobe, Weber finally begins to speak about his own work. "In *Freischütz,*" Weber says, "there are two principal elements that can be recognized at first glance: the hunting life and the force of the demonic powers [finst're Mächte], personified by Samiel. My first task in the composition of the opera was find the most significant tone and sound-colors [Ton-und Klangfarben] for these two elements."[15] The idea that this fundamental opposition was the kernel from which *Freischütz* developed has been very attractive, but it does not correspond to what we know about the compositional history of the opera.[16] Weber actually wrote quite a bit about the creation of *Freischütz* in his diary and in letters to his wife, and from these materials it seems that he began not with a depiction of the "demonic powers" or of the "hunting life," but with the A-major duet of Ännchen and Agathe at the beginning of the second act.[17] If we can make any generalization at all, it seems that Weber composed the significant arias for Agathe, Max, and Caspar first, and other sections later. The "Jägerchor" wasn't finished until 24 March 1820, almost three years after Weber began work on the opera.[18] Of course, Weber may have been conceptualizing musico-dramatic "characters" before he even began to write out notes— the creative genesis of Weber's operas, in any case, will always remain to some extent obscure. That Lobe's quotation does not necessarily describe the compositional process of *Freischütz* is ultimately less important than the truth that it contains, for the fundamental opposition between the "normal," natural world of the hunters and Samiel's hellish domain has been an important part of the presentation and interpretation of *Freischütz* since its premiere.

And yet this opposition is clearly not the only one at work in the opera. Max is saved from the clutches of Samiel not so much by the "naturalness" of the hunters as by the *himmlische Mächte* that are in their own way every bit as supernatural as the ghosts that haunt the Wolf's Glen. The demonic forces find their antipode not only in the hunting life but also in the characters of Agathe and the Hermit. And Caspar is able to insinuate himself into Max's confidence precisely because he is the tenor's *Jagdgesell*, who has one foot securely planted in the world of the hunters. His drinking song "Hier im ird'schen Jammerthal" is in many ways a parody of the *volkstümlich* style that Weber employs for the hunters, and in his great triumph aria "Schweig, schweig, damit dich niemand warnt" he modulates from D minor to D major, the very key that Weber otherwise reserves for representations of village life (it is, for instance, the key of the hunters' chorus). In place of Lobe's (Weber's) binary opposition, then, we might posit a two-dimensional space in which to graph out the plot structure of *Der Freischütz* (figure 3.1).

Naturally, Max occupies the middle part of the graph where the two axes intersect, divided not only between the powers of good and evil, but between his identity as a hunter and his correspondence with the spiritualized worlds represented by Agathe and Samiel. We can chart the drama of *Freischütz* by tracing Max's progress around the four corners of this musico-dramatic domain: his frustrated assimilation into village life; the drunken allure of Caspar's false friendship; the spiritual temptations of the Wolf's Glen; and the redemptive force of transfigured Nature personified by Agathe.

This network of oppositions helps us understand not only the plot of *Freischütz*, but also its position in the history of German opera, for through it the "very nature and inner constitution of opera—as a whole contain-

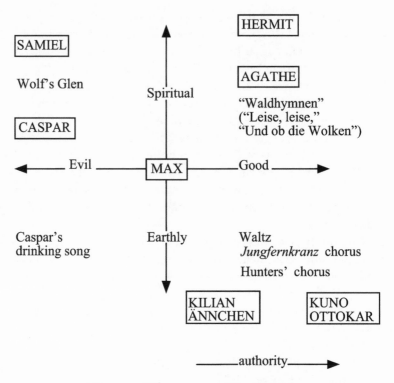

Figure 3.1   Plot structure of *Der Freischütz*

ing other wholes" could be turned from a liability into an advantage. The unique place of Weber's opera in the history of operatic style becomes clearer in comparison to Winter's work. The diverse characters and musical styles of *Das unterbrochene Opferfest* represent, so to speak, different genres that are competing for space within the same opera. As we have seen, the comic characters are largely independent of the principal plot, and their omission from *heroisch-tragische* versions of the opera, as Weber himself noted, served to tighten the drama of the work. The "comic" characters of *Freischütz* are in a certain sense equally independent of the supernatural drama concerning the fate of Max's soul. Ännchen, for instance, has no need of magic bullets to find a mate, and the musical contrast between her cheerful songs and the strange textures and harmonies of the Wolf's Glen is even greater than that which separates the music of the comic characters in *Das unterbrochene Opferfest* from the grand arias of Mafferu or Murney. But in *Freischütz*, unlike *Das unterbrochene Opferfest*, this contrast serves an essential dramatic purpose. Indeed, it is the very contrast between the musico-dramatic "quarters" of *Freischütz* that makes Max's progress from one to the other so compelling. Adopting Mosel's terminology, we can say that the character of the opera as a whole emerges precisely because the characters of the individual numbers and *handlende Personen* are so strongly differentiated from each other.

These same types of relationships between contrasting musico-dramatic spheres can of course be seen in other German operas of the generation before *Freischütz:* the opposition between Sarastro's world of light and the Queen of the Night's dark realm in *Die Zauberflöte* is the most notable example. Weber was not so much creating a new approach to opera composition as he was investing established techniques with new significance and dramatic power. And if the overall framework of the opera depends on earlier models, so too did Weber use specific musical ideas from earlier operas in his characterization of the individual musico-dramatic spheres. Scholars have long been aware of this type of borrowing, noting, for instance, that the monotone chorus in the *wilde Jagd* portion of the Wolf's Glen scene comes almost directly out of an earlier dialogue opera, *Das wütende Heer* (music by J. André and text by C. F. Bretzner).[19] These types of direct borrowings, however, are less interesting than the more general tropes and conventions that Weber employed to create the multiple "characters" of *Freischütz*. It is Weber's use of these tropes and conventions that establishes the links not only between *Freischütz* and the German operatic past, but also between Weber's work and contemporary trends in French and Italian opera.

Caspar

Of the three most important characters in *Freischütz* (Max, Caspar, and Agathe), it is Caspar who seems most firmly rooted in the conventions of late-eighteenth- and early-nineteenth-century German opera, and the outlines of his personality must have been quite familiar to audiences in Weber's time. Thomas Baumann notes that the character type of the bass villain is already present in the figure of the Bailiff in J. A. Hiller's dialogue opera *Die Liebe auf dem Lande*.[20] Caspar is the most notable example of what Bernd Göpfert calls the *Charakterbass*, a voice type closely related to the figure of Don Alfonso in *Cosi fan tutte* and parodied by the role of Osmin in *Die Entführung aus dem Serail*.[21] Caspar's more immediate ancestors may be found in bass roles from the operas of Peter von Winter, such as the character of the Oberbrahmin in *Marie von Montalban* or the role of Maf-feru from *Das unterbrochene Opferfest*. Kühleborn from E. T. A. Hoffmann's *Undine* is cast in the same mold, as are certain characters from the late 1820s and early 1830s, such as Bois-Guilbert in Marschner's *Der Templer und die Jüdin* and the Obersteiger in Wolfram's *Der Bergmönch*. Like Caspar, all of these villains are secret manipulators who attempt to ensnare the more vir-tuous characters in sinister plans, plans that they reveal to the audience in large-scale arias. These arias, which include Mafferu's "Allmächt'ge Sonne, höre," the Oberbrahmin's "Fünf trübe Jahre sind verflossen," and Kühle-born's aria with chorus "Ihr Freund aus Seen und Quellen," are typically in the key of C minor (often modulating to the relative or parallel major at some point in the aria) and show such remarkable similarities to each other that we can regard them as an operatic topos. Each begins with a slow-tempo recitative-like introduction in which the voice line is characterized by large leaps and a wide range, sometimes extending up to two octaves. The bass must be given full opportunity to display his sinister lower range. In the middle part of the aria the villain gives vent to his feelings of anger and his hopes for revenge. Here he either formulates his evil plans (as in "Allmächt'ge Sonne, höre") or calls upon the powers of evil to assist his de-signs. This middle part of the aria is usually in a faster tempo than the intro-duction, and the final section of the aria is sometimes faster still. Here the villain celebrates his imminent triumph with elaborate coloratura melis-mas, often on the first syllable of the word "Rache." As in the introductory section, these melismas exploit the extremes of the bass range.

That Caspar's aria (no. 5) "Schweig, schweig, damit dich niemand warnt" fits very clearly into this mold can be seen from a brief comparison with Mafferu's aria from *Das unterbrochene Opferfest*. The first ten measures of "Schweig, schweig, damit dich niemand warnt" form the slow introduction, and while the low A with which Caspar concludes this section is perhaps not as spectacular as the low E-flat that Mafferu sings at the corresponding point in his aria, it accomplishes the same sinister effect. In the first part of the middle section of the aria, which stretches from measure 11 to measure 40, Caspar exults over Max's imminent doom ("Nichts kann vom tiefen Fall dich retten"). Weber depicts Max's fate directly through the contours of the vocal line, which descends first through scalar figures and then via whole notes to low A, the melodic destination of the two "deep falls." The second part of the middle section ("Umgebt ihm, ihr Geister"), which extends from measure 41 to measure 63, is dominated by a motive first heard in the over-ture (cello and bassoon parts, measures 141 ff.) and clearly associated with the "dark powers." Here Caspar calls upon these dark powers to aid him. As in Mafferu's aria, the final section ("Triumph die Rache gelingt") is in the parallel major and includes "Rache coloratura," through which both villains celebrate the victory they believe is imminent.

There are important differences between the two arias—the striking changes of tempo in the middle section of "Allmächt'ge Sonne, höre," for example, have no counterpart in Caspar's aria. Weber's decision to use D minor and D major for "Schweig, schweig, damit dich niemand warnt" marks another distinction between the arias of Caspar and Mafferu. Weber may have chosen this key in order to reinforce the tonal symbolism of *Freischütz* (see Abert's argument below), but the tonality also establishes links between Caspar's aria and another, related tradition of baritone villain arias, such as Count Almaviva's "Vedro, mentr'io sospiro" in *Le nozze di Figaro* and Pizarro's "Ha! welch ein Augenblick" in *Fidelio*.[22] Although the dramaturgy and musical form of these arias is not as closely related to "Schweig, schweig, damit dich niemand warnt" as "Allmächt'ge Sonne, höre" is, they too show many similarities with Caspar's aria. Mozart never formally establishes the key of D minor in "Vedro, mentr'io sospiro," but he strongly suggests the minor tonality at the end of the first (allegro maestoso) section of the aria. The rearticulation of D major at the beginning of the final "triumph" section is thus at least to some degree analogous to the modal shift in "Schweig, schweig, damit dich niemand warnt." The tonal plan of "Ha! welch ein Augenblick" is even more closely related to Caspar's aria, for in both arias the first section is cast entirely in D minor. In sum, the tonal structure and smaller-scale musical gestures of Caspar's aria link the villain of *Freischütz* quite strongly to operatic traditions with which both Weber and his audience would have been intimately familiar. Although it is unlikely that Weber modeled Caspar's aria directly on the villain arias in *Das unterbrochene Opferfest, Figaro, Fidelio,* or any other work, he was clearly immersed in an influential group of operatic conventions. Caspar is an original creation, but he acquires a distinct character (in Mosel's sense) largely through his connections to the past.

Agathe

For the character of Agathe, Weber also drew upon established musical and dramatic topoi, yet the conventions that link the heroine to figures in other operas are more diffuse than those through which Caspar is characterized. Her position within the drama links her to certain virtuous bourgeois characters in the German dialogue operas of Hiller and Weisse, such as Löttchen in *Löttchen am Hofe,* but Agathe's most important music in the opera, her scene and aria "Wie nahte mir der Schlummer" (no. 8), has little in common with the short musical numbers that typically characterize heroines from German operas of the 1770s and 1780s. Agathe's aria is far more closely related to the two-tempo (slow-fast) *rondò* form common in late-eighteenth-century *opera seria* and in the *parte serie* of late-eighteenth-century *opere buffe.* Some better-known examples of this form come from the operas of Mozart and include "Bester Jüngling, mit Entzücken" from *Der Schauspieldirektor,* Donna Anna's "Non mi dir, bell'idol mio" from *Don Giovanni,* Fiordiligi's "Per pietà, ben mio perdona" from *Così fan tutte,* and Vitellia's "Non più di fiori" from *La clemenza di Tito.* In late-eighteenth- and early-nineteenth-century operas the *rondò* aria was usually reserved for the prima donna and the primo uomo and appeared in moments of great tension or dramatic urgency, often near the end of the act.

The term *"rondò"* is potentially confusing, for the more familiar instrumental "rondos" from the classical period have a different formal structure than these *rondò* arias.[23] Early *rondò* arias do indeed have a formal structure based upon the return of the first vocal melody (in her article on the *rondò* aria in the late eighteenth century, Lühning uses the term "Ritornellrondo" for this type), but by the late eighteenth century the term had acquired a different meaning. Manfredini, in his *Difesa della musica moderna* (1785), describes the form in the following manner: "Those arias resembling in part the rondo are not all true rondos, but sublime and grand airs containing two motives or subjects, one slow, the other spirited, each stated only twice; these arias are certainly better than what used to be called an aria cantabile, because they are more natural, more true, and more expressive."[24] In many ways Manfredini's description of the *rondò* fits "Wie nahte mir der Schlummer" quite well. The well-known melody with which Weber sets the words "Leise, leise, fromme Weise" is clearly the "first motive or subject," which returns only once more in measures 41–60 with the words "Zu dir wende ich die Hände." The second subject appears in the vivace section with the words "Süss entzückt entgegen ihm" (measures 118–25) and again in measures 162–69 with the words "Himmel, nimm des Dankes Zähren." Despite its radical differences from the *rondò* arias with which Manfredini must have been familiar, this is a "sublime and grand air" that invokes the conventions of the late eighteenth century. Like Donna Anna, Fiordiligi and Vitellia, Agathe expresses her innermost feelings and motivations in a grand *rondò* that identifies her as the prima donna of *Freischütz.*

If the *rondò* form of her aria established Agathe's connections to figures from late-eighteenth-century opera, its expansive dimensions also provided Weber with excellent opportunities for the art of characterization that was so central to his concept of operatic reform. Nowhere is this art of characterization more aptly demonstrated than in the two main subjects of the aria. In the first subject, "Leise, leise, fromme Weise," Agathe sings a kind of *preghiera* to a God who manifests himself in the mysteries of the natural world, similar in many ways to her third-act cavatina "Und ob die Wolke sie verhülle." Organized in two symmetrical eight-measure periods, the vocal line of this section eschews any outward virtuosity and, apart from an appoggiatura grace note in measure 23, stays entirely within the compass of an octave. The muted string accompaniment, with its undulating eighth notes, creates a mood of serenity and peace. Above all, it is through the slow tempo that Weber depicts Agathe's attitude of rapturous solemnity. If the first subject of the aria embodies Agathe's purity and religious devotion, so does the second subject express her excitement and joy at the prospect of seeing her beloved once more. In the quarter note rocking bass line we can almost hear the beating of her heart that Agathe verbalizes in the previous line of text, and the syncopated chords in the upper strings add to the sense of anticipation. Agathe never sings the type of bravura coloratura that characterizes many of Mozart's heroines, but her vocal line in this vivace section is decidedly more active than that of the first section. The dramatic contrast implied by the two contrasting tempos of the late-eighteenth-century *rondò* is thus fully evident in "Wie nahte mir der Schlummer."

Weber certainly uses the two conventional subjects of the *rondò* to depict Agathe's personality, but those sections of her aria in which the composer departs from the formal structure of the *rondò* make an even more important contribution to her characterization. During the late eighteenth and especially during the first decades of the nineteenth century, a typical way of expanding the structure of the *rondò* was by inserting a brief recitative or arioso section between the two halves of the aria, a section that would later come to be known as the *tempo di mezzo*. Weber incorporates just such a section into "Wie nahte mir der Schlummer" (measures 61–106, beginning with "Alles pflegt schon längst der Ruh"). This *tempo di mezzo* itself falls into two parts: an arioso section stretching from measures 61 to 73, and a more loosely organized recitative section in measures 74–106. The andante tempo of the first subsection functions as a transition between the two main subjects of the aria, while the second subsection creates the dramatic shift between the inward piety of "Leise, leise, fromme Weise" and the outward excitement of "Süss entzückt entgegen ihm." Within the context of the late-eighteenth- and early-nineteenth-century *rondò*, this *tempo di mezzo* is exceptionally long, but what makes "Wie nahte mir der Schlummer" even more unusual is the way Weber incorporates this kind of arioso-like music into what were normally the more symmetrically structured sections. In each of these sections Weber interrupts the two subjects of the aria with music that qualifies, threatens, or modifies the two principal "effects" that these subjects represent. The mood of the first "interruptive" section (measures 35–40, beginning with "O wie hell die gold'nen Sterne") seems to flow directly out of the first subject. But the solemn beauty of the night is threatened by dark clouds lurking on the horizon, and as Agathe notices the distant storm Weber deflects the tonality from E major toward E minor. If the threats to the serenity of the first subject manifest themselves in the natural world, those that undermine the joy of the second subject are of a more inward kind. The interruption of the vivace, which begins with "Konnt' ich das zu hoffen wagen?" is significantly longer than the section that comes between the two statements of the first subject, stretching from measure 126 to measure 161. Agathe at first questions the joy that stirs in her breast, but reassures herself with the thought that good fortune will soon return to her beloved. As this happy thought appears (measures 137–41) her vocal line regains some of the energy of the second subject, energy which dissipates with the more serious doubts Agathe voices in measures 141–51. All of her hopes may be nothing but delusion, she sings, as the tonality moves via an A minor chord to the Neapolitan tonality of F major in measure 150, the most harmonically distant point from the E-major tonality of the vivace. As this chord resolves, Agathe dedicates her tears to heaven ("Himmel, nimm des Dankes Zähren für dies Pfand der Hoffnung an") and then returns to the second statement of the second subject in measure 162.

These interruptive sections constitute perhaps the most noticeable structural difference between Mozart's *rondò* arias and "Wie nahte mir der Schlummer," and they are an important key to the difference of character that separates Agathe from the heroines of *Don Giovanni* and *La clemenza di Tito*. Donna Anna and Vitellia are figures of power, and it can be argued that it is their determination that sets the plots of *Don Giovanni* and *La clemenza di Tito* into motion. Agathe, in contrast, is completely passive— she can only respond to action and never initiate it. Despite her love for Max, her father will award her to whoever wins the shooting contest. She is powerless to prevent Max from going into the Wolf's Glen, and even her desperate plea in the final dialogue of the opera ("Schiess nicht, Max! Ich bin die Taube!") goes unheeded. The kinds of doubts and fears that Agathe expresses in the interruptive sections of her aria would be out of character (in every sense of the term) for Donna Anna and Vitellia, but in "Wie nahte mir der Schlummer" they are the vehicle through which the *rondò* is transformed from an expression of power into a psychological study. Character, we might say, is created through the tension between the aria and the structural conventions that inform it.

Max

This same type of creative tension between innovation and convention may also be seen in the other large-scale *rondò* in *Der Freischütz*, Max's aria "Durch die Wälder" (no. 3). The aria is set up by a peasant's dance, which functions as a dramatic transition from the public space of the first two numbers to Max's interior world. Nothing could be more regular than the tonic-dominant harmonies and the symmetrical phrase structure of the peasant's dance, and nothing could be more distant from Max's emotional state. Weber uses the contrast between this music and the shifting, irregular rhythms of the recitative ("Nein, länger trag' ich nicht") to illustrate Max's alienation from the community. Although there are no sharps or flats in the key signature, the recitative suggests C minor, the key that Weber associates with the *finst're Mächte*, and the key in which the aria will end. The first subject of the *rondò*, in E-flat major, begins with a brief ritornello in which the flutes and clarinets play the melody (measures 24–27). Here the woodwind texture serves as a reference to the sphere of Agathe—indeed, the entire cantabile section is for Max an idyllic fantasy, in which he has already overcome the central problem of the plot. There is no full restatement of the theme (as described in Manfredini's definition of the *rondò*), but Weber hints at a recapitulation of this first theme in the pickup to measure 48 with the words "freute sich Agathe's Liebesblick," and the entire cantabile is rounded off by a restatement of the principal theme in the woodwinds, beginning with the pickup to measure 59. "Agathe's Liebesblick," or rather the soaring lyricism with which Max describes it, offers another alternative to the *finst're Mächte*—not the highly rhythmicized, rough-hewn world of Kilian and the Bauerntanz, but the refined *Innigkeit* of romantic love.

Just as in Agathe's aria, the intermediate section of Max's aria (the *tempo di mezzo*) is quite extensive and falls into two distinct parts. In the first subsection ("Hat denn der Himmel mich verlassen," measures 64–79) Max's faith begins to falter, and as it does so, Samiel appears in the background along with his distinguishing leitmotiv (measures 68–72). The second sub-section of the *tempo di mezzo* (andante con moto, measures 80–107), in which Max thinks again of Agathe, represents a partial return to the idyll of the cantabile. But instead of recapitulating the E-flat major of "Durch die Wälder," Weber places this section in G major, so that the entire section may be said to function to some degree as a dominant preparation for the C minor of the final section. We know that the dark premonitions of evil depicted in the opening recitative and the first part of the *tempo di mezzo* have been only temporarily subdued.

In the final part of the aria the *finst're Mächte* that have lurked around the edges of Max's consciousness take center stage. This allegro falls into three subsections: measures 108–31, measures 132–59, and measures 160–95. The first subsection encompasses what Manfredini would call the second subject: the complex of C-minor motives that also forms the first theme of the overture. Just as in the overture, this theme group is followed by a second theme in E-flat major ("O dringt kein Strahl durch diese Nächte"), the key of the cantabile ("Durch die Wälder") and its idyllic hopes. In the overture Weber also uses the "Süss entgegen ihm" music to bring the overture to a triumphant close. But in this allegro, no ray of light penetrates the dark-ness. The major key is illusory and is quickly deflected toward E-flat mi-nor. As Max vainly struggles against the dark powers that threaten to over-whelm him, his music moves further and further away from the "demonic" C-minor tonality. The point of greatest harmonic distance from the C-minor tonic comes in measures 152–55 with the words "Lebt kein Gott?" words that Weber sets with a dramatic upward leap of an augmented sixth. We may indeed understand the chords underlying these words as incom-plete augmented sixth chords in E-flat minor, a harmony which is then reinterpreted as V/V in C minor (bass motion A–G–C). This return to C mi-nor marks the beginning of the third and final subsection of the aria. Al-though Weber repeats the text of the first part of the allegro ("Mich fasst Verzweiflung"), this section does not include a recapitulation of the "second subject" that Manfredini's model of the *rondò* prescribes. Nevertheless, the third subsection of the allegro does represent a return to the C-minor to-nality and the thematic complex with which it is associated. Max ends the aria even more firmly in the grip of the demonic forces, unable to resist the sinister plot that Caspar will unfold in the following scene.

As in the arias for the other two main characters of *Freischütz* (Caspar's "Schweig, schweig" and Agathe's "Wie nahte mir der Schlummer"), Weber creates character in Max's aria through what we might call a "referential network."[25] Caspar's aria, as we have seen, derives much of its meaning through reference to a particular tradition of villains in French and German operas of the late eighteenth and early nineteenth century. Agathe is also related to a common character type from these traditions, yet in her aria Weber creates a distinct personality largely through his departures from the operatic convention of the *rondò*. Max also sings a *rondò*, but the structure of "Durch die Wälder" is less important for Max's characterization than for the referential network that links his aria to other music in the opera. The C-minor music of the allegro, with its clear references both to the overture and to the *finst're Mächte* of the Wolf's Glen scene, is only the most obvious example of this network. Max's aria is connected not only to the C-minor world of evil, but also to the hope of redemption. The motive that Max sings in his vain protest against the dark powers ("O dringt kein Strahl"), for instance, is related both to the overture and to a theme from Agathe's aria ("Himmel, nimmt des Dankes Zähren," measures 155–57). It is no accident that Weber uses the clarinet to accompany this section in Max's aria, for it is the instrument that is most closely associated with Agathe. Together with the flute (and later the bassoon), the clarinet also plays the ritornelli in the cantabile section, helping to make Agathe a musical as well as a textual reference point in Max's aria.

That the C-minor tonality of the allegro is a reference to the dark powers depicted in the overture and in the Wolf's Glen scene is clear—less obvious are the referential meanings of E-flat major. In the aria, as in the overture, E-flat major is associated with Agathe and the hope of redemption that she represents. When the Hermit appears in the third-act finale, he sings in E-flat major, and we are reminded of the special significance that this key holds in *Die Zauberflöte*. The dramatic significance of C minor and E-flat major in this opera may help make Weber's choice of a key signature of no flats or sharps for the introductory recitative of the aria ("Nein! länger trag' ich nicht") more comprehensible. Perhaps Weber was suggesting a key progression of C major–E-flat major–C minor for the aria: in other words, the retrograde of the key progression of the overture and, in the most general sense, of the entire opera. If the key progression of C minor to C major represents Max's liberation from evil, then the move from the putative C major of the recitative to the C minor of the allegro represents the reverse. Just as the E-flat major second theme group in the exposition of the overture may be said in some sense to represent a partial or incomplete "response" to the first theme group (a response which is finalized by the C-major recapitulation of this material at the end of the overture), so too does the E-flat major of Max's cantabile ("Durch die Wälder") or the second subsection of the allegro ("O dringt kein Strahl") offer only temporary respite from the demonic power represented by C minor.

The Geography of *Freischütz*

If the plot of *Freischütz* is essentially the story of Max's fall and redemption, then this aria encapsulates its first half, emerging directly out of the D-major *Volkstümlichkeit* of Kilian and the peasants and leading through vain hopes of happiness to the demonic world of the *finst're Mächte*.[26] But this fall, of course, is not merely metaphorical. Weber narrates the drama not only through the sequence of musical "characters," but also through the sequence of tableaux in which the action takes place.[27] In order to understand this sequence we must turn our attention from the individual numbers to the form of the opera as a whole. The musical score describes six tableaux in *Der Freischütz* (table 3.1).

Each of the six tableaux is different, but the action essentially takes place in two types of areas: in the forest (first act; second-act finale; third act, scenes 1 and 6) and in the forester's house (second act, scenes 1–3; third act, scenes 2–5). As we might expect (given the gender dualities of early-nineteenth-century society), Weber and Kind populate the interior scenes predominantly with female characters; it is the men who dominate the exterior scenes. Indeed, Max is the only male character who sets foot into the female/interior realm. The narrative moves between these two groups in order to produce two symmetrical structures: an outside–inside–outside pattern for acts 1 and 2 that is repeated in act 3. The first scene of the third act, however, is often cut in performance. (It is not even included in the 1904 G. Schirmer piano-vocal score of the work.) Without this scene, a different and perhaps more interesting symmetry emerges, one that encompasses the entire opera:

Outside–Inside–Outside (Wolf's Glen)–Inside–Outside

These five tableaux also correspond to the different times of day in which the action takes place: midday (act 1); evening and the beginning of the night (first part of act 2); then Wolf's Glen for the darkest hour (between midnight and one); morning of the next day (first part of act 3); and full daylight (end of act 3). This circadian pattern is underscored by the keys

Table 3.1   Stage Setting Descriptions for *Der Freischütz*

First act (musical nos. 1–5)	An open space before an inn in the forest (Platz vor einer Waldschenke)
Second act, scenes 1–3 (musical nos. 6–9)	An antechamber in the forester's house, with two side doors (Vorsaal mit zwei Seiteneingängen im Forsthaus)
Second-act finale (Wolf's Glen scene, musical no. 10)	A fearsome gorge, for the most part overgrown with dark wood, surrounded by high mountains (furchtbare Schlucht, grössentheils mit Schwarzholz bewachsen, von hohen Gebirgen umgeben)
Third act, first scene[1]	A small wood (kurzer Wald)
Third act, scenes 2–5 (musical nos. 12–14)	Agathe's chamber, furnished in an ordinary and yet charming way (Agathens Stübchen, allerthümlich, doch niedlich verziert)
Third act, scene 6 (musical nos. 15 and 16)	A beautiful romantic landscape (eine romantisch schöne Gegend)

1. The entr'acte (musical no. 11) might almost be counted as part of this tableau; even if the curtain is drawn, its D-major tonality and references to the hunt (employing the music that Weber will later use for the hunting chorus) connect it clearly not only to the nature-world of act 3, but also to the opening scene of act 1.

in which the "outdoors" tableaux begin: D major (first-act introduction)–F-sharp minor (Wolf's Glen)–D major ("Jägerchor").

All of these symmetries frame and foreground what is surely the most extraordinary scene in the opera, the finale to the second act. Just as the Orpheus operas of the early seventeenth century, or later works such as Gluck's *Orfeo ed Euridice*, Beethoven's *Fidelio*, or Wagner's *Das Rheingold*, *Freischütz* thus pivots around a central scene in which the hero or heroine must descend. He or she needs to go down to hell, into the deepest part of the dungeon, to dark Nibelheim, in order to bring something back to the "normal world." Yet Max is no Orpheus figure. He does not find his missing spouse in the Wolf's Glen, but rather the tools of the Devil. The closer parallel is with *Das Rheingold*—like Alberich's ring, the magic bullets have great potential power, but they are also cursed.

If these operas each reconfigure a common mythological trope, then they also present composers with a common musical problem: the lower world must be in some way set apart from the other scenes. The Wolf's Glen, of course, is not literally "underground"—the stage directions make clear that it is in a wild part of the forest. Nevertheless, it fulfills the same function (at least in this regard) as do Nibelheim, Hades, or the dungeon in the stories of *Das Rheingold, Orfeo ed Euridice,* and *Fidelio.* Here *Freischütz* follows a distinction that we can also find in Gluck and Beethoven, a distinction that is further intensified in *Das Rheingold:* in descending into the underworld the hero or heroine leaves behind not only light and warmth, but also, at least to some degree, melody. If commentators from both the nineteenth and twentieth centuries have stressed the innovations of the Wolf's Glen scene, it also may be placed firmly within the conventions of operatic style. The otherworldly chanting of the invisible spirits near the beginning of the scene, for example, can be seen as a distant relative of the menacing, repetitive rhythms of Gluck's Furies. The strange, piercing woodwind timbres and unstable harmonies that Beethoven uses to depict the atmosphere of the dungeon at the beginning of Florestan's aria "Gott, welch Dunkel hier" have direct parallels in some of the textures of the Wolf's Glen scene, and it is surely no accident that both Beethoven and Weber use the technique of melodrama in the underworld. In the operatic depths, texture threatens to overwhelm melody, and nondiegetic sounds from outside of the genre may impinge upon the normal sounds of opera. The sounds that accompany Caspar's hellish manufacturing are, in this sense, precursors to the pounding of Nibelheim's hammers.

The Wolf's Glen

The need to set apart the Wolf's Glen from the other scenes in the opera returns us once again to the problem of *Charakter* that Weber enunciates in his review of *Undine.* Max and Caspar need to inhabit a singular musical environment in the finale of the second act, but the unique character of this scene must also be integrated into the character of the opera as a whole. Weber meets this challenge in a variety of ways. The strange textures in the first section of the second-act finale—tremolo strings, monotone chorus, fortissimo woodwinds, and so forth—may be the most blatant signifiers of the "otherness" of this scene. Through the descending line in the basses and bassoons (measures 2–12), followed closely by the ascending major-sixth gesture in the upper woodwinds, Weber opens a tonal space between high and low sounds—a potent metaphor for the yawning gulf into which Max will later descend. The Wolf's Glen, indeed, is full of strange sounds that we hear in no other scene, and in no other section of the work does orchestral texture play such an important role in the narration of the drama.

The orchestration of the second-act finale was one of the most controversial aspects of the opera, and few early-nineteenth-century reviews fail to mention it. In his biography of his father, as we might expect, Max Maria von Weber for the most part glorifies the reception of *Freischütz,* but he also includes this interesting passage concerning some negative criticism that the opera received:

> The critics admitted, it is true, the great musical importance of the work, the heart-stirring quality of its melodies, the ability with which Weber jested at all the rules of art without offending them, the originality of the instrumental effects, the breath of genius which breathed over the whole. . . . They even recognized the wondrous talent with which the strange, weird, supernatural effects had been treated without overstepping the bounds of the line of beauty, the marked character, and the contrasting tenderness. But they never could quite forgive the audacious novelty, and complained that classical repose was sacrificed to effect, that the originality was often monstrous, that the characterization bordered on caricature, that musical impossibilities were "music no more."[28]

Max Maria is primarily referring to the ambivalent review in the Berlin *Vossische Zeitung,* long thought to have been by E. T. A. Hoffmann.[29] The review is by no means wholly negative, but it clearly states that "the characters are cast as stereotypical forms, and a good-old-boy, an ingenue, a pious lover, a wild good-for-nothing, and so on, run around each other without giving us any reason to wish to get to know them better."[30]

If comments such as these can be read as a challenge to (or even as an inversion of) the rhetoric of *Charakter,* so too does another strand of *Freischütz* criticism challenge Weber's ideal of a more integral relationship between text and music. In his discussion of *Freischütz* the playwright Franz Grillparzer did not so much criticize the opera itself as the aesthetic ideals upon which it was based:

> It follows that music should above all strive to attain what is attainable, that she should not, in order to enter a competition with the speaking arts over the exact signification of concepts, give up those qualities with which she surpasses those arts. Music must not strive to make words out of tones, for like every other art, she ceases to be art when she goes out-

side of natural form. For music, this form is the beautiful melody, just as for all of the plastic arts it is the beautiful shape. If the poet who wants to attain the sound of music in his verses is a fool, so too the musician who wants to equal the poet's definitiveness of expression with his tones is deranged. Thus Mozart is the greatest composer and Maria Weber—is not the greatest.[31]

Grillparzer does not single out the Wolf's Glen scene as a specific instance of Weber's misguided attempt "to make words out of tones," but it seems likely that he would have cited the orchestral effects of the second-act finale as a prominent example of music "going outside of natural form." Weber was clearly pushing the early-nineteenth-century concept of "character" to its utmost limits, and perhaps beyond them. If, as I have argued, "leaving melody behind" signified the hero's descent into the underworld, then melody nevertheless was a central, perhaps *the* central element in the operatic language of the early nineteenth century. Grillparzer's sense that Weber had transgressed its rules was echoed a decade later by Richard Wagner, in his youthful essay "On German Opera":

> Weber never understood the management of Song, and Spohr wellnigh as little. But Song, after all, is the organ whereby a man may musically express himself; and so long as it is not fully developed, he is wanting in true speech. In this respect the Italians have an immeasurable advantage over us; vocal beauty with them is a second nature, and their creations are just as sensuously warm as poor, for the rest, in individual import.[32]

These criticisms of *Freischütz* touch upon what is perhaps the most ironic aspect of Weber's compositional career. The same aesthetic principles through which he intended to create a more organic opera—the integral relationship between text and music and the idea of "character"—instead presented him with what Carl Dahlhaus called the "danger of discontinuity."[33] This ironic opposition between "discontinuity" and "organic unity" has been central to *Freischütz* criticism since its premiere. Indeed, the extent to which scholars have attempted to demonstrate the organic unity of *Freischütz* may in some ways be seen as a measure of the acuity of Grillparzer's critique.

If the strange textures of the Wolf's Glen scene seemed for some critics to transgress the integral connection between words and melody that was essential to opera, they also served as an example of Weber's attempt to integrate the individual scenes of the work into an organic whole. The finale to the second act, as even the most casual listener may hear, is full of direct quotations from other sections of the opera, and some of the strange textures that "characterize" the Wolf's Glen are expanded versions of gestures heard in other scenes. The Samiel motive itself, for instance, first heard as Caspar invokes Samiel in measures 43 and following, is reinforced by trombones playing the bass line and ends in a thunderous C-minor cadence. The piccolo trill in the "drinking motive" (measures 127 ff.) comes from Caspar's drinking song "Hier im ird'schen Jammerthal"; here the gesture becomes an even more potent symbol of the demonic. The horn calls in E-flat major that announce Max's arrival (measures 154–58) are first heard in the overture (measures 92–96) and are further related to the adagio maestoso section of the third-act finale, in which the Hermit appears. Max's vocal line for the words "Ha! Furchtbar gähnt der düst're Abgrund," which follows immediately after these horn calls, is a close approximation of the clarinet melody that follows the horn calls in the overture, a melody which may further allude to the melody that Max sings to the words "O dringt kein Strahl" in his first-act aria. To accompany Max as he takes his first tentative steps into the Wolf's Glen (measures 191 ff.), Weber uses material first heard toward the end of the C-minor theme group in the overture (measures 91 ff.). After he sees the image of Agathe throwing herself into the flood (measures 247 ff.), we hear more of the C-minor music from the *finst're Mächte* sections of the overture and from the finale to Max's aria. The dark powers return in full force with the C-minor section beginning in measure 373 (presto). Caspar casts the sixth bullet, and, as the stage directions indicate, "the entire sky turns to black night. Thunderstorms clash against one another. Flames leap from the earth. Strange lights appear on the mountains, etc."[34] At this point, of course, Weber directly quotes the most distinctive music from the overture and Max's aria—here the dark powers acquire material form.

That the music associated with Samiel and the C-minor music of the *finst're Mächte* should appear in other parts of the opera as well as the Wolf's Glen is hardly surprising. Samiel's presence has been felt since the overture, and the casting of the bullets is only the most violent manifestation of his baleful influence. More interesting is the tonal organization of this scene: first, the way that Weber integrates this C-minor music into the harmonic pattern of the finale, and second, the way in which he integrates that harmonic pattern into the tonal structure of the opera as a whole. Scholars and critics have long been fascinated with this aspect of Weber's musical style, taking their cue perhaps from the composer himself, who, speaking about his composition of the cantata *Kampf und Sieg*, wrote: "Before I began with the representation of the individual [numbers], I tried out a large-scale plan of the tonal picture through the determination of the principal colors in each of the individual parts, that is to say: I wrote out exactly the sequence of keys whose successive effects promised to be successful."[35] Many commentators have drawn attention to Weber's large-scale tonal planning in *Der Freischütz,* but perhaps the most influential account of this technique may be found in the article "Carl Maria von Weber und sein *Freischütz*" by Hermann Abert (1926). Abert's article is far from a one-sided celebration of *Freischütz*'s greatness and originality—he freely acknowledges, for example, Weber's debts to earlier *Singspiel* and French *opéra comique.* But the emphasis of his article falls on Weber's long-range tonal planning. Echoing, perhaps, the putative quotation from Lobe cited above, Abert refers to the familiar contrast within *Freischütz* between the keys of C minor and D major, but then extends this contrast so that it encompasses other, more distantly related keys:

> [I]n this contrast we can see the tendency for the individual keys to achieve their effects not merely by themselves, but through the entire circle to which they belong. One can thus speak of entire key-spheres within which the character of the principal key predominates, key-spheres that underlie the corresponding turns in the course of the plot. In the exposition (numbers 1–3), for example, the principal key of D already appears together with its two dominants G and A. . . . Because the villain Caspar "puts on the forester's coat" he also belongs to this *volkstümlich* D major, but bends it in no. 4 first toward B minor, and then toward D minor. . . . The second act contains no D-major piece, and yet the sphere of this key is still at work in its dominant A major (no. 6) and its secondary dominant E major (no. 8): Agathe also belongs to the sphere of the *Volk,* yet with a subjective, heightened sensitivity. The F-sharp minor of the Wolf's Glen eventually refers back to the A major of the beginning of the act, for despite its nocturnal eeriness, it is the key of Nature that is still not disturbed by evil.[36]

Abert's exegesis, of course, is at least as much a prescription for listening to *Freischütz* as a description of the opera, and in many ways tells us more about the agenda of early-twentieth-century German musicology than it does about Weber's music. That Abert should focus on the network of key and motivic relationships which link the various numbers of *Freischütz* together is hardly surprising, for in this era of Lorenz and Schenker it was precisely through the demonstration of its organic unity that *Freischütz* could take its place in the canon of German masterworks next to the symphonies of Beethoven or the operas of Wagner. Large-scale tonal planning is indeed important to the drama and symbolism of *Freischütz*, but it is surely not the only criterion in Weber's choice of keys for particular numbers or passages. The music to which Agathe sings the phrase "Süss entzückt entgegen ihm," for instance, appears quite naturally in the tonic key of her aria, E major. In the overture, however, Weber places this same music in E-flat major so that it functions as the relative major of C minor. While it is possible to interpret this tonal contrast in terms of the large-scale "key complexes" at work in the opera as a whole, the more localized function of the two keys within Agathe's aria and the overture is surely much more significant.[37]

Even if the tonal symbolism of *Freischütz* is not as all embracing as Abert implies, there is little doubt that it plays a large role in the meaning of the second-act finale. If the unusual textures of the Wolf's Glen scene help to set it apart from the "normal world," so do the harmonic procedures that Weber employs. Instead of the tonic-dominant polarity that informs the *volksthümlich* numbers, Weber uses tonal centers related by tritones and diminished thirds. Abert describes these procedures in the following terms:

> Two tonally stable F-sharp minor passages at the beginning and the end [of the finale], that depict the secretive whorling and burbling of nocturnal forest life, enclose a large middle section in the tritone-related key of C minor, the key of the witching hour, in which the wild succession of natural powers, each more powerful than the last, is unleashed. This section also contains short episodes in a minor and E-flat major that are themselves tritone related. The entire succession A–C–E-flat–F-sharp thus produces the same diminished-seventh chord that appears in the 26th bar of the overture and that stands for the figure of Samiel.[38]

The harmonic organization of the finale is not quite as clear-cut as this passage implies. The passages that accompany the casting of the second, third, fourth, and fifth bullets, for example (measures 293–371), often suggest other tonal centers (B-flat major, D minor, A-flat major), and it is often the A pedal of the Samiel music, rather than the key area of A minor, that dominates a particular section. Nevertheless, Abert's observation is persuasive. *Freischütz* listeners may not necessarily hear the tonal centers of the Wolf's Glen scene "spelling out" the diminished-seventh chord associated with Samiel, but they are aware, I think, that these tonal centers bear unusual relationships to one another. The contrast between the harmonic procedures of the Wolf's Glen and those of the daytime world of the hunters' chorus, the first-act waltz, or the "Chorus of Bridesmaids" is clear. And yet the harmonic organization of this scene, which helps to distinguish the Wolf's Glen from the "normal" world, emerges directly from the referential network through which Weber links this music to the rest of the opera. The Wolf's Glen scene, to put it another way, projects a harmonic language that is at once unique and an integral part of the opera as a whole, and thus provides an ideal example of the principles of *Charakter* at work.

These principles may also be seen to inform the formal structure of the scene. At first glance this structure seems to have little in common with the musical forms that Weber uses in the other sections of the opera. In his book *Carl Maria von Weber und die deutsche Nationaloper,* Wolfgang Wagner analyzes this scene and sees little connection to the formal models of the late eighteenth and early nineteenth centuries. Wagner draws attention to the ways in which the finale references the tradition of operatic storm scenes and describes the formal structure of the scene as "episodic." Indeed, the "mythic numbers" of three and seven (numbers that Caspar invokes immediately before he casts the first bullet) seem to have more to do with the formal organization of the scene—Max has three visions at the edge of the abyss, and the casting of the bullets conjures forth seven manifestations of the powers of darkness. But alongside, or "underneath" these mythological structures, the second-act finale can be seen to follow a four-part form closely related to the structure of Agathe's and Max's arias and, further, to the *pezzo concertante* of contemporary Italian opera:

1. preparation (measures 1–154): Caspar speaks with Samiel;
2. Max's hallucinations (measures 155–257);
3. transition (measures 258–75): Caspar and Max;
4. casting the magic bullets (measures 276–430).

Sections 1 and 3, which contain melodrama and dialogue, thus fill the same function as the recitative and arioso sections in the large double-aria form that Weber uses for Max and Agathe. Section 2, in which Max sees three visions—the eagle's wing, his mother in her grave, and Agathe throwing herself into a river—is hardly a cantabile in the musical sense, but by offering a potential release from the powers of darkness it does serve a similar dramatic function as "Durch die Wälder" does in Max's first-act aria. Likewise, although the final section of the Wolf's Glen scene may not show the musical outlines of a traditional fast section, it nevertheless fulfills the same dramatic expectations: reconfirming and intensifying the character of the musical number by an increase of tempo and dynamics.

Ambivalent Symbols

The formal outlines of the Wolf's Glen scene may resonate with those from other numbers in the opera, but ultimately it is through dramatic imagery that the finale is most effectively integrated into the rest of the work. This integration is most apparent during the final section of the scene, in which Caspar is casting the magic bullets. The stage directions for this section, which are nearly as extensive as those for all the other parts of the opera together, describe a series of demonic manifestations, each more terrifying than the last (see table 3.2).[39]

Perhaps the most striking thing about these images is the extent to which they partake of the same mythology of the hunt that informs so much of the "normal world" in *Der Freischütz*. The images of the black boar trampling through the forest, the galloping horses, the "wilde Heer," and above all the figure of the Black Huntsman himself form a kind of evil inversion of the joys of the hunt celebrated in the third-act "Jägerchor"—in the second verse of this latter number the hunters refer explicitly to "felling the boar." This hunting imagery had enormous resonance for early-nineteenth-century Germans, as Susan Youens writes in her book *Schubert, Müller, and "Die schöne Müllerin"*:

> A "Jäger," after all, was the military term for a fusilier, and those who wrote the poetry of German nationalism *redivivus* during the Napoleonic years invoked the *Jägerkorps* with all the white-hot jingoistic fervor of those attempting to overthrow one of the great tyrants in European history. "Heimat" and "Wald," "Waidwerk" and "Jäger" (home forest, hunting, hunter) became multivalent terms, laden with political associations no English translation can adequately encompass. . . . At this fraught juncture in European history, the German *Jäger* becomes a nationalistic emblem, a masculine-heroic model of irresistible bravery and sexual appeal.[40]

Youens's specific concern, of course, is with the figure of the hunter in *Die schöne Müllerin*, but her remarks help illuminate the extent to which this hunting imagery was responsible for the success of *Freischütz*. This imagery, she points out, had its dark side as well. Youens describes many late-eighteenth- and early-nineteenth-century hunting songs that depict the

Table 3.2   Stage Directions for the Casting of the Magic Bullets

	The contents of the ladle begin to ferment and hiss.
Eins	
	Night birds come down; they gather around the fire, hopping and fluttering about.
Zwei	
	A black boar comes crashing through the bushes and darts wildly across.
Drei	
	A storm arises, bends, and breaks the tops of the trees, sparks and fire fly, and so forth.
Vier	
	One hears rattling, the crack of whips, and the trampling of horses.
Fünf	
	Barking and neighing are heard in the air. Shadowy forms of hunters, mounted and on foot, with stags and dogs rush through the air.
Sechs	
	The entire sky turns to black night. Thunderstorms clash against one another. Flames leap from the earth. Strange lights appear on the mountains.
Sieben	
	At that instant the storm begins to abate; in the place of the dead tree stands the Black Huntsman, grasping at Max's hand.

savagery of the hunt, and others in which the hunter's prey turns out to be his beloved. One is reminded here of the dialogue that precedes the third-act finale of *Freischütz*, in which Agathe cries, "Don't shoot Max, I am the dove!"[41] That Weber and Kind would use both sides of this hunting imagery problematizes the statement from Lobe quoted above, in which Weber supposedly identifies "the hunting life and the force of the demonic powers, personified by Samiel" as the "two principal elements" in *Freischütz*. For if the hunting life embodies uncomplicated masculine vigor in numbers such as the "Jägerchor," then it seems that the "demonic powers" can just as easily adopt its symbolism.

As in *Die schöne Müllerin*, these hunting references form a subset of the nature symbolism that informs nearly every scene in the opera. The "wilde

Heer" in the second-act finale, for instance, seems almost to be a part of the fearful storm that rages around Max and Caspar, and when the hunters describe their prey in the "Jägerchor," their joy is inseparable from their delight in the wild nature through which their horns resound. Nature is never far from the character's thoughts and forms a constant point of reference in Kind's libretto. But just as the "Jägerchor" and the Wolf's Glen scene show two different faces of hunting symbolism in the opera, so too is nature more generally associated not only with peace, purity, and goodness, but also with fear, anxiety, and evil. Indeed, for some commentators, the meaning of the opera seemed to lay precisely in its multivalent depiction of the natural world. For Hans Pfitzner it was above all in the symbol of the forest that this multivalency was embodied. In his essay "Was ist uns Weber," he therefore identified the *deutsche Wald* as the true *Hauptperson* of the opera:

> The heart of *Freischütz* is the indescribably inward and refined sound of nature-feeling. *We might say that the principal character of Freischütz is the forest,* the German forest in the brilliance of summer, alive with the sounds of horns and the pleasures of the hunt, the forest in midnight storm and dark, notorious chasm, in the first flash of morning joy, in the familiar rustling that steals into the evening stillness of the forester's house. In comparison to Nature the human characters play, so to speak, a secondary role. As with Eichendorff, they are put into the landscape only as accessories.[42]

It seems likely that Pfitzner was acquainted with Richard Wagner's remarks to the Paris public concerning *Der Freischütz* (1841), in which Wagner claims that the poem of *Freischütz* seems to have been written by the Bohemian forests themselves. The specific German character of the tale, Wagner says, lies precisely in its depiction of Nature.[43] In these passages, both Pfitzner and Wagner are placing *Freischütz* within a long cultural tradition that locates the national essence of Germany in its forests. Like so many other aspects of German cultural identity, this tradition was oppositional in its structure, pitting the German forests against the Mediterranean city, the greenery of the north against the masonry of the south. As Simon Schama points out in his book *Landscape and Memory,* this rhetoric is ancient. "The armies of the Caesars may have fought the battles," he writes, "but it was the prose of Tacitus that ordained the conflict, for generations, for centuries to come, on and on: wood against marble; iron against gold; fur against silk; brutal seriousness against elegant irony; bloody-minded tribalism against legalistic universalism."[44] The image of the forest in *Freischütz*, then, is never neutral, but rather is resonant with meanings in which ideas of "national character" figure very deeply indeed.

Inscape and Landscape

Pfitzner invokes Eichendorff, but another point of confluence would be between *Freischütz* and the landscape paintings of Caspar David Friedrich, a comparison that has been made by many commentators on the opera.[45] In many of Friedrich's landscapes nature appears to dwarf the human characters, who are often seen only from behind. Moreover, in these landscapes, as in *Der Freischütz*, the forest can serve a variety of different symbolic purposes. In paintings such as *The Cross in the Mountains* (Dresden, Gemäldegalerie Neue Meister) or *Winter Landscape* (London, National Gallery), the shapes of the fir trees and their positioning on the canvas clearly resonate with images of the cross or a gothic cathedral. Yet in others, such as *The Chasseur in the Forest* (private collection, Bielefeld, Germany), the trees appear dark, foreboding, and mysterious, akin perhaps to the *Schwarzholz* that grows in the Wolf's Glen.[46]

Friedrich's paintings of the weird, wind-scoured rocks of the *sächsische Schweiz* may be the most obvious parallel with the scenery of the Wolf's Glen, but his painting *Morgen im Riesengebirge* (Berlin, Nationalgalerie, Galerie der Romantik) has, in my view, a more profound resonance with the meaning of the opera as a whole. Friedrich composed the painting from sketches that he made on a walking tour of the Riesengebirge (on the southern border of Silesia). It is divided into two nearly equal parts: a rocky, mountainous landscape, treeless, half-shrouded in fog and mist that seems to rise from the valleys, and a cloudless sky, glowing with a pale golden light. In the foreground of the picture, a rocky outcrop rises; it is topped by a crucifix. This crucifix is the only point in the picture where the horizon line is bisected. A woman, clad in white, seems to have just reached this lonely peak; with one hand she grasps the base of the crucifix, and with another, the hand of her companion, a man in black who appears to be following her up the mountain. When this painting was first shown at the Dresden Academy exhibition of 1811, a reviewer from the *Journal des Luxus und der Moden* identified this figure as Friedrich himself and suggested that both the male and female figures had been painted by Friedrich's friend Kersting, who had accompanied him on his tour.[47] The painting reads almost like a visual representation of the ideology behind *Der Freischütz*. As in Weber's opera, the world is divided into two zones: one of clarity and light, the other shrouded in mist. The crucifix is the pathway from the earthly realm into the heavenly one, and it is the woman in white, the Agathe figure, we might say, who leads the man forward.

In his book on Friedrich, Börsch-Supan describes *Morgen im Riesengebirge* as a typical example of the artist's method. Friedrich did not paint *Morgen im Riesengebirge en plein air*, Börsch-Supan points out, but rather in his studio, from sketches he made while on his walking tour. The painting does not necessarily represent a particular spot in the Riesengebirge, but rather an "ideal landscape" that Friedrich assembled from various sketches and from his own imagination. That the painting represents such an "ideal landscape," rather than a particular image from the real world, reflects Friedrich's fundamental aesthetic philosophy. "The artist's goal," he wrote, "is not to faithfully reproduce air, water, rocks, and trees but to make these reflect his soul, his feelings. To recognize the spirit of nature, to allow it to penetrate the heart and soul, to both take it in and convey it—that is the task of the work of art."[48]

The metaphors of reflection and penetration that Friedrich uses to characterize the relationship between Nature and the painter's heart seem equally well suited to describe the relationship between Nature and the inner world of the characters in *Der Freischütz*. In an almost trivial sense we see the characters opening themselves to the spirit of Nature in numbers such as the "Jägerchor," where the hunters rejoice in the physicality of the hunt. More significant is the role of Nature in Agathe's second-act aria. The text for the aria is filled with images from the natural world, but one passage in particular seems to have special meaning—the music to which she sings "Welch schöne Nacht!" immediately before the adagio section of her aria. According to the stage directions, Agathe draws a curtain from before the balcony at this point, and "a bright starlit night is seen over the landscape." The chord progression beneath her F-sharp fermata (measure 14) seems a musical symbol of this act of opening, the very moment in which Agathe allows the "spirit of nature" to "penetrate the heart and soul." It is precisely this spirit, as Joachim Reiber points out in his book *Bewahrung und Bewährung: Das Libretto zu Carl Maria von Webers "Freischütz" im literararischen Horizont seiner Zeit*, that forms the connection between the human and the metaphysical realms.[49] Agathe's attitude is one of prayer, for she recognizes in Nature the power of the Almighty. But nature is also linked to the powers of darkness—in the first interruption of the cantabile, Agathe sees that "dort am Wald auch schwebt ein Heer dunkler Wolken dumpf und schwer."

Morgen im Riesengebirge by Caspar David Friedrich

Kind's choice of words is significant here; the image of the "Heer" (horde) of clouds will reappear as the "wilde Heer" of huntsmen that haunt the Wolf's Glen. Agathe perceives a natural world that is numinous not only with goodness, but also with evil.

And yet we might ask at this point whether Agathe is merely passively describing these numinous powers. We may also read the "dunkler Wolken" as the projections of her own anxieties, as an example, to use Friedrich's words, of Agathe making the natural world reflect her soul and her feelings. The demonic manifestations in the Wolf's Glen present us with a similar dichotomy between "reflection" and "penetration." On one hand they seem to emerge from Max's own tortured emotional state—we have already seen how Weber uses some of the C-minor themes from the overture for both the final section of Max's aria and for the section in which he sees Agathe jumping into the river. And yet the libretto makes it clear that the events in the Wolf's Glen have physical effects that are felt by other characters in the opera—the two hunters in the first scene of act 3, for example, discuss the terrible storms that they heard the night before, and Caspar is as terrified of the demonic manifestations as Max is.

That music alone cannot properly distinguish between events that are "really happening" and those that a character only imagines to happen is, in light of Friedrich's dictum, in no sense a disadvantage. For there is in *Freischütz* ultimately no distinction between "reflection" and "penetration" —the human soul and the natural world are mirrored battlegrounds in which the powers of good and the powers of evil rage against one another. The relationship between inscape and landscape, to put it another way, is not one of metaphor but of identity. It is perhaps in this relationship that the central character of *Freischütz* abides.[50]

Freischütz as National Opera

There is an idea that an isomorphic relationship between an ideal landscape and the emotions of the characters that inhabit it might be read as a modulation of Pfitzber's *bon mot,* but it can also be understood as a further application of the idea of *Charakter*—not simply to the individual numbers of an opera, or even to the work as a whole, but to the symbolic language that the opera employs. But my discussion of this symbolic still locates *Charakter* in artworks, and not in the history of their reception. Weber's own criticism, however, shows that he was interested not only in the character of individual musical pieces, but also in what I am tempted to call the character of his audience. The "Musico-Dramatic Articles" that Weber wrote for the *Abendzeitung*, for instance, represent an attempt to cultivate new ways of listening and a "new German public" for his new German opera. Here again Weber was a part of a larger critical, compositional impulse. Those engaged with the search for a German opera in the early nineteenth century, to put it another way, imagined a confluence between the character of the work itself and that of the nation to which it was addressed. This confluence has generated an enormous amount of commentary in the nearly two centuries since *Freischütz*'s premiere. If the idea of *Charakter* as developed by Koch, Körner, Humboldt, Mosel, and Weber himself can, as I have argued, be used to understand the structure and meaning of *Der Freischütz*, then certainly the idea of national character has been central to the reception of the opera. As Reiber points out, the idea that *Freischütz* was "the German national opera *par excellence*" has been a part of the reception of the work since its premiere, which was, as he says, "surrounded by the aura of a national event."[51] And yet, Reiber continues, the extraordinary fervor with which the German public greeted *Freischütz* was largely due to a number of factors that had little or nothing to do with the work itself.[52] Compositions such as *Kampf und Sieg* and *Leyer und Schwert*, with words by the patriotic poet Theodor Körner (Körner died fighting against Napoleon in the War of Liberation), had already established a connection between Weber and the reawakened forces of German nationalism in the eyes of the listening public. Weber's work as head of the German opera in Dresden and his music criticism also helped to establish his reputation as a "champion of German art." In the summer of 1821 in Berlin, moreover, *Freischütz* was in direct competition with Spontini's *Olimpia*. Spontini had made many enemies in his position as *Kapellmeister* in Berlin; his presence, alongside that of Weber, tended to polarize the critical public. Max Maria von Weber describes this unusual environment in his biography of his father:

> It was under these circumstances that "Der Freischütz" was destined to make its appearance on the Berlin stage. . . . The national party looked forward to the event with anxiety and hope. . . . The allies of the court-party, at the same time, who had the most influential portion of the press under their thumb, treated this hope with scorn, and drew their ranks closer together to discharge a deadly fire at the enemy. It was always the destiny of Weber, who arrived at a time of transition in the history of art in Germany, to see his works produced under the influence of excited party-spirit. He himself felt that this new venture must either raise him

to a high pinnacle, and render enormous service to the cause of German art, or be carried to the grave with scorn and mockery. There was no middle course. It was to be a battle for life or death.[53]

We may question the extent to which Max Maria is a trustworthy narrator of the circumstances surrounding the premiere of his father's most famous work. His words may not be an objective account (whatever that might mean) of events in the early 1820s, but they are a fine example of the reception of *Freischütz* in the later nineteenth century. That the premiere of *Freischütz* was deeply conditioned by political attitudes is beyond doubt, but in succeeding generations it became, if anything, an even more important center around which discourse about national identity in music might gravitate. Like Max Maria's account of *Freischütz*'s premiere, much of this discourse employs what we might call the "military metaphor," a metaphor whose roots stretch back at least as far as the nationalistic music criticism of men such as Spazier and Fink. Here *Freischütz* is not an opera; it is a weapon aimed against the foreign. In the years surrounding and immediately after the unification of Germany, the discourse surrounding *Freischütz* seems to have taken on an increased urgency—here the premiere of *Freischütz* appears not only as a musical analog of the War of Liberation, but also perhaps of the Franco-Prussian War. Emblematic of this new critical tone is the description of *Freischütz*'s premiere by Friedrich Wilhelm Jähns's monumental *Weber in seinen Werken*—words that seem to recall the style and ideology of Ernst Moritz Arndt:

> Just as Germany on this very day (18 June 1815) liberated itself from the yoke of foreign domination, so too, exactly 6 years later, did German music liberate itself from the domination of foreign artistic elements, elements that were particularly influential at this time. Weber, the straightforward German, was directly confronted by the well-defended Spontini, but behind Spontini stood the perhaps even more dangerous Rossini, armed with alluring and ear-flattering sounds. In this victorious battle Weber won consciousness for the German people, and earned for them their own place in musico-dramatic art.[54]

The nationalistic coloring of Jähns's words might be partly explained by his particular historical position, but we may also find echoes of his tone in the work of other music historians, from Hans Pfitzner to Siegfried Goslich and Ludwig Schiedermair. In his 1930 work *Die deutsche Oper*, for instance, Schiedermair wrote:

> The warriors returning from the front [Schiedermair is referring to the
> War of Liberation] received it [the *Singspiel Der Freischütz*] with rejoic-
> ing; the younger generation regarded it as a deadly axe stroke against the
> Italian opera. But many German works, that shared not only the patriotic
> mood of *Freischütz* but also its artistic power, would have to follow before
> the Italian fortresses in Berlin (1824/41), Munich (1825), Dresden (1832)
> and Vienna (1848) would finally fall.[55]

Here Schiedermair has carried the metaphors of battle and liberation to
the point of absurdity—his image of German operatic history as a kind
of Thirty Years' War between the Germans and Italians is at best a gross
simplification. But even if *Freischütz* was not a "deadly axe stroke," it nevertheless has played a very significant role in German culture. Like the symphonies of Beethoven, *Freischütz* served a quasi-ceremonial purpose for a
variety of different German regimes. Here the performance history of the
opera in Dresden provides a specific example of this broader phenomenon.
Frequently seen during the Nazi period, *Freischütz* was the last opera performed in the Semper opera house before Goebbels and Hitler shut down
the theater late in 1944, as a consequence of their declaration of "total war."
The opera house was of course demolished (along with most of the rest of
the city) in the bombing attacks of February 1945, but an interim theater
opened soon after the war's end, naturally enough with a production of
Freischütz. The East German government then helped to sponsor the reconstruction and modernization of the prewar opera house. It was *Freischütz*
that was chosen to ceremonially inaugurate the rebuilt theater, forty years
to the day after it was destroyed.[56]

   That *Freischütz* could serve the ceremonial function of a "national opera"
under so many different regimes is due to a variety of factors, not least
of which is what I am tempted to call the "process of elimination." *Die
Entführung aus dem Serail* and *Die Zauberflöte* were perhaps too closely
connected to eighteenth-century traditions of the *Singspiel,* and Mozart's
cosmopolitanism made his works seem less "national." If Mozart's Italian
masterpieces seemed to alienate him from the history of German opera, so
too did *Fidelio* seem to stand apart, more allied to Beethoven's symphonic
oeuvre or to the French operas of Cherubini than to national German operatic tradition. Wagner, despite his grandiose creation of a "national theater" at Bayreuth, has been too closely associated with nineteenth- and
twentieth-century racist ideologies and the genocidal war to which they
contributed for his music dramas to be regarded as "national operas" in the

late twentieth century. Weber is a far less abrasive and controversial figure than Wagner, and his biography has made a much more appealingly "national" context for the reception of *Freischütz*. His work as a conductor and critic on behalf of German opera, his relationships with friends, family, and colleagues, and his premature death in London have all made him well suited for idealization, a tendency that may be traced at least as far back as Wagner's speech at Weber's graveside in 1844.

Freischütz and the Problem of "National Character"

That the political environment of the early 1820s; the nationalistic agenda of late-nineteenth- and twentieth-century music historians, biographers, and critics; and the cultural needs of various German regimes have to a great extent determined the place of *Freischütz* within the canon of "national works of art" seems beyond a doubt. Indeed, the idea that *Freischütz* epitomizes the national character of Germany has become a commonplace in the immense literature surrounding the opera. Exploring this idea, however, takes us very far from the discourse about "character" with which I began the chapter. Herder and Mosel, Koch and Weber himself, we are reminded, did not locate *Charakter* in the reception history of an artwork, but in the work itself. The discourse of *Charakter*, to put it another way, was essentialist. If we want to understand the place of *Freischütz* in the search for a German opera, we are obliged (insofar as it is possible) to assume the ideological patterns of this discourse and ask the following question: Is there something about *Freischütz* itself (apart from its reception history) that embodies the "character of the nation"?

This question, of course, may be asked of a number of other "national" operas, such as Smetana's *The Bartered Bride* and Moniuszko's *Halka*. *Freischütz* thus constitutes a case example of what we might call the problem of "national character" in music, a problem that Carl Dahlhaus addressed in his influential history of nineteenth-century music. "A historical analysis of national character in music," Dahlhaus writes,

> faces several difficulties: uncertainty regarding the imprint of the individual in the national; extrinsic motivation due to political necessity; and the negligible effect of adopting folk music. This may tempt us to avoid these difficulties by defining national music in reference to its function rather than its substance. This change in logical status entails nothing less than jettisoning Herder's and Hegel's thesis of the "national spirit" as a

hidden agent in history, and seeking the national side of music, not just in its ethnic and melodic-rhythmic substance, but to a greater extent in a historical function in which aesthetic and political elements merge.[57]

For Dahlhaus, in other words, there is essentially no such thing as national character in the work itself—the national character of a piece of music emerges as a result of historical circumstances. Applying Dahlhaus's thesis to *Der Freischütz*, we would say that the opera acquired its status as a national work of art not so much because of its musical form, its key structure, or the way in which it represents the forest, but simply because it served a specific historical function. This view, of course, locates "national character" exclusively in the reception history of a work of art and largely overlooks ways in which a composer might self-consciously create "national character" in his or her works. In his book *Carl Maria von Weber und die deutsche Nationaloper* Wolfgang Wagner uses Dahlhaus as a point of departure by touching precisely upon this weakness in his argument: "One can also completely invert Dahlhaus's thesis: Weber's individual style was not elevated into a national style, but rather Weber himself used precisely those things that were regarded as 'national' to create his own individual style."[58] Wagner's inversion of Dahlhaus's thesis reminds us that if we jettison Herder's and Hegel's ideas about "national spirit," we jettison one of the most important ideological influences on Weber's work and, indeed, on the entire search for a German opera.

Perhaps the best way to answer the question about the presence of "national character" in *Freischütz* is to "cut the Gordian knot" by redefining what we mean by "the work itself." In this context, the work of Jean-Jacques Nattiez offers a promising alternative to more conventional definitions of the musical work. Nattiez begins his book *Music and Discourse: Toward a Semiology of Music* with an arresting hypothesis:

> the musical work is not merely what we used to call the "text"; it is not merely a whole composed of "structures." . . . Rather, the work is also constituted by the procedures that have engendered it (acts of composition), and the procedures to which it gives rise: acts of interpretation and perception. . . . The *essence* of a musical work is at once its genesis, its organization, and the way it is perceived.[59]

Nattiez's redefinition of the musical work might be read as an attack on conventional patterns of music scholarship, but in a curious way it echoes the early-nineteenth-century discourse about *Charakter* with which I began this chapter. Koch, we remember, felt that the *Charakter* of a musical piece was the result of many factors: "meter, tempo, rhythm, the type of melodic figures and how they are used, the form, the accompaniment, modulation, style," and so forth. Koch is speaking primarily about what Nattiez would call the "organization" of the work, whereas Nattiez himself is concerned with what we might call (for lack of a better term) the work's ontology. But despite these differences, Nattiez and Koch use rhetorical gestures that are remarkably similar. For each scholar, the "work itself" emerges from disparate elements; it is essentially composite and combinatorial.

Folding Nattiez's hypothesis into the discourse of *Charakter*, we could then say that the national character of *Freischütz* is both the topic and the result of a dialogue between "acts of composition" and "acts of interpretation and perception." Here we might imagine a recursive relationship: Weber adopted preexisting signifiers of national style, but through "acts of composition" he changed and developed these signifiers. After the premiere of *Freischütz*, certain of its features were themselves adopted, through "acts of interpretation and perception," as preconditions of the national style, and perhaps, as elements in the ever-changing definition of the nation itself. This recursive relationship is always fluid and continually redefining its terms. Still, in order for a "national style" to become a reality or, in the words of Daniel Sanders, to "feel itself to be a unity," there must be a certain continuity of expectation and convention. The recursive relationship between "acts of composition" and "acts of interpretation" must, to use a musical metaphor, have a certain degree of consonance. Weber himself, of course, was prominent at many different points in this relationship; he helped shape "national character" in German opera not only as a composer, but also as a critic and conductor. What is interesting about this recursive process, however, is not merely the ways in which Weber's criticism informed his compositional practice (and vice versa), but the ways in which the dialogue of national character escaped his control. Weber's failures (if we want to call them that) are as compelling as his successes, for in them we hear the "dissonance" between composition and interpretation that would forestall the search for a German opera. For this reason we must turn from *Freischütz* to its "ill-fated sister," Weber's *grosse romantische Oper Euryanthe*.

4 *Euryanthe:* Reconfiguration and Transformation

The Plot Structure of *Euryanthe*

The origins of *Euryanthe* may be traced back to a letter that Weber received from the impresario Barbaja on 11 November 1821, inviting him to write a new opera for Vienna. Barbaja may have envisioned something along the lines of *Der Freischütz*, which had just enjoyed an enormously successful premiere. Weber had something else in mind. The similarities between the structure of *Freischütz* and *Euryanthe* as well as between the individual numbers in the two operas cannot obscure the fact that *Euryanthe* belongs to a fundamentally different operatic genre than its predecessor. Weber called *Euryanthe* a *grosse romantische Oper,* a description that requires some elucidation. The term, as Tusa points out, was remarkable for its "commixture of two genres, 'grand opera' and 'romantic opera,' that for the most part had previously been kept apart,"[1] and was hardly common during the first decades of the nineteenth century. (According to Hermann Dechant, the first work to be called a *grosse romantische Oper* was Hoffmann's *Aurora,* written in 1811–12.[2]) In the context of an operatic title, both *"grosse"* and *"romantische"* were "combinatorial" terms, which suggested various things about the relationship between text and music, the subject matter of the opera, and even the general character of the work (see the discussion of operatic genre in chapter 1). The precise definition of *grosse Oper* during this period was far from clear, but the "genre boundaries" of *romantische Oper* were perhaps even more elusive. The notoriously slippery adjective "romantic" seems to have been applied to opera in two primary senses, senses that were themselves interrelated. First, the term suggested that the subject matter of the opera would have something to do with the marvelous, the supernatural, or the fantastic. Weber's description of his *Silvana* as a *Romantische Oper* seems to have come from this sense of the word, and the poet and composer in E. T. A. Hoffmann's famous story of the same name also use the term in this manner. But the term also had less distinct associations, bound up with the more general idea of "romantic music." Weber's use of the term in this sense appears perhaps at its most succinct in his introduction to Cherubini's *Lodoiska*, in which he describes the temperament of the composer as typically "romantic":

> A serious composer, often to the point of gloomy brooding; always choosing the most sharply defined means, hence his glowing palette; laconic and lively; sometimes apparently brusque; throwing out ideas which in fact have a close inner connexion and when presented with their full harmonic flavour are the distinguishing feature of this composer and explain the depth of his musical character, which, in the vast contours and masses conjured up by his imagination, still takes full account of every apparent detail: that is Cherubini.[3]

In this passage, of course, Weber is describing a romantic *composer* and not a romantic *opera;* nevertheless, it is the music itself that is the subject of his prose. It is the expressiveness of Cherubini's music, and not its "fancifulness," that is truly romantic. In Weber's description the term is associated with another group of ideas—seriousness, inner organic connection, harmonic richness, depth, and imagination—ideas which (as we have seen) were also central to the search for a German opera. A *romantische Oper* in this sense was not so much one which featured a marvelous or fantastic plot, but rather one in which music played more than an adjunct role in the drama, an opera whose music served as a gateway into the sublime.

Each of the two adjectives in the subtitle for *Euryanthe* thus served to differentiate the new opera from its illustrious predecessor. The term *große Oper* suggested that dialogue would be replaced by recitative, but by using this term Weber was also placing *Euryanthe* in a different context, connecting it to the serious operas of Gluck and Mozart rather than to the traditions of German dialogue operas. The context of "grand opera" implied first that *Euryanthe* would maintain a serious and elevated tone throughout—the folksy *Singspiel* scenes that relieve the tension of *Freischütz* would have no place in the new opera. The differences between *Freischütz* and *Euryanthe* are in this sense analogous to the transformation of *Das unterbrochene Opferfest* from a *heroisch-komische* into a *heroisch-tragische* opera—the deflating comedy of Ännchen's "Einst träumte meiner sel'gen Base" would be eliminated from *Euryanthe* just as surely as Pedrillo and the other comic characters were excised from the revised version of Winter's opera. The idea of a *romantische Oper* intersected with this idea of "genre elevation." The music of *Euryanthe,* Weber seems to be suggesting, should be heard in a different way than that of *Freischütz.* If the "serious" music of *Freischütz* (to use Hoffmann's words again) "served to bring before our eyes the wonderful apparitions of the spirit-realm," the work nevertheless was "pulled back to earth" by the traditions of the *Singspiel*. The music of *Euryanthe*, by contrast, would be thoroughly transcendental, sublime, and "romantic," purged of the earthly dross that had "weighed down" his earlier work.

Weber's ambition to write a "grand opera" may also have led him away from the *Schauerromantik* of *Freischütz* toward more conventional story lines. *Euryanthe* returns to the more familiar plot tropes of serious opera, in which the path to romantic fulfillment is blocked not by supernatural powers but by human villains motivated by jealousy and greed. For the libretto of the opera Weber turned to Wilhelmine von Chezy, a Dresden poet whom he met through his membership in the Dresden *Liederkreis*.[4] Chezy derived her libretto from her own version of the medieval romance *Roman de la violette*, which she had translated as *Geschichte der tugendsamen Euryanthe von Savoyen* for Friedrich Schlegel's *Sammlung romantischer Dichtungen des Mittelalters* in 1804. The familiar story of the falsely accused wife (or fiancée) may also be found as the tale of Ginevra in Tasso's *Orlando Furioso*, in the novella *Bernabò da Genova e la moglie Zinevra* in Boccaccio's *Decameron*, as well as in Shakespeare's *Cymbeline*. Scarlatti based his opera *Griselda* on the same subject, which also forms the basis for Schumann's only opera, *Genoveva*. (For a synopsis of the plot of *Euryanthe*, see appendix 5.) The chivalric world of the Middle Ages, personified by the king and the chorus of noblemen and ladies, provides the background for the story, filling the role that the huntsmen and peasant women play in *Der Freischütz*. The supernatural element in *Euryanthe* is furnished by the ghost of Adolar's dead sister, Emma. Emma never sings herself, but she is associated throughout the opera with distinct and highly chromatic music, labeled as "Vision" in the manuscript sources. But the principal drama centers around four main characters: Adolar and Euryanthe (tenor and soprano), who are engaged to be married; Lysiart, the villain who falsely accuses Euryanthe of infidelity; and Eglantine, the false friend of Euryanthe, secretly in love with Adolar, who uses her intimacy with the heroine to further her own evil designs. Lysiart lusts for Euryanthe and, through his treachery, hopes to claim her for himself. The virtuous characters are thus love objects not only for their "legitimate" counterparts, but also for the evil pair, thus creating "crossing" threads of desire that disrupt the sentimental order, as may be seen in figure 4.1. It is these crossing threads of desire that motivate the villains, who set the plot in motion by their evil machinations.

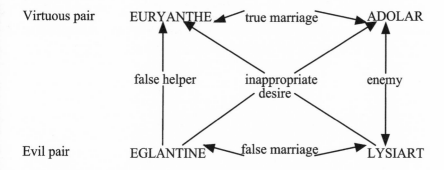

Figure 4.1   Plot structure of *Euryanthe*

Charakter in *Euryanthe*

Chezy's libretto has come under intense critical attack since *Euryanthe* first appeared, but it appealed to Weber, in part because it offered such a diversity of "character" and "situation."[5] As in *Der Freischütz, Charakter* functions in *Euryanthe* not only on the level of the individual musical numbers, but also in "sound worlds" that come to stand for a particular emotional or spiritual condition.[6] Sometimes these sound worlds manifest themselves in distinct melodies or harmonic progressions (such as Eglantine's "deception motive" that I will examine below), akin in some respects to the Wagnerian leitmotiv. But far more often, Weber characterizes the various musico-dramatic spheres of the opera in much less direct ways. They are best described as musical colors that "emerge out of a combination of features": melody, harmony, rhythm, and orchestration all help differentiate them from one another. Weber's practice here is clearly an extension of that which he uses in *Freischütz,* and with a few changes, I may plot out the sound worlds of *Euryanthe* on the same type of graph that I used in the previous chapter.

We may use figures 3.1 and 4.2 to visualize some of the key similarities between the two works. By using the same basic structure for the two graphs, I have tried to show how a similar set of binary oppositions informs both *Freischütz* and *Euryanthe*—oppositions that are very much a part of the operatic criticism of the period. In the first chapter I described some of the

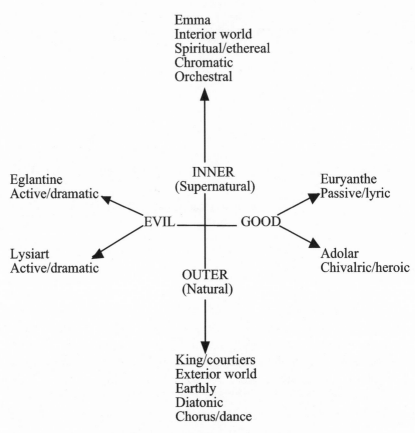

Emma
Interior world
Spiritual/ethereal
Chromatic
Orchestral

Eglantine
Active/dramatic

INNER
(Supernatural)

Euryanthe
Passive/lyric

EVIL———— GOOD

Lysiart
Active/dramatic

OUTER
(Natural)

Adolar
Chivalric/heroic

King/courtiers
Exterior world
Earthly
Diatonic
Chorus/dance

Figure 4.2   Musico-Dramatic axes in *Euryanthe*

most immediately apparent connections between *Freischütz* and *Euryanthe* (the similarity of the hunters' choruses and the close relationship between the characters of Euryanthe and Agathe, for example). Despite the genre distinction between *Singspiel* and *grosse romantische Oper*, Weber uses many of the same musical forms and large-scale structures for both *Freischütz* and *Euryanthe*. But these connections also extend to the large-scale forms and musical language of the two works. Both operas, for instance, include a prominent supernatural element, which Weber characterizes by unusual orchestral textures and highly chromatic harmonies. The courtly world, which sets this "supernatural music" in relief, is quite different from the *Volksthümlichkeit* of *Freischütz*; nevertheless, Weber adopts many of the same musical strategies in the large choral scenes of both operas. In both works, moreover, Weber is at pains to depict the dichotomy between good and evil in musical terms. Weber, in short, not only recycled much of the musical and dramatic material of *Freischütz* for his *große romantische Oper*, but also reproduced many of its fundamental ideological dualisms.

But if the graphs illuminate some of the similarities between the two works, they also suggest some of the ways in which *Euryanthe* is distinct from its predecessor. Some of the differences between the graphs are relatively superficial. I have redesignated the vertical axis of the graph, for instance, to represent a dichotomy between "inner" and "outer"—a dichotomy which includes (but is not limited to) the opposition between the supernatural and the earthly that is so important to *Freischütz*. In the graph for *Euryanthe* both ends of the horizontal axis are forked, in order to represent the differences between the male and female characters that, as we shall see, are so important to the musico-dramatic meaning of the opera. Still, these changes do not obscure the common dualistic framework that both operas share. The most striking difference between the two works lies not in these dualisms themselves, but in the way in which they become manifest in the individual characters. The struggle between good and evil in *Freischütz*, as we have seen, is played out in Max's soul; this struggle is "both print and seal" of the cosmic struggle that resonates powerfully and mysteriously in the natural world. Max occupies the center of the graph, where the forces of good and evil, the natural and supernatural worlds, intersect and do battle with each other. The inner torment of which Max sings in his first-act aria plays a large part in *Euryanthe* as well. The villains, in particular, are given ample opportunity to display the conflicts that rend their souls. But the sophisticated musical language that Weber employs to depict their inward struggle functions (in comparison with *Freischütz*) on the periphery of the drama rather than in its center. The same types of tensions so apparent in *Freischütz* also inform *Euryanthe*, but here they operate primarily in the external realm, in the relationships between the various characters. What is at stake is not the future of Max's soul, but Adolar's wealth, Euryanthe's honor (even her very life), and the future of their love. This fundamental difference between the dramaturgical structure of the two works is ultimately more important than the formal distinction between *Singspiel* and *grosse romantische Oper*, or the contrast between the background of the Bohemian forest and that of the medieval court.

We might best compare *Freischütz* and *Euryanthe*, then, by hazarding a distinction between *Charakter* and musical style. The distinction is admittedly tenuous, for the two terms inform and overlap one another. But if we define style as a set of musical strategies—conventional forms, harmonic procedures, melodic types, large-scale tonal planning, and so forth—then we can say that Weber's musical style in the two works is quite similar. The challenge of writing a *grosse romantische Oper* naturally stimulated Weber to develop his style in new directions—in many sections of *Euryanthe,* for instance, we can see the composer attempting to efface the boundaries between musical numbers and move toward a more through-composed style. But the novelty of *Euryanthe* lies less in these stylistic innovations than in the ways in which Weber deploys his stylistic vocabulary to create new kinds of dramaturgy. The difference between *Freischütz* and *Euryanthe,* we might say, is one of *Charakter,* not one of musical style; it has to do not so much with the individual features of Weber's music than with the ways in which he combines those features and the dramaturgical ends toward which they are directed. We may thus approach *Euryanthe* as Weber's effort to reconfigure and transform the musical and dramatic strategies that he had successfully deployed in *Freischütz* in order to create a distinct *Charakter* on every level of the artwork: for each of the individual characters, for the various "sound worlds" in which they operate, and within the opera as a whole. By exploring each of the four musico-dramatic spheres of *Euryanthe,* we may uncover the distinct character of Weber's most ambitious work and the extent to which this transformation and reconfiguration could fulfill the search for a German opera.

Inner and Outer Worlds

As in *Freischütz,* Weber denotes the supernatural by a group of gestures and motives that are clearly distinguished from the rest of the music in the opera. The counterpart of Samiel's motive in *Euryanthe* is the music associated with Emma's ghost. Like Samiel's motive, this "spirit music" first appears in the overture, where it functions as a kind of episode in between the exposition and the development sections of a sonata-allegro form. Originally Weber had wanted to have a *tableau vivante* during the overture, in which the ghost of Emma would actually appear at this point (I have reproduced an orchestral score of the spirit music in the overture as example 4.1).[7] Weber clearly sets this spirit music apart from its surrounding musical environment by changing its tempo key and particularly its orchestration. Here in the overture, for instance, Weber scores the spirit music for viola and eight muted violins, split into four parts. The unusual texture makes a particularly stark contrast with the tutti that precedes it. Weber obscures the phrase structure by the abundant use of chromatic leading tones—clearly the unresolved "wandering chromaticism" of this music symbolizes Emma's unquiet ghost. As is the case throughout the opera, the key in which Weber sets this passage functions not only to provide a sharp contrast with the surrounding music, but as a dramatic, or indeed, one might say, metaphysical symbol. Except for its final appearance in the last number, Emma's music always appears in a highly chromaticized B major. Here Schubart's widely read *Characteristik der Töne* provides some context for Weber's key choice—Schubart describes B major as "[s]trongly colored, indicating wild passions, assembled from the shrillest and most piercing colors. Anger, fury, envy, frenzied rage, despair, and every burden of the heart," Schubart continues, "lie in its domain."[8] The half-cadence on F-sharp, with which Emma's music usually ends, leads us even further into what Schubart refers to as the "colored" keys, away from the purity of C major.

Although both Emma and Samiel represent the supernatural, Weber treats their appearances within the respective operas in quite different ways. Unlike Samiel's motive, Emma's spirit music is constructed so that it can be easily combined with a vocal line in a style that approximates accompanied recitative. Samiel, of course, actually takes physical form, but Emma appears only through the imaginations of the other characters. In this sense she participates in the plot more fully than Samiel does. That she has no corporeal presence on the stage does not prevent Weber from portraying her redemption, a process that is articulated by the voice of the orchestra alone. Since Samiel represents the "evil principle," his motive is not subject to change. The highly chromatic harmonies and asymmetrical phrase structure of Emma's music, on the other hand, make it well suited to development—indeed, Weber never reproduces it in exactly the same form (a table summarizing the appearances of Emma may be found as table 4.1). After the overture, it next appears when Euryanthe quotes Emma's words in the recitative that follows Eglantine's "O mein Leid ist unermessen" (no. 6). Here it is primarily the orchestral texture of the passage that forms a recognizable link with the spirit music of the overture; Weber alters the rhythm of the original statement of Emma's music in order to make it more serviceable as the accompaniment to a recitative. Emma's music also appears when Eglantine sees her ghost during the *Hochzeitsmarsch* (no. 23), although here Weber shortens and modifies the music to end on a C-sharp major chord rather than on F-sharp. In terms of the tonal symbolism described above, this represents an intensification of the "coloration" effect, further distancing Emma from the redemption symbolized by C major. This redemption

Example 4.1 Emma's spirit music (from the Overture)

comes only in the third-act finale, when Adolar sees a vision of his sister's ghost finally laid to rest ("Ich ahne Emma"). Here the wandering chromaticism is finally "diatonicized" and transformed so that it resolves on a "pure" and "innocent" C. Weber's transformation of the Emma music thus shows the same kind of tonal symbolism and large-scale tonal planning that Abert described in his analysis of *Freischütz*. Like the C-minor music of the *finst're*

Mächte in the overture to *Freischütz,* Emma's B-major music eventually finds its way to C major.

The antipode to Emma's spirit world is the natural music for king and court, hunters and happy peasants. This is the world of normalcy, characterized by clear-cut phrase structures and frequent use of what Schubart would have called the "uncolored" keys: F major, D major, and G major. It includes numbers such as the introduction number 1 ("Dem Frieden Heil!"), the choral sections of the first-act finale number 9 ("Jubeltöne, Heldensöhne" and "Fröhliche Klänge"), and the beginning of the second-act finale number 14 ("Leuchtend füllt die Königshallen"). The music does not symbolize the inner world of the imagination, but rather the outer world of ceremonial action. These pieces often represent what Marx would call *wirkliche Lebenserscheinungen:* dramatic situations (such as courtly dances) that would be accompanied by music even if *Euryanthe* were a play. This type of music is the counterpart to the *volkstümlich* numbers of *Freischütz,* and as we have seen in the case of the two hunters' choruses, the connection between *Freischütz* and *Euryanthe* is sometimes quite strong. These two choruses form an extreme example of musical and dramatic correspondence between the two operas, a correspondence that is rarely so direct. The stately, ceremonial character of the choral music from the introduction of *Euryanthe* ("Dem Frieden Heil!"), for instance, has little to do with the raucous peasant celebration with which *Freischütz* begins. But in both operas the relatively simple and straightforward musical style of the "natural music" forms an essential foil to the more dramatic material sung by the principals. The internal torment to which Max gives voice in his first-act aria, for instance, is brought into sharper relief because it emerges out of a peasants' waltz, just as Lysiart's accusation of Euryanthe in the second-act finale is made more effective because it has been preceded by the dramatically static music of the court.

Ironically, it is the functional similarity of the "natural" sound world in *Freischütz* and *Euryanthe* that implies some of the most important differences between the two works. In both operas Weber uses this "natural music" to represent local color, the sense of time and place that forms such an essential backdrop to the plot. But of course, the local color of *Euryanthe* is a radical departure from that of *Freischütz.* The rustic world of a forest village has been replaced by the aristocratic world of a medieval court. Even those numbers in *Euryanthe* that most closely resemble their counterparts in *Freischütz,* the hunters' chorus and the scene with chorus, number 21 of *Euryanthe* ("Der Mai bringt frische Rosen dar"), have had their rough edges

Euryanthe: *Reconfiguration and Transformation* 125

Table 4.1   Emma's Spirit World in *Euryanthe*

Number	Dramatic Context	Key	Harmonic Context
Overture	—	B major (complete statement)	Preceded by an augmented sixth chord in B-flat, which is reinterpreted as a dominant seventh chord based on F-sharp. This chord then resolves into B minor.
No. 6	Euryanthe tells Eglantine the secret of Emma, and why she still haunts her own grave.	B major (complete statement)	Preceded by a brief recitative, loosely in E-flat minor. Followed by a recitative based around diminished seventh chords that resolve into an E-major chord.
No. 23	On her way to her marriage with Lysiart, Eglantine sees Emma's ghost rising out of the grave.	B major (incomplete, half-cadence on C-sharp major)	The "Hochzeitsmarsch" in D major, but the spirit music here is immediately preceded by a brief recitative based around a diminished seventh chord. Ends with a half-cadence on C-sharp, which leads to a cadence on E major.
No. 25 (finale)	Adolar sees Emma's ghost redeemed by the tears of an innocent.	C major (modified and foreshortened)	Preceded by "Hin nimm die Seele mein," with choral accompaniment, in C major. Followed by final chorus in E-flat major.

sanded down. The hunters of *Euryanthe* sing a neatly turned lyric in praise of the natural world—no "Jo ho, tra la la" interrupts their poetry. "Der Mai bringt frische Rosen dar" occupies the same dramatic position as the *Jung-fernkranz* chorus in *Freischütz,* but its irregular phrase structure (5 + 4 + 3 + 3 measure phrases) and the tinges of chromaticism in its melody present a more refined and sophisticated image than that of its model. The *Volks-tümlichkeit* of these numbers does not approach that of their counterparts in *Freischütz,* and they make up a much smaller proportion of the opera.

To fill *Euryanthe* with rustic peasant scenes, Weber may have felt, might have compromised the "grandness" and "seriousness" of the opera. But by replacing much of the *Volkstümlichkeit* of *Freischütz* with ceremonial num-

Example 4.2   Der Mai bringt frische Rose dar

bers for the king and court, Weber was distancing himself from some of the most popular music of his earlier work. The unsophisticated surface of numbers such as the "Lasst lustig die Hörner erschallen" chorus or the peasants' dance from the first act of *Freischütz* doubtless had particular appeal to the *Mittelstände* of nineteenth-century Germany, who defined themselves against the foreign and the aristocratic. To quote Arndt once again, it was after all the German princes who, by catering to foreign powers, had caused the decline of medieval Germany. The favorable light in which Weber placed this foreign, aristocratic world must have seemed at odds with the nationalism of his aesthetic agenda.

Using a medieval French court rather than a Bohemian forest as the backdrop for *Euryanthe,* then, involved far more than simply substituting aristocratic gowns for dirndls and lederhosen or rewriting a few choral scenes. We get more of a sense of the distance between *Freischütz* and *Euryanthe* by comparing the stage settings for the various tableaux. The "open space before a forest inn" or the "beautiful romantic landscape" in which the characters of *Freischütz* operate is much different from the castle gardens of *Euryanthe.* Instead of the forester's hut, the interior tableau of Weber's *grosse romantische Oper* is a colonnaded hall in the king's castle. The world of *Euryanthe,* to paraphrase Simon Schama's argument in *Landscape and Memory,* is primarily one of masonry, not greenery.[9] That is not to say that

Weber and Chezy never reference the natural world in their most ambitious work. In the third-act scene and cavatina "So bin ich nun verlassen / Hier dicht am Quell," as we shall see, brook and forest mirror Euryanthe's emotions just as surely as the dark clouds that Agathe sees in "Leise, leise" reflect her inner anxieties. Many early librettos of *Euryanthe* describe a violent storm brewing in the background during Lysiart's second-act aria, making the connection between the villain of Weber's *grosse romantische Oper* and the *finst're Mächte* of *Freischütz* even more explicit.[10] The natural world does play a role in *Euryanthe,* but no one could claim, as Pfitzner did of *Freischütz,* that the German forest is its true hero. In the transition from *Singspiel* to *grosse romantische Oper* Weber left behind not only *Freischütz*'s rough-edged crowd scenes, but also what I have called its central metaphor: that inscape and landscape not only reflect, but embody one another.

The Villains

The inner-outer axis that stretches between the sound worlds of Emma's spirit music and the ceremonial music of the court is striking, but it is ultimately less important to the musical and dramatic structure of the opera than the moral axis that stretches between the good and evil pairs. Occasionally Weber expresses this moral contrast in a musical language that is as clear-cut as that of *Das unterbrochene Opferfest*—in many ways, Eglantine, Lysiart, Adolar, and Euryanthe are the descendants of familiar character types in the German opera of the preceding generation. The "ancestry" of the two villains is particularly evident. That Weber himself thought of Eglantine as belonging to the same "character family" as Elvira, for instance, is made clear from his remarks on the coloratura conclusion to her aria "Bethörte! die an meine Liebe glaubt":

> the conclusion of Eglantine's aria should be sung with fiery brilliance, and any singer who cannot achieve this would be well advised to simplify the passage rather than allow the passionate character of the whole number to suffer. In the same way a singer who cannot bring the right vengeance-breathing manner to Elvira's aria in *Das unterbrochene Opferfest* will prejudice the work less if she omits the aria altogether than if she makes it sound like an easy-going singing exercise.[11]

It is surely no accident that Weber wrote Eglantine's aria in the same key as Elvira's aria "Süss sind der Rache Freuden."[12] Indeed, E major characterizes Eglantine throughout the opera, not only in her monologue aria, but also for instance during the third-act finale, as she confesses her crime to the king and court ("Triumph! gerochen ist mein Schmach!"). Lysiart's big aria at the beginning of the second act is likewise in the same key (C minor) as Mafferu's "Allmächt'ge Sonne, höre." Both arias begin with the same type of orchestral gesture, a tremolando C-minor chord, marked "fortissimo," and follow the same basic formal plan, passing through a slow movement to end in a coloratura allegro section in which the villains express their hopes for revenge. Despite these similarities, Lysiart and Eglantine are far more complex figures than their counterparts in *Das unterbrochene Opferfest.* Their evil stems not so much from jealousy as from unrequited love, a love similar to the love that Adolar and Euryanthe hold for each other. Indeed, they function in many ways like twisted shadows of the good pair, bearing Euryanthe and Adolar within themselves as buried parts of their own personalities. Unlike the villainous Caspar of *Der Freischütz,* Lysiart and Eglantine are not completely dark figures, but rather are "mixed" characters—their souls are battlefields between good and evil.

If the moral axis at work within the opera as a whole is to some extent encapsulated within the two villains, so too do their characters embody what I have called the "vertical axis" of the *Euryanthe*'s dramaturgy: the contrast between inner and outer. The juxtaposition of styles in the music for Lysiart and Eglantine expresses not only the conflict between good and evil, but also the conflict between private and public selves. The personalities of the two villains can be peeled back like the layers of an onion. To Euryanthe, for instance, Eglantine shows the face of a devoted friend, even imitating, in their first-act duet, the yearning lyricism of Euryanthe's sound world. But beneath this deceptive surface is a burning hatred born of unrequited love. Deeper still, perhaps, in that part of her soul from which she sings her slow movement, this love still glows. The various levels of her personality are dissonant with each other: she is a character at war with herself. Lysiart's personality is similarly complex. During the finale of the first act, for example, when he arrives at the castle of Nevers in order to invite Euryanthe to the royal court, he is acting as the king's messenger. Hoping to make a good impression on Euryanthe, he adopts the musical language and the flowery words of the courtly world, singing an elegant duet with the woman he is about to deceive. Both his envy and his unrequited love are hidden behind the mask of a courtier. Lysiart is of course trying to woo Euryanthe, and the knight's response to his "five-measure *Romanze*" make it clear that Lysiart's *courtoisie* is false—motivated by evil and not by love. But after hearing the slow movement of Lysiart's aria we are unsure that his

Example 4.3   Lysiart's courtly façade in the first Finale

courtly facade does not reflect a genuine love for Euryanthe that lies even deeper inside of his character, beneath the evil persona that he shows to the king and court.

That this chivalric facade was also important to the drama of the opera as a whole is made clear by the favorable review of the opera printed in the 1825 *Berliner allgemeine musikalische Zeitung.* Herr Forti, the famous bass who portrayed Lysiart in the Vienna premiere of *Euryanthe,* had come to Dresden for a series of guest roles and had temporarily replaced Herr Mayer in the role of the villain: "As Lysiart, Herr Forti knew exactly how to cover the essential evil of his character with genuine chivalry. The circumstances whereby Adolar lets himself be led astray by Lysiart and Eglantine into thinking that his angelically pure Euryanthe is faithless thus became more probable, and [the drama in general] was therefore more effective and gripping."[13] The duplicity of the villains, as this reviewer recognized, underpins the plot, and the music that portrays their conflicted nature therefore assumes particular importance within the opera as a whole.

The personalities of the two villains are most fully explored in two arias: Eglantine's scene and aria (no. 8), that comes just before the first-act finale, and Lysiart's comparable scene at the beginning of the second act. In both arias, Weber depicts the struggle between good and evil, between the yearning love and the bitter vengeance that constitute the inner and outer parts of Eglantine's and Lysiart's personalities. In no other place do opposing musico-dramatic characters come into such sharp and violent conflict. Just as in *Das unterbrochene Opferfest*, the contrast between good and evil is cast as a conflict between musical styles, only here this conflict is played out within the frame of a single aria. Weber uses moral dualism as a structural principle.

Both arias follow the same musico-dramatic pattern, a formal plan that is related to some of Mozart's two-part arias such as "Dove sono" from *Le nozze di Figaro* (for a comparative overview of their structure, see figure 4.3).[14] Each opens with an orchestral introduction that is built respectively around "characteristic music" of the two villains. The next section is an introductory recitative that serves as a transition between this music and the uncharacteristic lyricism of the slow movement, in which Eglantine and Lysiart adopt the personae of the good pair. The closed musical phrases of this section give way in the transition to a more loosely structured musical style, similar to the introductory recitative. Here Eglantine and Lysiart reclaim their villainous nature and turn to thoughts of hatred and revenge. These emotions are fully explored in the fast movements that end each aria.

Eglantine's aria takes the form of an extended monologue, in which she reveals the motives behind her decision to betray Euryanthe. It begins with a brief orchestral introduction, in which we hear Eglantine's characteristic motive: a serpentine sixteenth-note descent whose slippery chromaticism seems to embody deceit. Throughout the first section of the aria, during which Eglantine gloats over her deception of Euryanthe, this motive is interwoven between her dramatic outbursts. As Eglantine's thoughts begin to shift, her motive begins to lose some of its chromatic nature. Eglantine hopes that her devious plot will enable her to win Adolar's love, as her motive briefly suggests a C-major tonality. This musical and dramatic transformation helps to set up the slow section of the aria (beginning with measure 21), the lyric passages in which Eglantine imagines a blissful future as Adolar's lover. Although the borders between the musical sections are not as

Measures	1–39	40–61	62–96	97–113	114–35	136–56	157–263	264 ff.
Lysiart's aria	Orchestral prelude	"Wo berg ich mich?"	"Schweigt, glüh'nden Sehnens"	"Was soll mir ferner Gut und Land?"	"Und er sollte leben?"	"So weih' ich mich"	"Zertrümmre, zertrümmre, schönes Bild"	Postlude and transition
Formal sections	Prelude	Introduction	Slow movement		Transition		Fast movement	Postlude and transition
Eglantine's aria	Orchestral introduction	"Bethörthe! die an meine Liebe glaubt!"	"O! der Gedanke"		"Hinweg, wahnsinn'ge Hoffnung!"		"Er konnte mich um sie verschmäh'n!"	Postlude and transition
Measures	1–5	6–20	21–43		44–53		54–130	131 ff.

Figure 4.3   Comparative overview of Lysiart's and Eglantine's arias

distinct as they would be in a more typical two-part aria (or indeed, as they are in some of the other arias in *Euryanthe*), this section functions as a "first movement" adagio, that will contrast with the allegro fiero with which the aria ends. As she imagines herself in Euryanthe's place Eglantine adopts some of the musical language of her nemesis. The chromatic voice-leading of the passage "fand ich den Tod" recalls the yearning love of the "good pair," as do the arching, lyrical melodies of phrases such as "Nur einen Augenblick."

Weber begins this section with a sweeping lyrical melody in the lower strings (measures 21–23, closely related to the vocal melody in measures 23–27). The upward thrust and diatonic implications of this melody seem to mark it as a gesture of purity and hope, the musical opposite of the opening chromatic descent. As Eglantine's thoughts drift further into romantic fantasy ("Nur einen Augenblick an seiner Brust") the melody reappears, first in the cellos (measures 38–40) and then transferred (I am tempted to write "transfigured") to the flute in measures 41–44. A derivation of Eglantine's characteristic chromatic descent returns at measures 46 and 49 in the next section of the aria, which functions as a transition between the slow and fast movements ("Hinweg"). Eglantine banishes the vain thoughts of a future with Adolar and dedicates herself wholly to revenge and to evil.

In the final section of the aria, marked "allegro fiero," Weber manipulates the various motives associated with Eglantine to create a complex musical image of her personality. The section begins with a motive that is very closely related to the lyric melody of the slow movement (measures 54–57, cf. measures 22–23), and which is also associated with the vocal line in measures 60–62 and measures 64–66. The melody is directly repeated in both the orchestral and vocal parts in measures 104–107. These motivic connections to the slow movement of the aria serve dramatically to underscore the connection between Eglantine's romantic fantasy of Adolar and the dedication to revenge that this fantasy motivates. Weber's choice of B major as a local tonic for both of these motives reminds us that they are each indicators of "wild passions, frenzy, and the burdens of the heart" (to paraphrase Schubart), despite their contrasting tempi and expressive markings. The accompanimental figures in measures 62–63 and again in measures 66–75, on the other hand, clearly recall the serpentine descent with which the aria opened. Eglantine's resolution is born not only of her disappointment in love, but also from the devious flaw in her personality. The dotted rhythms and jagged outlines of Eglantine's melodies, in turn, emphasize her relationship to Lysiart and place her firmly in the sound world of evil as the implacable enemy of Euryanthe and Adolar's love. Her distance from the hero and heroine is further underscored by the explosions of "rage coloratura" that punctuate this final section (measures 90–91 and 121–27), music that both recalls the villain arias of *Das unterbrochene Opferfest* and anticipates the final allegro of Lysiart's aria (see below).

This aria follows the same pattern as Eglantine's but is written on a much larger scale—it is in fact the longest aria in the entire opera.[15] The orchestral introduction is dominated by a leaping, dotted-rhythm major-seventh motive. Unlike Eglantine's characteristic serpentine descent, this motive does not recur throughout the entire opera, even though it does bear a strong similarity to other orchestral motives associated with Lysiart. Within the context of this aria it functions in much the same way as the opening motive in Eglantine's aria. In the recitative section which follows the orchestral introduction, for example, this major-seventh motive forms the main element of the orchestral responses to Lysiart's dramatic outbursts, just as Eglantine's characteristic motive answered her gloating lines in the first part of her first-act aria.

The slow section of Lysiart's aria (beginning with "Schweigt, glühn'den Sehnens" in measure 62) is clearly set apart by an abrupt change in tempo, meter, and key. Just as for Eglantine, Lysiart's evil stems not so much from a fundamentally perverted nature as from his unrequited love for the paragon of nobility and virtue, in this case Euryanthe. And just as Eglantine adopted the lyrical voice of Euryanthe in her slow section, so Lysiart here sings the "troubadour music" of Adolar. The recitative-like nature of the final part of the slow movement, "Was soll mir ferner Gut und Land," makes it function as a transition to the next section of the aria (an alternative analysis of the aria could begin the "transition" here, rather than with "Und er sollte Leben?"). Here Lysiart asks himself a series of questions that slowly change his romantic yearning into bitterness and anger. Weber sets these lines with the same type of alternating musical structure that he used for the introductory recitative. He subtly depicts Lysiart's emotional shift in the orchestral motive that punctuates his lines, a motive in which lyric and dramatic elements are commingled (measures 97–99, 100–101, etc.). The first part of the motive is a sweeping melody reminiscent of Lysiart's lyric vocalism. But the motive ends sharply, with dotted rhythms that recall the "characteristic" music of the orchestral introduction. At first this ending employs the conjunct motion typical of the first part of the slow movement, but in the later statements (measures 105–107 and 110–11) it is transformed into a leaping motive more characteristic of Lysiart's evil, aggressive side.

At the beginning of the transitional section proper Lysiart's thoughts shift decisively toward anger and hatred. Over a turbulent accompaniment of sixteenth notes and tremolo chords, Lysiart dedicates himself to the death of Adolar. In the second section of the transition, "So weih' ich mich den Rachgewalten," Lysiart sings a powerful, sweeping melody over a surging thirty-second note chromatic scalar accompaniment. He gives himself over to the forces of evil and revenge and establishes both the dramatic mood and the C-minor key of the final allegro movement. The tempo and tonality of this section represent a return to the orchestral introduction, but now Lysiart's characteristic key and tonality have been transformed and intensified by his brief excursion into the yearning love of Adolar's world. This section provides a particularly striking example of the way in which Weber invokes the conventional rhetoric of the late eighteenth and early nineteenth century to paint a complex musical and dramatic portrait. Despite his rage, for instance, Lysiart sings in ¾, a meter that Schilling (1838) describes in the following manner:

> Among all the odd-numbered meters, ¾ has the most well-measured gait, yet it is no image of rest; on the contrary, its rhythm often has something disquieting about it, and yearns toward the even-measured meters as towards an unreachable completion. It is therefore best suited to the expression the secret pain of unhappy love. Quiet hope, innermost melancholy, grief and sorrow and soft lamentation belong to its sphere. ¾ is the most natural meter of unsatisfied yearning.[16]

Like the slow-movement of the aria "Schweigt, glüh'nden Sehnens," the triple meter of "So weih ich mich" establishes connections between Lysiart's condition and the "unsatisfied yearning" of which Adolar sings in his first-act romance. It is this yearning, this "secret pain of unhappy love," that is at the center of Lysiart's personality. Both Schilling and Schubart, for instance, characterize Lysiart's "home key" of C minor not as the key of hatred, but of "declarations of love, as well as complaints about an unfortunate love.—All the pining, longing, and sighing of a love-drunk soul lie in this key."[17] Just as Eglantine's romantic fantasy of Adolar motivates her dedication to revenge, so too is the ultimate source of Lysiart's hatred his yearning love for Euryanthe. The dilemma of Lysiart and Eglantine—"love-drunk souls" twisted into evil by the cruelties of fate—is so similar that we may almost see them as male and female versions of the same character.

The spiritual kinship of the two villains is further accentuated by the similarity between the final movements of each of their arias. Just like Eglantine, Lysiart erupts into rage coloratura (measures 196–97, 239–40, and 250–51). The links between Lysiart's vivace feroce and his orchestral introduction are perhaps not as strong as those that Eglantine's serpentine motive creates between the two outer sections of her aria, but the combination of a leap followed by a half-step that characterizes so many of the motives in this final section (the orchestral accompaniment in measures 186–89 and 235–38, or the vocal line in measures 231 and 233, for example) hearkens back to the melodic gesture with which the aria opened. The arias of the two villains are quite similar to each other, not only in their dramatic contour and overall form, but also in many more small-scale details of musical construction.

It is interesting to note that the musical form Weber uses for these two arias was not suggested by the poetic forms of the libretto—the music in some ways works across the grain of other symmetries suggested by the text layout of the two arias. In the earliest librettos both texts are divided into recitative and aria, but this division does not necessarily conform to Weber's musical divisions, or at least not in ways that we would ordinarily expect. The recitative of Eglantine's aria text follows no regular meter or rhyme scheme, although the seventh and eighth lines, with eleven syllables each, are metrically paired. These lines mark the beginning of Eglantine's "slow movement," when she fantasizes about a love with Adolar. The music for the aria section of Eglantine's text corresponds to the final section of her music (the allegro fiero). Its meter and rhyme scheme may be described as *ababacc*, with an exclamation ("Weh!, Weh!") between the fifth and sixth lines. The *a* and *c* lines have eight syllables each, and the *b* lines are seven syllables long.

Lysiart's *Recitativ* divides into three parts. The meter and rhyme patterns of the opening section (corresponding to the music I have labeled as the introduction in my formal diagram) are irregular, but the second section of the text (the four lines from "Schweigt glüh'nden Sehnens" through "Ganz Wahrheit is sie, ganz Natur") follows a regular *abab* rhyme pattern, with alternating lines of nine and eight syllables. The third section of the *Recitativ* (stretching from "Was soll mir ferner Gut und Land" through "Sie liebt ihn, ich muß untergeh'n") returns to the irregularity of the first section. Many of the lines rhyme ("ohne *sie*," "ent*flieh*," "Mein wird sie *nie!*"), but no regular pattern emerges. Likewise, many lines are eight syllables long, but other lengths (five, seven, eleven syllables) interrupt the metric rhythm. Lysiart's aria text is divided into two quatrains. The meter and rhyme pattern of the first quatrain (corresponding to the music for the second part of the transition) is *abba*, with nine-syllable *a* lines and eight-syllable *b* lines. The four lines of the final quatrain (the vivace) are all six syllables long and follow an *abcb* rhyme pattern.[18]

Although Weber's musical divisions articulate these textual divisions, it is clear that his overall musical plan for the two arias did not emerge from the structure of the libretto. The important musical division in Lysiart's aria between "Sie liebt ihn!" and "Und er sollte leben" (measures 113 and 114) occurs in the middle of a line of text and is indicated in the printed libretto only by a dash. And although the tempo indications of Eglantine's aria correspond to the division between recitative and aria in the text, there is little in the meter or rhyme patterns of the recitative to suggest its musical subdivisions. Weber, it seems, was following his own formal strategies for the villain arias, casting them in a musical structure designed to foreground conflict, opposition, and duality. Despite Weber's reputation as a champion of German opera, his formal procedures in these two arias are in many ways quite similar to those found in contemporary Italian opera. Weber's use of the Italian terms "scene" and "aria" might in fact tempt us to see the aria as an example of Italian influences in *Euryanthe*—the form of both the villain arias is akin to the early-nineteenth-century Italian double aria. The tonal and thematic connections between the introduction and the transition of Eglantine's aria, for instance, evoke comparable models from Rossini operas —they correspond to what Basevi would call the *tempo d'attacco* and the *tempo di mezzo*. We would not be too far off the mark if we were to label "Schweigt, glüh'nde Sehnens wilde Triebe" as Lysiart's cantabile, and use the term *cabaletta* to describe the final section of his aria. The large-scale formal patterns of *Euryanthe* are also quite similar to some Italian models. The introductory tableau of *Euryanthe*, for instance (made up of the first four numbers), is comparable to the Rossinian *introduzione* (such as the beginning of *Il barbiere di Siviglia*), which also contains an aria for the tenor. The *Charakter* of *Euryanthe* might have been distinct from Italian opera, but many of its musical forms are remarkably similar to the Rossini operas with which it competed during the 1820s.

While it is clear that Weber was certainly quite influenced by contemporary Italian opera, the extent and nature of that influence is often difficult to determine. It may be, for instance, that the expansive, multi-sectional nature of the transitional section in Lysiart's aria represents a conscious or subconscious attempt on Weber's part to obscure the Italian origins of the aria's form. Weber uses a wide variety of formal models in *Euryanthe*, from the strophic *Romanze* of Adolar (no. 2) to Adolar's two-part aria in the second act (no. 12) to shorter arias without strong internal contrasts, such as Euryanthe's cavatina or Eglantine's "deception aria" "O mein Leid ist unermessen" (no. 6). In the eclectic world of early-nineteenth-century German opera, the sectionalized "Italianate" structure of the two villain arias would most likely be read as the indicator of a complex, conflicted personality, and not as a reference to a particular national style. The structure of the villain arias, it should be noted, is closely related to that of "Leise, leise,"—it is perhaps more accurate to trace the form of all these arias to the eighteenth-century *rondò* rather than to the Rossinian double aria. But regardless of the relationship between *Euryanthe* and contemporary Italian opera, it is interesting to see the champions of both the *Vorbild* and the *Gegenbild* adopting similar solutions to problems of musical style and structure. Lysiart's conflicting emotions and the diverse musical idioms with which he expresses them are united not by the creation of a completely new operatic style, but rather in much the same manner as they are united in contemporary Italian opera, through the conventions of musical form.

When we compare Weber's use of the double aria or *rondò* form in *Freischütz* and *Euryanthe* to similar scenes in early-nineteenth-century Italian opera, however, we notice an important distinction. In contrast to arias such as "Ah, segnar invan io tento" (*Tancredi*) or "Casta Diva" (*Norma*), the Weberian double aria or *rondò* is always a monologue. No chorus comments on the action, for the aria is devoted exclusively to portraying the character's inner emotional life. It is interesting in this context to compare Lysiart's "Wo berg ich mich" to the villain aria in *Freischütz:* Caspar's "Schweig, schweig, damit dich niemand warnt." Both arias begin with a slow-tempo recitative and end with a fast movement dedicated to thoughts of revenge. But the two villains are fundamentally different. Caspar is not in love with Agathe or any other soprano, and he sings no cavatina; his aria, in short, expresses gloating triumph but not the inner torment of a "love-drunk soul." In contrast to Caspar, Lysiart is a truly "Romantic" character, at war with himself, similar to inwardly conflicted characters in early-nineteenth-century German opera.[19] Indeed, the "tormented baritone" is common enough to be regarded as a topos of Romantic opera.[20] The three baritone villains in Marschner's *Der Vampyr* (Ruthven), *Der Templer und die Jüdin* (Bois-Guilbert), and *Hans Heiling* (Hans Heiling) are of this type, as are, at least in some sense, the figures of Telramund and the Dutchman.

Caspar does not essentially belong to this topos—the closest musical par-

allel to Lysiart's aria in *Freischütz* is not "Schweig, schweig, damit dich niemand warnt," but rather Max's aria from the first act. That both arias follow
the same basic formal structure (see figure 4.4) is perhaps less interesting
than the similar emotional structures that these two arias express. In each
of the cantabile sections Max and Lysiart dream of the heroine's love, and
in the final sections of their arias each gives himself over to the evil powers
represented by C minor. Both "Wo berg ich mich?" and "Durch die Wälder"
can thus be heard as encapsulations of the dramatic conflict between good
and evil, a conflict that is central to each of Weber's operas. Lysiart's fate, of
course, is the opposite of Max's—in *Euryanthe* there is no redeeming feminine love to save him from the clutches of the evil powers. But despite the
difference in their vocal ranges it is Lysiart, rather than the tenor Adolar,
who is the true musico-dramatic successor to Max.

This "dramaturgical shift" constitutes one of the most important differences between *Freischütz* and *Euryanthe*. In Weber's *grosse romantische Oper*
the villains get the most opportunities for vocal display, and their inner
drama is in many ways more interesting than the outer drama of Adolar and
Euryanthe. It is not surprising, then, that contemporary reviews of *Euryanthe*
found the villains of the opera more compelling than the hero and heroine.[21] The lengthy review that appeared in the *Wiener Zeitschrift für Kunst,
Literatur, Theater und Mode* shortly after *Euryanthe*'s premiere, for instance,
had little good to say about Adolar and Euryanthe, but in general approved
of the characterization of Eglantine and Lysiart. The reviewer commends
Lysiart's aria for its "bedeutungsvoll" (meaningful) accompaniment and
"durchgreifenden, schauerlichen Charakter" (completely gripping and terrifying character), and singles out "So weih ich mich den Rach gewalten"
from the transitional section for particular praise.[22] Many modern writers
have also commented on the balance between the good and evil pair in
Euryanthe and in Weber's operas in general. In the *Oxford History of Music,*
for instance, Winton Dean writes:

> The obverse of [Weber's] achievement was a tendency to distance and de-
> preciate the characters, especially the agents for good, who in all Weber's
> operas (and some of Wagner's) appear intellectually and emotionally
> flabby by contrast with the evil or the doomed. Adelhart in *Silvana,*
> Caspar in *Der Freischütz,* Eglantine and Lysiart in *Euryanthe* are far
> more powerfully drawn, as individuals and therefore as symbols, than
> their virtuous counterparts.[23]

Measures	1–39	40–61	62–96	97–113	114–35	136–56	157–263	264 ff.
Lysiart's aria	Orchestral prelude	"Wo berg ich mich?"	"Schweigt, glüh'nden Sehnens"	"Was soll mir ferner Gut und Land?"	"Und er sollte leben?"	"So weih' ich mich"	"Zertrümmre, zertrümmre, schönes Bild"	Postlude and transition
Formal sections	Prelude	Intro-duction	Slow movement		Transition		Fast movement	Postlude and transition
Max's aria (preceded by the waltz, measures 1–58)	Orchestral intro-duction	"Nein! länger trag' ich nicht"	"Durch die Wälder"		"Hat denn der Himmel" (Samiel motive)	"Jetzt ist wohl ihr Fenster"	"Doch mich umgarnen finst're Mächte"	
Measures	59–63	64–81	82–121		122–37	138–65	166–253	(not present)

Figure 4.4   Comparative overview of Lysiart's and Max's arias

Adolar and Euryanthe

The balance between the forces of good and the forces of evil, as Dean implies, was a problem not merely in *Euryanthe,* but also in many other early-nineteenth-century German operas. In *Der fliegende Holländer* Wagner perhaps hit upon the most effective solution to this problem by making the tormented baritone the center of the plot.[24] But the plot of *Euryanthe* remains centered on the tenor and the soprano. Adolar is the hero of the opera, and in order to maintain the proper balance between the characters he must also have a complex solo aria, equivalent in some ways to "Bethörte! die an meine Liebe glaubt" and "Wo berg ich mich?" This aria is "Wehen mir lüfte Ruh'," which Weber places in the middle of the second act, as the young duke awaits Euryanthe's arrival at the court. The aria has some important formal similarities to the villain's arias. In the most general sense, all three arias are derived from the two-part slow-fast aria of the late eighteenth century. Like Lysiart's aria, "Wehen mir Lüfte Ruh'" begins with an extensive orchestral introduction that prefigures some of the aria's most important themes. Weber orchestrates the first section of this introduction entirely as a "chorale" of woodwinds, an orchestral color that is associated throughout the opera with the feminine, and more specifically with Adolar's yearning for Euryanthe (see the discussion of the *Romanze* and the introduction, below). The music that follows corresponds to the slow movement of both Eglantine's and Lysiart's arias, not only in tempo and musical form, but also in emotional meaning. Here too Adolar is longing for his love, only his longing will be fulfilled instead of turning into thoughts of revenge. The final movements of all three arias depict the fruit of the love expressed in the slow movements: evil and hatred in the case of the villains and *Seligkeit* for Adolar. All three arias share the contrast between inner and outer, or between static and kinetic, that is implied by the musical form.

But these superficial similarities mask the more important differences between the arias of the villains and that of the hero. Although the two sections of Adolar's aria are in different tempi, they share the same key (A-flat major) and, more important, the same general character. The private and public parts of Adolar's personality are clearly in harmony with each other. As we might expect, "Wehen mir Lüfte Ruh'" lacks those extensive, loosely structured, recitative-like sections that are so prevalent in the arias of the villains (particularly in Lysiart's aria). These are the sections in which Lysiart and Eglantine struggle with themselves, asking questions that reveal their tormented souls. Adolar sings only the barest of transitions between the slow and fast sections of his aria—it stops short of being seven measures long.[25]

If the complex form of Lysiart's aria expresses his conflicted nature, the simpler forms that Weber uses for Adolar's music stand at the opposite end of the spectrum. Both he and Euryanthe are "solid to the core": their outward actions reflect their inward purity. The misplaced love that motivates Lysiart and Eglantine is only voiced in the most secret places: in the slow movements of long arias that none of the other characters can hear. Adolar sings most extensively of his "motivating love" not in the slow movement of his aria, but in his *Romanze* "Unter blüh'nden Mandelbäumen" (no. 2). In contrast to the "love arias" of Lysiart and Eglantine, Weber places the *Romanze* in the most public of all musical spaces, between two ceremonial numbers. Like the "Ernster Reigen" of the preceding number, the *Romanze* is *wirkliche Lebenserscheinung*—Adolar in fact sings his troubadour melody in response to an invitation from the king. Its three-strophe structure and position in the opera recall Joseph's romance and, indeed, many other tenor romances from French and German operas of this period.[26] Apart from minor changes, mostly to facilitate the text declamation, the melody and harmonic structure of the three verses are exactly the same. Adolar is supposedly accompanying himself, and the pizzicato string accompaniment evokes the sound of his zither. But Weber combines this musical realism with more symbolic orchestration, interposing the woodwind choir between the phrases of Adolar's song as the object of his yearning becomes clearer. As Adolar moves deeper into his description of Euryanthe, the accompaniment thickens and intensifies. The climax of the *Romanze* comes at the end, as Adolar celebrates Euryanthe's constancy with the words "heil'ger Treue schönste Rose blüht in deiner Brust allein!"—words which he repeats in the two-measure fortissimo coda.

The musical style of the *Romanze* and its placement in the score help to underscore Adolar's close connection to the ceremonial world of king and court, a world in which Euryanthe also participates. In the finale of the first act, for example, when Euryanthe is overjoyed with the thought of seeing Adolar again, she acts as a kind of "leader of the chorus." But more often her voice is a private one. Unlike Adolar, Euryanthe makes her first appearance completely alone, in the cavatina "Glöcklein im Thale!" (no. 5). The slow and sustained lyricism of this music and the nature images that form the greater part of its text typify Euryanthe's sound world and prefigure her most extensive solo number, the scene and cavatina from the third act.

As with the other principals, Euryanthe's musical style has strong connections to German opera of the previous generation. If Elvira is the ancestor of Eglantine, then Euryanthe may trace her heritage back to Myrrha or, better still, to the music of Pamina in *Die Zauberflöte*. Slow and profoundly lyrical, her music conveys many of the same emotions that Mozart touched with "Ach ich fühl's." Except for a few isolated instances, Euryanthe eschews the dramatic coloratura that typifies the music of the villains. But this lyricism does not necessarily mean that Euryanthe's music is simple. Like Myrrha, Euryanthe is absolutely innocent, but she expresses this innocence in a style that is far more sophisticated than that of "Ich war, wenn ich erwachte."

Euryanthe's scene and cavatina, "So bin ich nun verlassen / Hier dicht am Quell" (no. 17), comes after she has been abandoned by Adolar, as she awaits a lonely death in the wilderness. Although the division of the number into "scene" and "cavatina" is easy to hear, it is probably less important than the numerous subdivisions which cut across the traditional musical form. Weber uses a highly unusual orchestration to depict Euryanthe's emotional state: strings with solo bassoon and a single phrase voiced for solo flute. Virtually every line of the text is given its own distinct melody and accompaniment. We might expect this type of musical correspondence in the *Scene*. Weber's musical evocation of the rustling brook and the glimmering moonshine in the sixteenth-note accompaniment to Euryanthe's recitative (measures 13–18) is effective, but it is hardly surprising. More unusual is the cavatina itself. "Hier dicht am Quell" falls into three sections that trace a pattern of departure and return. In the first section (measures 1–8) Euryanthe imagines her death, and the willow and brook that will be her only grave markers after she is gone. Her song begins simply, with two closely related two-measure phrases. In the next four measures Euryanthe repeats the opening couplet, but her melody and the chromatic accompaniment underneath it lead toward G minor and the more rapidly changing music of the middle section (measure 8, final two beats, to measure 16). Despite its occasional chromaticism, this section is clearly in D major, which sets up the expected return to the tonic in measure 17. Euryanthe imagines the words that the willow will speak to Adolar when he visits her grave. The return of the melody and key of the first section seem to underscore the surface meaning of the text: the music is finding peace and rest along with Euryanthe's soul. Euryanthe's song, however, is not completely about resignation, and with the second repetition of "sie fand von Lieb' und Leide Ruh'!" (measures 18–19) the music launches into more chromaticism. Yet as the imagined flowers tell the future Adolar of her constancy, the harmony slips back into the tonic key.

In the opening paragraphs of this book I described the music which follows this return to the tonic (the transition to the "Hunters' Chorus") as Weber's attempt to "smooth over and partially obscure the boundaries between the individual pieces of the number opera and move toward a solution of what he saw as the essential problem of the genre, namely, to bring unity to an art form that was a 'whole containing other wholes.'" This same tendency to efface conventional formal divisions may be observed not only between many of the individual numbers of *Euryanthe*, but also within them. Euryanthe's recitative "So bin ich nun verlassen," for instance, often approaches the rhythmic impulse and phrase structure of the "aria style," while the musical style of the cavatina proper seems to hover between aria and arioso. Weber seems to be consciously attenuating a central distinction of eighteenth- and early-nineteenth-century opera, that between recitative and aria. And while the harmonic pattern of departure and return gives "Hier dicht am Quell" a certain sense of balance, it would be misleading to classify it as a ternary-form aria. The form of Euryanthe's cavatina is better described as "characteristic" in the nineteenth-century meaning of the term: uniquely adapted to the specific needs of the drama.

Like the hunters' chorus "Die Thale dampfen die Höhen glüh'n!" Euryanthe's "Hier dicht am Quell" has a close counterpart in *Freischütz*, namely Agathe's "Und ob die Wolke sie verhülle." Weber titles both of these pieces cavatinas and places them near or at the beginning of the third act in their respective operas. Both pieces are in a slow tempo, and the two heroines sing in a predominantly lyric style. The relatively light orchestration that Weber uses for these two pieces is also quite similar, and although there is no exact counterpart to the solo cello that prefigures Agathe's melody in "Und ob die Wolke," Weber does use the bassoon and the flute as "characterizing instruments" in the scene from his *grosse romantische Oper*, most notably during the introduction to Euryanthe's recitative. In addition, certain harmonic details of "Hier dicht am Quell" recall similar procedures in "Und ob die Wolke." In measure 23 of "Und ob die Wolke," for instance, Weber uses an unexpected C-major chord (a major mediant relationship to the A-flat-major tonic of the cavatina) as Agathe sings "ewig rein und *klar*," a wonderfully expressive gesture that he repeats in measure 19 of "Hier dicht am Quell" as Euryanthe sings "sie fand von Lieb' und Leide Ruh'!" The two cavatinas, in short, employ the same general musical style, a style that seems to distill the essence of the Weberian heroine: vulnerable, tender, and yet radiantly spiritual.

The musical connections between the roles of Euryanthe and Agathe are not limited to their two cavatinas, but may be found throughout *Freischütz* and *Euryanthe*. The two roles belong to the same *Fach:* they lie in the same range and make similar demands on the singer. The soprano who portrays either Agathe or Euryanthe must be capable of long, sustained phrases; she must have a powerful and rich lower and middle register as well as the ability to spin out soft pianissimo notes in her upper range. Coloratura is almost negligible in the two roles: only in the fast section of "Leise, leise" does Agathe sing anything approaching *fioratura,* and Euryanthe eschews it altogether. Yet these similarities of musical style (to adopt the distinction that I made above) are only symptomatic of the deeper similarities of *Charakter* that link Agathe and Euryanthe. Both sopranos are close to nature and to God. During her moments of greatest stress, for instance, when Lysiart accuses her of infidelity during the second-act finale, or as Adolar does battle with the serpent near the beginning of the third act, Euryanthe's thoughts turns naturally heavenward, and her song becomes quite literally a prayer. Agathe's religiosity is even more explicit: she sings "Und ob die Wolke" while kneeling at an altar.[27]

But despite these similarities of musical style and *Charakter,* the role of Euryanthe is not simply Agathe in the "formal dress" of the *grosse romantische Oper.* If the similarities between the two cavatinas provide yet another example of ways in which Weber modeled *Euryanthe* on his previous success, so do the differences between the two numbers illuminate those between his *Singspiel* and his *grosse romantische Oper.* In contrast to the structural fluidity of "Hier dicht am Quell," "Und ob die Wolke" is cast in a clear ternary form. The phrase structure of Agathe's cavatina is also far more regular than that which Weber adopts in Euryanthe's scene, and although Weber is certainly attentive to the text in "Und ob die Wolke," he does not seem interested, as he is in the corresponding scene from *Euryanthe,* in giving each line of the libretto a specific musical character. In "Hier dicht am Quell" Weber approaches a through-composed style that has no real counterpart in *Der Freischütz.*

That the two cavatinas occupy similar places within the scores of the two operas, moreover, should not obscure the quite different roles that "Und ob die Wolke" and "Hier dicht am Quell" play in the drama of their respective works. Although Agathe is in an attitude of prayer, the text of her cavatina reads more like an inner dialogue, through which she reassures herself (and thereby the audience) that the heavenly Father watches over and protects all things. Euryanthe's cavatina, on the other hand, is essentially about resignation; if she finds solace in the natural world she is nevertheless the innocent victim of the villains' perfidy. This plot difference between the two cavatinas thus embodies a more essential distinction between the roles of Euryanthe and Agathe, a distinction that is created by the contrasting dramaturgical structures of *Euryanthe* and *Freischütz*. Agathe's function in the plot is symbolic as well as dramatic; she is (as she tells us immediately before the third-act finale) the white dove, an emblem of purity and spiritual power. "Und ob die Wolke" represents the most direct musical expression of this element of Agathe's character. Euryanthe may be just as innocent and pure as Agathe, but she remains "earthbound," embroiled in the machinations of the plot. There is no hermit figure in *Euryanthe* to cast his protective aegis over the heroine, and the supernatural powers that she invokes remain distant. This difference thus manifests a fundamental distinction between the two works. The plot of *Freischütz* unfolds in a mythical world, in which the forces of good and evil are embodied on the stage; it can be read as a kind of operatic morality play. Despite the presence of supernatural elements in *Euryanthe,* the opera remains a purely human drama.

Geschlechtsverhältnisse

That the figure of Euryanthe exists on the "all too human" stage of the *grosse romantische Oper* makes her in many ways a more telling reflection of world outside of the opera house. For if Euryanthe's music manifests some of the aesthetic ideals of early-nineteenth-century criticism, so does her personality manifest some of the most important aspects of its ideology. In this context, Euryanthe's piety and inwardness make her a kind of ideal woman—the embodiment of that same "domestic spirituality" that the young maidens of Memphis voiced in Méhul's *Joseph.* That Euryanthe is beautiful goes without saying, but her outward appearance is not as important as the qualities that Adolar celebrates in his *Romanze:* Euryanthe's chastity and loyalty. Euryanthe's chastity is of course the central issue in the opera. When Adolar and Lysiart bet all of their lands on Euryanthe's faithfulness, they are enacting what for early-nineteenth-century Germany was a self-evident truth: that women's purity and chastity was essential not only for a marriage, but for the life of a community. If Adolar cannot command the loyalty of his bride, to put the matter in the simplest terms, how can he be the lord of Nevers? The relationship between Adolar and Euryanthe is a thinly veiled metaphor for the relationship between a lord and his people.

The relationship between the sexes, and the way in which this relationship reflects and informs fundamental social and political structures, is also the subject of a lengthy article in what was probably the most important reference work in early- and mid-nineteenth-century Germany, the *Staatslexicon* of Rotteck and Welcker.[28] The first edition of this work appeared in fifteen volumes between 1834 and 1843. Welcker begins his article on *Geschlechtsverhältnisse* with the following words:

> The relationship between the sexes is the most general and weighty relationship in human society; its importance for political and legal theory is indisputable. This mysterious, basic relationship is the ever-renewing life source for the entire society, for the physical and moral education (or miseducation) of each of its members, in every generation. It must be established with justice and wisdom, it must be morally pure and healthy, for it is the basis of society.[29]

Welcker's concept of the "mysterious, basic relationship" between the sexes shows many similarities to the concept of *Charakter* that I examined at the beginning of chapter 3. Like *Charakter,* this relationship is a type of "essence" that escapes precise definition, operating on society "from the inside out" in much the same way that *Charakter* informs and brings unity to the entire work of art. For Welcker, the relationship between the sexes both models and determines the life of the state: there is therefore a direct connection between feminine chastity and "civic virtue":

> Wherever women become degenerate, civic virtue and strength will disappear as well. Only if the strongest of all sensuous drives are subordinated to the domination of moral good sense first in the family—the foundation and plant nursery, the prototype of the state association—can the permanent victory of [moral good sense] be hoped for in the state as well.[30]

The proper relationship between the sexes is based on a polar opposition that stems from the different procreative roles of men and women:

> The man's part consists in more active, outward excitement, the creation of individual life, whereas the woman, more passive, absorbs the vital influences necessary for the material development of the new life from

without, and following deep impulses, is concerned only with the inward development necessary for the continuation of the species.[31]

The relationship between the sexes, in short, functions for Welcker as the primary means whereby the natural order is imprinted onto society. In this context, the extensive nature descriptions in the arias of Euryanthe and Agathe take on new meaning. Apart from a few ominous clouds in "Leise, leise," Weber's heroines use these arias to describe a beautiful, spiritualized natural order, the same natural order that, through their chastity and virtue, will eventually triumph in the human societies of both *Freischütz* and *Euryanthe*.

If Euryanthe embodies the passive, chaste, loving ideal of femininity so essential to the life of the community, then Eglantine is in many ways its *Gegenbild*. Struggling against natural law, she is what Welcker would call a *Mannweib*, dangerously mixing active and passive roles that should be kept separate. Her misplaced, "active" love of Adolar helps set the plot in motion, and she makes the betrayal of Euryanthe possible by stealing the poisoned ring from Emma's tomb (second scene of act 2, immediately following Lysiart's aria). Eglantine's crime is essentially that of exposure: she makes Euryanthe's private secret public. The exchange between Lysiart and Eglantine that immediately precedes their duet reveals much about Eglantine's "mannish" character:

EGLANTINE: You overheard my secret?
LYSIART: As atonement, Forest offers you his hand.
    I will change these chains into a garland of roses
    You shall rule over all these rich lands.[32]

Lysiart identifies himself through the territory over which he rules and offers Eglantine lordship over Adolar's lands—their betrothal is part alliance and part business transaction.

Interpreting the opera through the gender ideology of early-nineteenth-century Germany, we could say that the loveless marriage between Lysiart and Eglantine is doomed because the two villains are too much alike. As Welcker writes:

> [The two sexes] can, in accordance with the most universal law of nature, simultaneously maintain their own essential definition and maintain their fundamental attraction and harmonious union for their common life-purpose only when they are in polar opposition and connection.[33]

This polar opposition finds concrete expression in *Euryanthe,* most notably in the sound world of the king and court, where it helps define the "normalcy" against which the "abnormal" events of the plot unfold. It is most clearly seen in music from the very beginning of the introduction, an antiphonal chorus for the ladies and the knights of the court. The ladies begin by singing the praises of peace, accompanied by a brief orchestral ritornello, scored for woodwinds and marked "dolce e grazioso." The knights respond with virtually the same melody, but here it is more thickly harmonized in *Männerchor* style. More important, the woodwind ritornello is replaced by one for brass and timpani (only the bassoon carries over from the earlier orchestration).[34] The polar opposition between the sexes thus operates within the opera on a musical as well as an ideological plane, forming a kind of "third musico-dramatic axis" in addition to those between inner and outer and between good and evil that I have discussed above.[35] It is precisely this polar opposition—the foundation of harmony between the sexes—that the villains transgress. As we might expect, the second-act duet that follows the betrothal of Lysiart and Eglantine ("Komm denn, uns'rer Leid zu rächen") is not about love, but revenge. The extensive imitative passages that make up the bulk of this duet can be read as a musical symbol for the villains' dilemma: they are possessed by the same thoughts of hatred and revenge and yet are unable truly to unite.

Lysiart's aria and the villains' duet set up a pattern—an aria for a male figure followed by a duet between him and his partner—that Weber repeats in the next two numbers of the opera: Adolar's "Wehen mir Lüfte Ruh'" and the duet between the hero and the heroine ("Hin nimm die Seele mein," no. 13). Weber uses this parallelism to accentuate the contrast between the "degenerate" relationship of the villains and the ideal relationship of Adolar and Euryanthe. Weber casts "Komm denn, uns'rer Leid zu rächen" in B major, whose implications we have already had the occasion to discuss (see the discussion of Eglantine's aria, above). The aria does indeed depict "anger, fury, envy, and frenzied rage, assembled from the shrillest and most piercing colors." "Hin nimm die Seele mein," by contrast, is in the "pure, innocent and simple" key of C major.[36] In contrast to the villains, Euryanthe and Adolar sing predominantly in parallel thirds and sixths, a musical symbol of unifying love. This same theme will recur in the final scene in the opera as a symbol of Euryanthe and Adolar's complete reconciliation, an idealized love between the hero and heroine that is based very much on the "polar opposition" between the sexes. In order for this opposition to operate,

Euryanthe must be the passive counterpart to Adolar's active nature. But if Euryanthe's absolute passivity is an ideological necessity, it also tends to undermine the drama of the opera. Euryanthe's spotless virtue and inability to act robs her of her operatic nature. The balance between music and drama is disturbed.

This balance is the subject of some interesting remarks in A. B. Marx's *Die Music des neunzehnten Jahrhunderts und ihrer Pflege.* In this passage, that shortly precedes his comments on *Euryanthe,* Marx focuses on the fundamental problems of the German opera:

> In the German opera, the purely dramatic element has never been able to attain full ascendancy; the musical element, or the expression of individual sensations, has always been predominant. It is not difficult to point out the cause of this. The two requisites of dramatic life and truthfulness—natural freedom and unrestrained energy of action, or, in place of it, that piquante *petite guerre* of intrigue which keeps our western neighbors active and alive, even in times of political depression—were not to be found in our nation. . . . And the more fully the genius of musical art revealed itself to the German, and its mysteries filled his soul, the more he was drawn away from the external sphere of active life into the internal region of dreaming and brooding contemplation.[37]

Innigkeit and the "mysteries of the soul" typify the German people, we might paraphrase Marx, and in music Germans found the art form that was most suitable to these qualities. Euryanthe herself embodies all of those typically German characteristics, and her spiritualized language, rich in nature metaphors, resonates deeply in German music and literature from this period. However "characteristic" Euryanthe's inward song may be, however, it did not prove to be viable as the center point of an opera. Making the passive heroine the center of the drama made sense within the context of the rhetoric of the *Bildungsbürgertum,* for it was precisely this figure who incarnated those feminine virtues upon which the health of the entire society rested. But if Euryanthe's passive virtues were important for the creation of a new German nation, they were far less effective as the center of an operatic drama—the strategy rarely resulted in a genuine popular success. Schumann, for instance, used a plot quite similar to that of *Euryanthe* for his only opera, *Genoveva.* Schumann's libretto has far fewer logical problems than Chezy's, and the opera contains much beautiful music, but it also failed at the box office.

In the libretto of *Euryanthe* these aesthetic problems are exacerbated by the many places where the plot lacks plausibility. The biggest problem occurs in the finale of the second act, when Lysiart presents Emma's ring as proof that he has enjoyed Euryanthe's love and threatens to reveal the terrible story behind it. Euryanthe admits to breaking her oath of secrecy, but adds "Doch treulos bin ich nicht." The rest of the assembled company, including Adolar, immediately assume the worst and accuse her of betraying Adolar's love. Inexplicably, Euryanthe does not try to explain the situation. Instead of defending herself actively, she turns to God and prays that he will reveal her innocence. Presumably Euryanthe must know that Lysiart could have only discovered the secret of the ring from Eglantine, and indeed, she makes this connection in the third act, when the king asks her directly about her "crime" (no. 19, duet with chorus). The ideological need to make the heroine completely passive results in a heroine whose actions, in many instances, are simply not believable. Lapses of logic, however, have not stood in the way of other opera plots. Euryanthe's irrational behavior would be readily forgiven if she were always given the most exciting or impressive music to sing. But in a musical style that placed such high value on the "organic" correspondence between text and music, Euryanthe's absolutely passive nature tended to make her musical characterization monochromatic. The role of Euryanthe thus presents an absolute contrast with the prima donna roles of contemporary Italian opera, in which a priority was placed on the diversity of musical gesture. In these operas, it is the prima donnas who get to sing the complex double arias. If Euryanthe's absolutely passive nature left a hole in the middle of the opera's dramatic structure, so too did her prayer-like cavatina, as beautiful as they are, fail to make her the musical center of the work. In Weber's *grosse romantische Oper,* to sum up, gender ideology came into direct conflict with the musical and dramatic demands of the operatic stage.

Reception

Early-nineteenth-century critics did not speak about a conflict between ideology and aesthetics, but they did realize that the work was on the borders of contemporary operatic conventions. And although the music was greatly admired by many writers and composers, its lack of popular success could not be denied. Despite Weber's predictions it never came close to the popularity of *Der Freischütz.* Indeed, after the third performance Weber admitted that the opera was perhaps too long and reluctantly "laid hold of the knife." [38] As we might expect, these cuts concentrated on the recitatives, in particular in the long conversation between Eglantine and Euryanthe between number 5 and number 6. Weber also eliminated twenty-two bars from Euryanthe's third-act scene and cavatina (from "Was rieselst du im Haine" through "mir blühet keine Heimath mehr!"). After Weber left Vienna late in 1823 *Euryanthe* was subjected to another series of cuts by the *Kapellmeister* Conradin Kreuzer. These were far more extensive than the ones that Weber himself authorized. It is perhaps best to quote Jähns on this topic:

> It was he [Kreuzer] who struck out the place in Lysiart's aria #10 "Was soll mir" up through "Entflieh!" as well as the beautiful introduction to Adolar's aria, from the sixth measure on; it was he, who by transposing the Introduction of the third act into c minor, cut out its last 22 measures, including Euryanthe's recitative up to Adolar's entrance with "Hier ist der Ort," and further, the entire duet "Du klagst mich an." [Kreuzer] eliminated measures 5–10 in Euryanthe's cavatina "Hier dicht am Quell," as well as Adolar's gripping phrase in the third Finale from "Nein! gibt ihm frei!" up to the entrance of the hunters' chorus behind the scene. And it was Kreuzer who tore from the work one of its most brilliant jewels, the entire #8, Eglantine's great Scene and Aria "Bethörthe"— altogether 352 measures, in other words, twice again as much as Weber himself cut, taken together nearly an eighth of the opera.[39]

It is significant that many of Kreuzer's cuts concern the two villain arias. Jähns's tone of outrage is unmistakable, but considering the "Italianate tastes" of the Vienna audiences, Kreuzer's cuts make perfect sense. Indeed, they bear some similarity to the revisions that were made to *Das unterbrochene Opferfest* during its transformation into *Il sacrifizio interotto*. For audiences accustomed to the vocal pyrotechnics of Rossini's heroines, it must have been easy for the soprano who sang Eglantine to overshadow the heroine, the same "problem" inherent in Winter's score. Despite the "inward beauty" of Euryanthe's two cavatinas, she has nothing to compare with "Bethörthe! die an meine Liebe glaubt." If eliminating "Süss sind der Rache Freuden" helped to shift the balance between the two sopranos decisively toward the virtuous heroine, so too did Kreuzer's decision to cut Eglantine's largest aria help focus the drama more firmly on Euryanthe. By abbreviating the middle section of Lysiart's aria, Kreuzer also helped to diminish the dominating musical and dramatic position of the villains, as well as to heighten the similarity between "Wo berg ich mich" and the contemporary Italian double aria. Kreuzer's cuts may thus be seen as an effort to repair the most serious fault of the opera, the imbalance between the virtuous pair and the villains.

Despite these cuts, interest in the opera began to fade quickly in Vienna, and after twenty performances the opera was withdrawn. *Euryanthe* fared little better in its premieres in Cassel, Frankfurt, and Prague, and by the spring of 1824 Weber was to have doubts about the future of what he regarded as his greatest opera.[40] The harshest words may have come from the poet Grillparzer:

> Yesterday again at *Euryanthe*. This music is *disgusting*. This inversion of euphony, this rape of the beautiful would have been punished by the state in the good old days of [ancient] Greece. Such music is illegal; it would create monsters, were it ever possible that it gradually could find public acceptance. . . . This opera can please only fools, or lunatics, or scholars, or street thieves and assassins.[41]

Although most critics treated *Euryanthe* more favorably, it never achieved more than a very modest place in the German operatic repertoire—it was far less popular than now-forgotten works such as Marschner's *Der Templer und die Jüdin* or Kreuzer's *Der Nachtlager in Granada*. No other German opera from the first half of the nineteenth century (except perhaps *Der fliegende Holländer*) was more of a disappointment.

The failure of what was supposed to be the prototype of a new German operatic genre caused serious problems for those critics and scholars who were anxious to chronicle the triumph of German art. Heavy criticism fell, as we might expect, on the librettist. In the pages of nineteenth-century Weber biographies such as Benedict's, Chezy emerges as a ludicrous figure, pressuring Weber for money, embarrassing everyone by her inappropriate behavior at performances of the opera. That Helmine von Chezy was a little-known female poet made her a convenient scapegoat for those who would explain *Euryanthe*'s lack of success, such as the historian Julius Cornet:

> [After the premiere of *Freischütz*] Weber was still drunk with victory and full of holy ambition. He quickly chose . . . the libretto "Euryanthe" from Madame Chezy; he manfully defended himself against the Italian trio in Germany—against Rossini, Spontini, and Morlacchi through his words, his writings, and his actions, even while the Neapolitan impresario was rewarding the Italian trillers with a 300 pct. profit. Weber—as he himself admitted to me—often regretted the over-hasty choice of libretto.[42]

Euryanthe: *Reconfiguration and Transformation* 153

Attacks on the libretto of *Euryanthe* became so intense that Chezy felt compelled to defend herself in an article in the *Neue Zeitschrift für Musik* (1840).[43] As we might expect, Chezy emphasizes Weber's role in creating the libretto and blames the poor reception of the work on the unfavorable circumstances surrounding its premiere. The idea that *Euryanthe* would have succeeded if it had only been performed in another city or with a different cast also surfaces in Cornet, as well as in the pages of other histories.[44] Wagner's famous critique of *Euryanthe* in his early essay "Die deutsche Oper" (1834) perhaps comes closest to the mark:

> Freischütz is Weber's best work. . . . But turn to his Euryanthe! What splitting of hairs in the declamation, what fussy use of this or that instrument to emphasize a single word! Instead of throwing off a whole emotion with one bold freehand stroke, he minces the impression into little details and detailed littlenesses. . . . And since the audience is bound to admit in the end that it hasn't understood a note of it, people have to find their consolation in dubbing it astoundingly *learned,* and therefore paying it a great respect—O this wretched erudition—the source of every German ill![45]

The basic kernel of Wagner's critique is present in the earliest reviews of the opera. The Vienna review from which I have already quoted puts the matter more simply: the music is far too complicated and there is too much recitative. Chorley, hearing a Dresden performance of the opera in 1839, was tremendously excited by the music, but nevertheless criticizes certain "advanced" elements Weber's style. "The airs are constructed on unusual and arbitrary forms of rhythm," Chorley writes, referring perhaps to the diverse meters of the libretto, and "there is no prophesying, by the best-practised listener, of the change or chord which is next to come."[46] Ironically, the very qualities through which Weber hoped to establish a distinctively German operatic style caused audiences the greatest consternation. The same ideological structures and musico-dramatic innovations that made *Euryanthe* the embodiment of early-nineteenth-century critical ideals made it a failure at the box office.

As Wagner indicates, *Euryanthe* tended to earn the respect of nineteenth-century audiences rather than their love. The one notable exception was the city of Dresden. Here the opera held an important, if not dominating, position in the repertoire into the middle of the nineteenth century.[47] The first performance at the German opera, which Weber conducted on 31 March 1824, with the famous soprano Wilhelmine Schröder-Devrient in the title role, was a remarkable success. "I have never seen our public so taken, so full of enthusiasm," he wrote to his friend Lichtenstein:

> The excitement increased with every act. At the end I was called out, and then everyone, by a veritable storm. There is now complete agreement about how much higher this opera stands than *Freischütz*. Tieck, among others, was supposed to socialize after the opera, but explained that his spirit was too full, and said (to others, naturally) that there are things in this opera for which Gluck and Mozart would have envied me.[48]

Euryanthe remained popular in Dresden largely because of its particular association with Weber (and with Schröder-Devrient, who starred in most of the Dresden productions during this period).[49] Indeed, the work took on a special meaning in the city as an emblem of its "Germanic" operatic history and came to symbolize the achievement of German art. Nowhere is this clearer than in the special boldface, enlarged-type announcement of the twenty-fifth anniversary of the Dresden premiere, printed in the *Dresden Anzeiger*.[50] The announcement appeared together with a historical article, in which the quasi-ceremonial role that the opera had begun to play in Dresden is very clear. The article, for instance, reprinted a poem recited by Fräulein Wüst (singing the role of Eglantine) to Wilhelmine Schröder-Devrient at a performance of the opera in 1837, just before the prima donna was to take a long leave of absence from the stage. The hate between the characters of Eglantine and Euryanthe, runs the gist of the poem, is exactly the opposite of the love that Fräulein Wüst bears toward her colleague and the joy that she feels in the service of a great work of German art. The author of the article also reminds his or her readers that *Euryanthe* was the first opera to be performed in the new *Hoftheater*.[51] Needless to say, Morlacchi's *Tebaldo e Isolina* was not given this type of treatment, nor was *Les Huguenots*, which actually received more performances during this period. These works were merely operas. *Euryanthe* was a memorial to the past.

Conclusion

The performance and preservation of *Euryanthe* as a "commemorative piece" in Dresden during the early nineteenth century prefigures its reception in the late nineteenth and twentieth centuries. For although the work quickly passed out of the active repertoire, *Euryanthe* assumed a symbolic importance far greater than its limited popularity would seem to warrant, as the work in which the theories of the pro-German criticism were put into practice. The stylistic "advances" of *Euryanthe*—its through-composed, "organic" structure, its text declamation, its imaginative use of texture and harmony—do indeed correspond to many of the goals voiced by the pro-German critics and have led many scholars, both in the nine-teenth and twentieth centuries, to see the work as the archetypal German Romantic opera. This stance toward the work is evident as early as A. B. Marx's *Die Musik des neunzehnten Jahrhunderts und ihre Pflege,* in which *Euryanthe* stands for both the positive and the negative attributes of an en-tire genre. "In none of his works has Weber proved himself so fertile as in this," he writes,

> nowhere else has he, or any of his predecessors or contemporaries, adapted so ingeniously and happily the tone of expression to the time and place to which the drama refers. But by this time the thoughts and ideas of the people had already taken another direction. The middle ages, with its spectral apparitions and mysterious voices, its mingled idoliza-tion and degradation of women, the whole circle of its ideas had become strange to the people. . . . *Euryanthe* was and remains a failure.[52]

The ideological changes to which Marx is referring were critical to the development of German opera, but like all such changes, they are extremely difficult to trace. For some writers the death of Goethe in 1832 marked the end of an era, the transition from a Romantic to a realistic zeitgeist.[53] Other historians have spoken about the "historicalization" of art, music, and lit-erature.[54] We can certainly see these forces at work in Dresden in the large number of new journals devoted to historical or geographic subjects, and in the tremendous popularity of the new "historical" genre of French *grand opéra.* German audiences of the 1830s seem less concerned with the "myste-rious spirit world" that is so deeply explored in *Euryanthe* and more in-volved in the active sphere of politics and history. Yet the medieval setting of Wagner's *Tannhäuser* did not impede its success with Dresden audiences of the mid-1840s. The "spectral apparitions" of the Middle Ages may have been temporarily out of fashion, but the medievalism of Weber's opera can only partially account for its lack of success. And while nineteenth-century critics often complained that the work was too learned or complicated, they also recognized a great deal of beautiful music in the score.

Why then did *Euryanthe* fail? Chezy's libretto must bear a large part of the blame, and the shifting tastes of opera audiences were also an important factor. But the variety of reasons responsible for *Euryanthe*'s failure may best be understood within the same ideological framework that surrounded its birth: Weber's search for a distinctive German operatic character. That search led Weber into a problematic relationship not only with the conventions of French and Italian opera, but also with the heritage of the *Singspiel*. Despite *Euryanthe*'s stylistic innovations, these conventions are clearly present in many places throughout the score. What is novel in *Euryanthe* is not so much its musical forms as Weber's effort to infuse these forms with dramatic meaning. The same level of musico-dramatic detail that makes *Euryanthe* such a rewarding object of study made these forms unwieldy, overburdened by the demand that every note of the score should be fully "characteristic." That demand, as Wagner was to recognize thirty years later, would require a more radical departure from the conventions of early-nineteenth-century opera.

5 Epilogue: Institutions, Aesthetics, and Genre after Weber's Death

Der Streit der deutschen und italienischen Oper

It is well known, writes the Dresden correspondent for the *Berliner allgemeine musikalische Zeitung* in a report from 1825, that the city is divided into two parties. The first party, he says, is "the party of Weber":

> who have now won a small victory through their exemplary patriotism. This party will have nothing but Weberian *tours de force*. Elsewhere one knows little of the mighty leaps of Euryanthe, but they are the only things that satisfy this party: here one should subscribe to the view that it is the *non plus ultra* of all successful performances. The strange harmonies and broken melodies, the exaggerated accents, which appear on every page, are to them the expressions of a prudent genius. All of the powers of the German opera are spent on this music, yet there is another type of opera, which affects the hearts of its audience with less vain stimulation. The biased partisans of the first party are not pleased by this music, especially when their opera is giving something mediocre. The second musical party in Dresden is the Italians, who have just lifted themselves up with a new successful production.[1]

This quotation encapsulates many of the cultural and aesthetic issues that informed the German operatic milieu in the years immediately after *Euryanthe*'s premiere. *Euryanthe* may not have been the culmination of the search for a German opera in the aesthetic sense, but these years were profitable ones for German operatic institutions, not only in Dresden, but throughout the nation. In Dresden, as in most other German cities, the 1820s and 1830s were a time of transition, when the last vestiges of the predominantly Italian-language court companies that were so important during the eighteenth century were being replaced by German-language operatic institutions. Many late-nineteenth- and early-twentieth-century historians, as we have already noted, described this development in terms of conflict, as an institutional struggle running parallel to the aesthetic War of Liberation in which *Freischütz* figured so prominently. Max Weber, for instance, drew on his father's diaries and letters to paint a picture of the composer constantly battling with Francesco Morlacchi, his counterpart in the Italian opera. Recent scholars have tried to find a more balanced understanding of the period. In his introduction to the Garland reprint of Morlacchi's *Tebaldo e Isolina*, for instance, Philip Gossett warns against taking histories of the conflict between the "native and the foreign" at face value. Many Italian composers, he writes,

> continued to spend at least part of their careers attached to foreign insti-
> tutions: Rossini and Paër in Paris, Spontini in Paris and Berlin, Donizetti
> in Vienna, Nini in St. Petersburg, Mercadante in the Iberian peninsula.
> For perfectly obvious reasons (quite apart from aesthetic considerations),
> they were often treated with hostility, even loathing, by local musicians.
> In the historical mythology generated by these confrontations, the cul-
> tural "imperialists" emerge as caricatures, whose sole purpose was to
> prevent the development of local musical culture.
>   Nowhere is this myth more prevalent than in histories of the Dresden
> musical world in the 1810's, the Dresden of Francesco Morlacchi and Carl
> Maria von Weber.[2]

The "mythology of conflict" between the German and Italian companies has come under attack in the last few decades, most notably in an article by Eberhard Kremtz entitled "Das 'Deutsche Departement' des Dresdner Hoftheaters."[3] Kremtz emphasizes the support that Weber received at court and points out that the king himself approved the idea of the German opera. The conflict between Weber and Friedrich Hellwig (regisseur of the court theater), Kremtz believes, was at least as significant as that between Weber and Morlacchi. In Dresden the "Streit der deutschen und italienischen Opern" was probably played out more in the imaginations of music critics than in the day-to-day affairs of the theater.

The border between native and foreign was even blurrier in other German cities that did not share the institutional division between Italian and German companies that characterized the Dresden opera. In Vienna during this time, for instance, the Kärntnerthor Theater was leased to impresarios (such as Barbaja), who often produced *stagioni* of Italian operas. The rivalries that plagued the Munich opera during the 1820s and 1830s had more to do with overlapping responsibilities than with nationality. Perhaps the closest analogy to the institutional structure of the Dresden opera comes from Berlin, where in 1807 the royal opera and the Nationaltheater had merged to form the Königliche Schauspiele. The two companies formed a part of one institution, but their repertoires were kept separate. That the "mythology of conflict" could inform much of the rhetoric concerning opera in Berlin is clear not only from the criticism surrounding the premiere of *Freischütz,* but also from the critical response to the "Rossini season" of 1826. Here, as in other German cities, the taste for Italian opera was likened to a disease, or mercilessly ridiculed in texts such as Rellstab's *Henriette, oder Die schöne Sängerin.*[4] The title refers to the soprano Henriette Sontag, who enjoyed enormous success during this period as an interpreter of Italian operatic heroines. As we might expect, the critic A. B. Marx was deeply distrustful of Sontag's popularity and found something not quite canny in her singing:

> What does Art matter, for those who are so infatuated with the vision
> of grace that they glow with feverish heat, whose sighs are sunk in deep
> dreams, who through the nightingale-tones of her voice imagine them-
> selves in Elysian fields, who, enticed by the magic of her siren-like move-
> ments have lost their very selves? What value can the philosophy of Art
> find in her who breathes only in the world of feelings, whose vision,
> entranced by her own gods, has not yet been able to lift up true wisdom
> to God? How many priests can she win over by her uninhibitedness, out
> of those who have not yet been possessed by the devil of desire? What
> value is she to artistic truth, she who has sworn by the flag of the full
> box-office, and who has chained her own flesh to the cohorts of the hard
> dollar?[5]

The dichotomies that Marx presents—between health and disease, chastity and lasciviousness, "artistic truth" and commercial success—have no doubt become familiar to the reader. Their inflammatory tone had little to do with the institutional development of German opera, and it is clear that both contemporary criticism and subsequent histories distorted the relationship between the native and foreign to serve their own agendas. But the mythology of conflict is more than a distorting lens that interferes with our perception of the past. The myth is itself a "fact of music history" that shapes and testifies to the intersection of opera and national identity. Despite its continued popularity, foreign opera became for many German critics a universal *Gegenbild,* not only for music and drama, but also for the proper role of art in human life. For the "nationalist" musicians, what was seen as the superficial triviality of French and Italian opera came to incarnate the more general social and spiritual forces that were threatening to undermine the integrity of German culture. And although later biographies of Weber certainly overexaggerated the division of the city into the partisans of the German and Italian opera companies, there is no doubt that the city served as a lightning rod for nationalist music criticism. The idea of the institutional conflict between the two Dresden companies as the arena for a broader aesthetic and ideological struggle found clear expression, for example, in an article by A. B. Marx entitled "Streit der deutschen und italienischen Oper in Dresden." "Throughout Germany today," he writes, "there is a competitive struggle of patriotic sensibility against the all-penetrating Italian opera and its offshoot, the neo-French."[6] The Italian opera has had such success in Germany, he continues, because Germans

> tend to overvalue the foreign, and to justify their opinions with phrases like "Art is general among all peoples" and "All peoples love and hate, sing and dance." [These types of thoughts] even confuse the greater number of our artists, who are generally not well enough educated to stand on their own. They hinder themselves by trying to learn from the foreigners what this one or that one lacks. Thus it is the duty for everyone for whom it is possible to bring forth his or her own light, and change this hateful twilight into bright day.[7]

In a footnote, Marx traces the Dresden proclivity toward Italian music to the conversion of its dukes in order to become kings of Poland. Even Sebastian Bach, he points out, could not get a job at the Saxon court.

Marx's comments only serve to introduce the remainder of the article, the "Scherz und Ernst" by Richard Otto Spazier, from which I have already quoted in chapter 1. In Spazier's work the rhetoric surrounding the "Streit der deutschen und italienischen Oper" reaches an almost comic stridency. Unlike Marx, Rellstab, or Miltitz, Spazier was strictly an amateur musician. To his contemporaries Spazier, a sometimes translator and a passionate spokesman for the Polish people, was better known as the biographer of his uncle, Jean Paul Richter. He is uninterested in issues of text declamation or musical form—the most important thing for him is the ideological struggle between the native and the foreign. In a particularly vituperative 1830 review of a performance of *Fidelio*, Spazier recapitulates the grievances of the German opera in Dresden and hopes for a brighter future:

> He who understands the conditions under which the German opera has labored since its foundation: opposed by a rival who alone attracted the attention of the public, who alone enjoyed support and favor [of the

court], for whose maintenance there was nothing too expensive, who did everything possible to maintain its position, so that German art had to clothe itself in leftover scraps, and, as has been said in another place, run behind a pompous dandy like a humiliated beggar—he who knows these conditions must regard [this performance of *Fidelio*] as the harbinger of the dawn that, thanks to the continuing efforts of our German artistic institution, is breaking over the long overclouded artistic horizon of our richly endowed city. The blooming and thriving of a German artistic institution . . . and the final removal of every foreigner from one of the German capitals, is not only a local, but a national interest.[8]

The Dresden Opera after Weber

Spazier's harsh tone may be explained partly by the extremely "overclouded" condition of the German opera company in the period 1825–30. The years immediately after the premiere of *Euryanthe* were not good ones for the German opera in Dresden. As his many biographers have noted, Weber's health was extremely fragile, and he had difficulty meeting the strenuous requirements of his job as *Kapellmeister*. Exhausted by his work with *Euryanthe* and by the disappointments of its premiere, often compelled to take on extra duties because of Morlacchi's frequent illnesses and absences, Weber composed almost nothing during the two years after his *grosse romantische Oper*. Moreover, it appears from contemporary reviews that the general quality of the performances at the German opera was in decline. Wolfgang Becker sums up his chronology of the opera under Weber in the following manner: "The ideal of the German opera and all of the thoughts with which it was associated, the ideal that lay at the base of Weber's work for the Dresden theater since its beginning, was completely lost during this year [1825]."[9] Weber left Dresden in February of 1826 to accept a lucrative commission in London (the opera *Oberon*). His subsequent death in London on 5 June only exacerbated the institutional difficulties of the company that he had founded.

The most pressing question was clearly who was going to succeed Weber as head of the German opera. The most obvious candidate was Heinrich Marschner. Marschner had lived in Dresden since the early 1820s and had been hired as Weber's assistant with the title of *Musikdirektor* in November of 1823 (immediately after the *Euryanthe* premiere). Weber was glad to have help, but Marschner was by no means his first choice. The personal relationship between the two men was somewhat cool—Weber may have regarded Marschner as more of a "commercial opportunist" than as a dedicated champion of German art.[10] In later histories of German opera Marschner appears as a kind of bridge between Weber and Wagner, as the composer who was best able to balance the aesthetic and ideological demands for a national operatic style with the need to produce popular works. But Marschner's most successful operas began to appear only in the late 1820s and early 1830s (*Der Vampyr,* composed in 1827 and first performed in 1828, *Der Templer und die Jüdin,* 1829, and *Hans Heiling,* 1833). In 1826 he was best known as the composer of *Singspiele* and incidental music, an arranger and editor rather than an original genius. Wolf August von Lüttichau, who had become the general director of the *Hoftheater* in 1825, needed a composer-conductor with a bigger name. Although Marschner made a vigorous push for the position of *Königliche Kapellmeister,* Lüttichau ignored his application, and Marschner left Dresden for greener pastures in August of 1826.

In the fall of 1826 there were thus two posts open in Dresden: Weber's former place at the head of the German opera and Marschner's old position as *Musikdirektor.* The man who was eventually to inherit Weber's position, Carl Gottlieb Reissiger, was originally hired in November of 1826 to replace Marschner. Lüttichau at first wanted to hire Johann Nepomuk Hummel for the higher-ranking position of *Königliche Kapellmeister.* But it proved difficult to lure Hummel away from his prestigious and lucrative post as *Kapellmeister* at the Weimar court. Negotiations stretched out through early 1827 and were further delayed by the death of King Friedrich Augustus in that year.[11] Since Morlacchi was frequently ill during this difficult time, Reissiger was often compelled to direct not only the German company, but the Italian company as well. By all accounts he was extraordinarily successful—Lüttichau specifically mentioned Reissiger's diligence and musical abilities in a letter to the new king in August 1827, recommending an increase in Reissiger's salary from one thousand to twelve hundred thalers.[12] Hummel decided to keep his position in Weimar, and so Reissiger appeared to be the best choice to head the German opera. In early May of 1828, he was granted the position of *Kapellmeister.*

The terms of Reissiger's contract reveal the extent to which the traditions of the eighteenth century still held sway in the Dresden of the late 1820s.[13] The contract refers to Morlacchi as the "oldest" or "senior" *Kapellmeister* and, just like Weber's contract of more than a decade earlier, demands that Reissiger take over Morlacchi's duties in the case of "illnesses and absences." Reissiger is required to compose a certain amount of church music every year, including a vesper service and a mass. In his biography of the composer, Kurt Kreiser claims that Reissiger was also compelled to wear livery during certain festival occasions.[14] Reissiger's oeuvre shows that he had mastered the idiom of the day, and he seems to have had moderate success as a minor composer of operas, songs, and choral works, supplying pieces for the growing market of bourgeois "household music."[15] But although he remained active as a composer through the 1830s, his output seems to have declined in the following decade. Reissiger's real genius lay in his organizational skills and in his ability to attract first-rate singers to the Dresden stage. By the end of the 1820s the German opera was flourishing, well on its way to becoming one of the most important houses in Germany.

Reissiger's success stands in marked contrast to the Italian opera, which, as Heyne points out, was already showing signs of stagnation during Weber's last years. In 1824 Morlacchi's company generated an income of only 8,241 thalers in comparison with 35,108 for the German opera company.[16] The correspondent for the Leipzig *Allgemeine musikalische Zeitung* described the decline of the Italian opera in an 1829 review of the Dresden opera season:

> In the few years since I have last heard it the Italian opera seems to have become much worse, and it is not a completely evil thing that it has been closed during the last three months. And the public, thanks be to God, is taking no more interest in this powerless music. I am even more pleased to report the beginnings of a lively participation of the court and the public in the direction of the German opera. I must also mention the strenuous exertions of the German singers, who had to perform two or three times a week during June, July and August. They put on only repetitions of old operas, but the singers and the orchestra were so well-prepared and accomplished that they sufficiently compensated for the lack of anything new. I will mention only the most successful performances of *Oberon, Euryanthe, Jacob und seine Söhne,* and *Libella,* as well as *Die Vestalin,* (given here in German for the first time) and the newly prepared production of *Fidelio.*[17]

These disparaging remarks about the Italian opera could stem from Spazier's highly biased pen (the review is unsigned), but they nevertheless hint at some of the reasons that Reissiger was successful. He conserved his resources by producing well-known operas, but he also seems to have reached out to the Dresden public. In addition to his duties at the opera, for instance, Reissiger was active as a director of the increasingly popular *Männerchorvereine,* in which many of Dresden's prosperous burghers sang.[18] Reissiger, in fact, rapidly became involved in many aspects of Dresden's musical and social life. Kreiser describes some of his activities in the following passage from his biography of the composer:

> In the Albina Gesellschaft, an association of artists and intellectuals, one could often hear his beautiful bass voice resounding. In the leading salons of Dresden society, the bankers Oppenheim and von Kaskel, and above all the salon of Major Serre, Reissiger was a musical *spiritus rector*. The daughters of Herr Kaskel were particularly musical, and Reissiger dedicated many songs to them.[19]

In modern parlance, Reissiger was a "networker" who rapidly ingratiated himself into Dresden's cultural elite. These were the men and women who attended the opera and sometimes provided scores or librettos for its performances. They reviewed these performances in the local press and corresponded with other people across Germany, helping to establish other contacts and to spread the fame of the German opera in Dresden.

The End of the Italian Opera

The Italian opera had no such network. Morlacchi never learned German adequately and remained highly dependent on his contacts at court. While Reissiger was harmonizing in the Albina Gesellschaft and giving music lessons to rich banker's daughters, Morlacchi was traveling through Italy, attending the premieres of his operas, hiring singers, and "refreshing himself under native skies," as the Dresden *Abend-Zeitung* puts it. During the eighteenth and early decades of the nineteenth century, this type of foreign connection brought composers wealth and success, but by the late 1820s it was becoming a liability, for economic and cultural power was beginning to pass out of the hands of the court circle and into the ranks of the upper bourgeoisie, the men and women with whom Reissiger was establishing contact. When the revolutionary unrest of 1830 spread from Paris across Germany, they made their bid for political power as well.

The 1830 revolution in Saxony began in September, when the police interfered with a bachelor party in Leipzig. Unrest quickly spread to Dresden and throughout the kingdom, and by 13 September King Anton was forced to replace the conservative cabinet minister von Einsiedel (who had been a supporter of the Italian opera and one of the foremost critics of Weber's efforts) with the liberal Bernard August von Lindenau. One of the most important demands of the liberals was met in November, with the establishment of the Communal Guard. But the most important result of the 1830 revolution in Saxony was the constitution that went into effect in September of 1831, creating a representative legislative assembly for the first time in Saxon history. The franchise that elected this assembly was of course severely limited by property and gender restrictions, and the nobility retained a great deal of political power. Nevertheless, contemporaries regarded the 1830 revolution as a great defeat for the aristocracy.

The financial power that the new legislative assemblies were occasionally able to wield had important consequences for operatic life not only in Saxony, but in other parts of Germany as well. The remarks of the Englishman Sir Arthur Brooke Faulkner, who traveled through Germany in the years 1829, 1830, and 1831, reveal a great deal about the effects of the 1830 revolutions on German opera companies. Faulkner visited Darmstadt in 1829, where the grand duchess was scandalized not only by the tight lacing of Wilhelmine Schröeder-Devrient's dress, but by the "loud plaudits" with which her costume was greeted by the public. "To understand [the grand duchess's] feeling in this respect," Faulkner writes,

> my compatriot must be pleased to consider that the Darmstadt opera is
> an amusement provided for the people by the sovereign—an appendage,
> in fact, to the grand ducal establishment. The royal family conceive [that]
> the public ought therefore to behave themselves as guests, rather than as a
> mere auditory who have paid full value for their entertainment, whereas
> they only contribute in part. If this plauditory indecorum, for it is consid-
> ered indecorum, be repeated, the public are threatened with having the
> opera shut up altogether, and no doubt this measure would not be long
> delayed if the dignity of the court were not committed to keep it going.
> In fact operas are a kind of indulgence which German sovereigns accord
> to their subjects pretty much on the same principle as we give a toy to a
> child to keep it quiet, or in good humour with its nurse.[20]

But the tables were turned after the bourgeoisie assumed political leadership. Visiting the city after the 1830 revolution, Faulkner writes:

> Whether as a measure of revenge or economy, is not quite apparent, but
> the opera—this once unrivalled opera—the very model of all operas, and
> the theme of praises all over Germany, is closed, and, some say, not to be
> opened again. The common opinion is, that this step was taken in conse-
> quence of a declared determination of the changers not to defray the
> debts incurred by the late grand duke for its support, the extent of which

may be inferred from the fact, that one of the singers was enabled, by her ascendency [*sic*] over her royal protector, to live in a style not exceeded by any of the grand ducal family. Her mansion, in the same square, fronts, or confronts, or, as people may prefer the reading, affronts the palace; a conspicuous monument of the licentious profusion of princes, and their criminal disregard of the decencies they exact from their subjects.[21]

For the newly elected assembly, the Darmstadt opera was a symbol of the aristocratic past, simultaneously offending their moral sensibilities, their liberal politics, and their pocketbooks. But the opera was also enormously popular, not only with the aristocracy, but with the other classes as well. Faulkner continues:

All ranks have become impatient of being deprived of their accustomed recreation of the opera. Music here, like tobacco or coffee, is one of the necessaries of life. My coachman, who is a citizen of Darmstadt, swears he finds it impossible to get on without his opera, and is quite sure the re-opening of the theatre must soon be called for by universal acclamation, though it were even on the condition of paying the whole of the grand duke's debts.[22]

The Darmstadt opera thus functioned in two ways: as a symbol of the aristocratic past and as a central source of entertainment for the city. In Dresden these two functions were to a large degree split between the Italian and the German opera companies. As the statistics quoted above make clear, Morlacchi's company was already losing popular support by the mid-1820s. When the newly elected legislative assembly imposed an austerity budget on the court in 1832, the ministry decided to economize by eliminating the Italian opera company. The venerable tradition of the Italian opera in Dresden ended on 31 March, with a production of *Don Giovanni*.

We must not overexaggerate the importance of this change, for it does not in any way mean that Italian opera ceased being performed in Dresden. Despite the claims and wishful thoughts of the pro-German critics, Italian opera remained extremely popular in Dresden and throughout Germany, particularly after the new operas of Bellini and Donizetti made their way across the Alps. French opera probably became more rather than less popular during the 1830s, when Dresden audiences discovered the *grands opéras* of Meyerbeer, Auber, and Halévy. The *Tagebuch der deutschen Bühnen* from 1833, the year after the Italian company closed its doors, lists ninety performances of "deutsche Opern, Singspiele, und Vaudeville" at Reissiger's company, compared with twenty-nine performances of Italian operas. But these statistics refer only to the performance language of the works and not the language of composition. Not only were operas still being performed in Italian during the 1830s, but more than half of the German-language repertoire consisted of translated works. The "institutional victory" of the German opera had not diminished the importance of foreign works in the repertoire. The difference was that now these operas were nationalized into the German opera just as the French *opéra comique* had been absorbed. *I Puritani*, in contrast to Rossini's operas of the 1810s and 1820s, enjoyed success in Dresden as *Die Puritaner*. Not only repertoire, but also singers were "naturalized" into the German opera. The *Charaktergemälde von Dresden*, written in 1833, describes the fate of Herr Zezi:

> Herr Zezi, earlier a member of the local Italian opera and now a member
> of the German one, may well be the most outstanding baritone that
> Germany possesses. With his exceptionally beautiful and sonorous voice,
> whose deep inwardness irresistibly dominates the feelings of the audience
> . . . [Zezi] approaches the ideal of manly beauty. Because his method
> belongs more to the German than to the Italian school, he is one of the
> most priceless acquisitions of our German opera institute. His "Wald-
> burg" in Bellini's noble opera *The Stranger* ["die Fremde"—the writer is
> speaking of *La Straniera*] will remain unforgettable for everyone.[23]

Herr Zezi's career symbolizes the fate of the Italian opera in Dresden. With the application of a few choice adjectives such as "deep inwardness" and "manly beauty," Herr Zezi's mellifluous voice was made the ideological property of the German camp. But this naturalization process is superficial— Herr Zezi is still scoring successes with foreign music. The "German" opera that emerged under Reissiger in the 1830s was in reality the successor to *both* Morlacchi's and Weber's companies.

Operatic Form

If the absorption of the Italian opera company marked the institutional victory of the German opera, its aesthetic triumph, as we have seen, was less spectacular. After Weber's death and the failure of his *große romantische Oper Euryanthe*, the search for a German opera lost its momentum— composers such as Marschner and Lortzing were more interested in creating popular successes than in manifesting the aesthetic principles of a new national style. This "retreat" from the artistic goals of the early part of the century has led many scholars to speak of a hiatus in the stylistic development of German opera, the "gap between *Freischütz* and *Lohengrin*," as Aubrey Garlington puts it.[24] It might be more accurate to see Weber, Hoffmann, and Spohr as the anomalies. As Carl Dahlhaus writes: "the carefree mixture of styles that Robert Schumann bemoaned as musical 'juste milieu' in the case of Heinrich Marschner had always been a feature of German Romantic opera, which was not in fact as German as it was made out to be by a nation that firmly asserted its cultural identity because it lacked a political one."[25] Although the operatic style of Marschner and Lortzing was clearly quite different from *Das unterbrochene Opferfest*, the "juste milieu" in many ways merely continued the eclectic traditions of composers such as Peter von Winter. The differences between the musical style of German and Italian opera in the 1830s were still similar to the differences between *Das unterbrochene Opferfest* and *Il sacrifizio interotto:* they had more to do with certain aspects of harmony and text declamation than with large-scale approaches to musical form. Like Winter's, Marschner's operatic style was filled with forms and idioms adapted and "naturalized" from Italian and French opera. Moreover, German opera composers had their greatest successes during the 1830s and 1840s with essentially the same form that Winter used in *Das unterbrochene Opferfest:* dialogue operas drawing on a wide variety of operatic traditions.

To some extent Weber's final opera, *Oberon,* represents this "retreat" from the aesthetic goals of the search for a German opera.[26] As with *Euryanthe,* Weber composed the work in response to a commission, in this case from the English director Charles Kemble. The libretto to the opera was written by James Robinson Planché and was based on a work by C. M. Wieland.[27] The plot unfolds against backgrounds far more exotic than the Bohemian forest or the court of medieval France, including a remote island and the palace of the Caliph of Baghdad. Supernatural events play a much larger role in *Oberon* than they do even in *Der Freischütz.* Characters are magically transported from one scene to another, they see supernatural visions of one another, and invisible spirits raise a powerful storm—the plot, in other words, is essentially a fairy tale. In many ways the story of the opera (and some of the music as well) recalls Mozart's *Singspiele* of a generation earlier. Like *Die Entführung aus dem Serail* (and like Weber's own *Abu Hassan*), *Oberon* contains many examples of operatic orientalism (in Edward Said's sense of the term): the diabolical villain, cruel harem guards, and "fair Arabian maids." The plot of *Oberon* includes many motifs and at least one scene that seem to be lifted almost directly from *Die Zauberflöte.* Instead of a magic flute or glockenspiel, the tenor hero receives a magic horn to help him in his time of need. As in Mozart's opera, the tenor sees an image of the soprano before he actually meets her, an image that causes him to fall instantly in love (in *Oberon* the soprano also sees a vision of the tenor). Like Tamino, he is accompanied by a baritone helper-figure who embodies, at least to some extent, the simple desires of the common man. In the third-act finale of Weber's opera the magic horn causes the slave guards to dance rather than to burn the tenor and the soprano at the stake, just as Papageno's bells cause Monastatos and his minions to dance in the finale of act 1 in *Die Zauberflöte* ("Das klinget so herrlich"). Similarities between the plots of *Oberon* and *Die Zauberflöte*, however, are not necessarily proof of direct borrowing. Planché and Schickaneder were drawing at least to some extent on common sources: the "oriental tales" of Wieland and, more generally, the mythological tropes upon which these tales were based. The exotic backgrounds and fairy-tale plot of *Oberon* may connect the opera to the traditions of the late-eighteenth-century *Singspiel,* but they also have an important place in the tradition of the English masque. Weber was surely aware of the similarities between *Oberon* and Mozart's German operas, but he did after all compose the work to an English text for the specific requirements of the London stage.

Like many of the *opéras comiques* of the first decades of the century, however, *Oberon* enjoyed its greatest success in German translation. During the late 1820s and into the 1830s and 1840s it was performed frequently in many German houses, where it became probably the most popular of Weber's works after *Der Freischütz.* The unusual history of *Oberon* gives it a somewhat anomalous position with regard to the nationalist operatic criticism that I have described above: it is the last work of the greatest practitioner of "national opera" but is still, at least to some extent, a "foreign" work. *Oberon* nevertheless shares many traits with the works by Marschner, Lindpaintner, Wolfram, and Kreuzer that typified German operatic composition in the decade after Weber's death. The opera adopts the musical form of the *Singspiel,* with dialogues separating the musical numbers rather than recitatives. As in *Freischütz,* however, Weber includes brief passages of melodrama, usually at those points in the libretto when some supernatural event occurs. Like so many German operas from this period, *Oberon* contains a great variety of musical forms. In some places, such as Rezia's aria "Ocean, thou mighty monster," Weber uses complex, multi-tempo structures, akin in form, if not in *Charakter,* to Lysiart's "Wo berg ich mich" or Agathe's "Leise, leise." On the whole, however, the musical numbers in *Oberon* tend to be more highly sectionalized than those in *Euryanthe* or even those in *Frei-schütz*. Indeed, in some ways Weber's last opera is more similar to early works such as *Abu Hassan* or *Preciosa* than it is to his operas of the early 1820s.

To characterize the music and drama of *Oberon* and other German operas of the 1820s and 1830s as a "retreat" into the styles of a previous generation, however, betrays a developmentalism that cannot do justice to the complexity of early-nineteenth-century German opera. Any history must foreground certain topics and ignore others, but a narrative that construes the German opera of this period as the progress from the sectionalized *Singspiel* of the late eighteenth century to the music dramas of Wagner is particularly problematic. Even more so than in other times and places, the German opera of the early nineteenth century drew on a diverse assortment of musical and dramatic conventions and was informed by a diverse group of theoretical ideas. The discourse of *Charakter* and the rhetoric of organicism may have been particularly influential and vibrant during this period, but they by no means determined the course of operatic history.

That the voice of the search for a German opera seems to grow more muted in the decade after Weber's death is not so much evidence of a "retreat" from a particular set of critical and compositional goals, but rather indicates a fundamental change in the institutional and cultural conditions with which these goals were entwined. In 1798 the idea of a central theater for serious opera staffed almost completely by Germans seemed unthinkable; in 1817 it still seemed unlikely to succeed; but by 1832 it had become a reality. The audience for opera in Germany was also changing. While it is virtually impossible to assess accurately the class background of opera audiences in the early nineteenth century, it does seem that the opera had moved out of the courtly, aristocratic world and into the new bourgeois public sphere. Here again Dresden provides a case example of a broader development. Morlacchi's core patronage group was the king and court, Weber's was the quasi-aristocratic membership of the *Liederkreis,* but Reissiger seems to have drawn his support from the members of the upper bourgeoisie and professionals who were gathering in singing societies and amateur groups. Even if we cannot pinpoint the class origins of Reissiger's audiences, we can be sure that these audiences were growing. The Morettische Haus was proving increasingly inadequate to the demands of opera and theater in the 1830s. Despite the enlargements of the late eighteenth and early nineteenth centuries, the theater still held only 814 people.[28] Moreover, operas of the 1820s and 1830s began to demand ever-more elaborate stage designs, beyond the technical capabilities of the old house. Plans for a new theater were being made during the mid-1830s, and the architect Gottfried Semper's design was eventually selected. The new theater, completed in 1841, provided the most advanced lighting and mechanical capabilities of the time and more than doubled the audience space to 1750 seats.[29] The size of Semper's new opera house is quite impressive when we remember that Dresden, like almost all German cities, was still quite small in the early nineteenth century, its population growing from 68,886 in 1820 to 82,014 in 1840. Opera was clearly a large and important part of public life.

National Ideology

Although this institutional transformation fulfilled some of the hopes embodied in the search for a German opera, it also to some extent eliminated the *Gegenbild* against which nationalist critics directed their attacks. The *Streit der deutschen und italienischen Opern,* for instance, meant something different after the German company in Dresden had absorbed Morlacchi's troupe. As the institutional circumstances of German opera changed, so too did the rhetoric of the native and the foreign and the discourse surrounding the *Charakter* of opera and the *Charakter* of the nation.

No one played a greater role in this transformation than the young composer who came to Dresden in 1842 to produce and conduct his *grand opéra Rienzi.* Wagner, of course, rather than Marschner or Lortzing, has always been regarded as the inheritor of Weber's goals for a national operatic style. This idea emerged within Wagner's own lifetime—we can probably trace it back to his years as the second *Kapellmeister* in Dresden, 1843–49. Despite his disparaging comments regarding *Euryanthe,* Wagner quickly realized that (at least in Dresden) Weber was a national hero, and that he would have more success emphasizing his connections to the former *Kapellmeister* rather than his differences. In many ways Wagner's mature musical style reflects some of the aesthetic goals of the search for the German opera, and many writers, starting with Weber's own student Julius Benedict, have traced Wagner's dependence on the older composer.[30] A discussion of these aesthetic influences would take us well beyond the scope of this work. What interests us here is not Wagner as composer, but Wagner as *Kapellmeister*—particularly the way in which his work at the German opera in Dresden reflected the ideological goals of the search for a German opera. Like so many other early-nineteenth-century artists and intellectuals, Wagner believed that the opera theater had an integral role to play in the construction of the nation, and if essays such as his 1848 "Entwurf zur Organization eines deutschen National-Theaters für das Königreich Sachsen" served his own personal ends, they also reflected the nationalist ideology of the early-nineteenth-century search for a German opera.

Wagner's plans to create a national theater in Dresden went unrealized, but he did have a powerful effect on the city's musical life, not only through his own operas, but also through a process that contemporary Germans might call *Vergangenheitsbewaltigung*. Wagner revived (and in the case of Gluck's *Iphigénie en Aulide*, virtually reconstructed) many older operas, particularly those of Gluck and Mozart, but also those of Peter von Winter. He also "managed the past" in other ways: through his famous Palm Sunday concert of Beethoven's Ninth in the old baroque opera house (1846) and through his speech at the reinterment of Weber's remains (1844). And although the repertoire of the Dresden opera did not yet reflect the "museum culture" of present-day opera, the processes whereby an operatic canon would be created were already at work. The biographical sketches of composers and historical backgrounds to various operas that Weber printed in his musico-dramatic articles, for instance, can be seen as the ancestors of modern program notes. And the reception of *Euryanthe* during the 1840s prefigures a concentration on the history of opera that would only become more marked through the rest of the nineteenth century and into our own. The operas of the late eighteenth and early nineteenth centuries, particularly those of Gluck, Mozart, Weber, and Beethoven, were the first ones to carve out a permanent place in the repertoire, and with every decade of the nineteenth century the relative position of older works would become more important.[31]

This reorientation away from the future and toward the past began already in the last years of the period I have considered and represents the most important ideological legacy of the search for a German opera in the early decades of the nineteenth century. It may be explained in part by the important changes in the social position of the *Bildungsbürgertum* with which the search for the German opera was so closely associated. When the German bourgeoisie was still marginalized during the very early years of the nineteenth century, its aestheticians concentrated on the future of German opera, just as its political theorists articulated a vision of a unified, liberal Germany to be realized at some point in the years ahead. But as the bourgeoisie moved into a position of cultural hegemony in the period after the 1830 revolutions, it began to concentrate on conserving and re-interpreting operatic history. Wagner's changes to the repertoire were part of an enterprise that stretches back at least to the period of *Joseph* and the *heroisch-tragische Das unterbrochene Opferfest*—the effort to "naturalize" or "nationalize" the German past. Out of the diverse and sometimes contradictory history of opera in Germany, conductors, critics, and scholars began to construct a "history of German opera" that eventually became more important than plans for a completely new type of genre. The search for a German operatic future blended with, and was eventually overtaken by, the search for a German operatic past.

The Semper Oper

Although Wagner would manifest his highest goals for a national opera in Bayreuth rather than in Dresden, the development of German opera was perhaps more accurately symbolized by another building project, roughly contemporary with the erection of the *Festspielhaus:* the construction of the second Semper opera house in Dresden during the years 1871–78 (the first Semper opera house had been destroyed by fire in 1869). The Anglo-American bombing raids on 13 and 14 February 1945 destroyed this opera house, along with most of the city. Rebuilt over an eight-year period under the East German regime, the opera house reopened ceremonially on the fortieth anniversary of the bombing attacks. The elaborate ornamentation of the original opera house was painstakingly reconstructed, preserving the building's character as a temple of art and a homage to Dresden's artistic past. The interior roof of the auditorium, for instance, is dominated by eight panels that radiate outward from the central chandelier and features pictures of the four "national muses" (French, English, German, and Greek—no Italian muse) along with the names of famous playwrights and composers. The eight composers that are featured reflect the late-nineteenth-century concept of the history of music theater: Gluck, Mozart, Beethoven, Weber, Spontini, Mendelssohn, Meyerbeer, and Wagner. In the stairwells and the main foyer are statues of the famous singers and actors from Dresden's past, as well as memorials to both Weber and Wagner. The interior foyers and vestibules feature the columns and rounded arches that characterize Semper's style, harmonizing with the exterior facade as well as with the shape of the building as a whole. In the rounded arches along the interior walls are lunettes that feature painted scenes from various plays and operas. *Euryanthe* is here, alongside *Freischütz, Rienzi, Tannhäuser, Jakob und seine Söhne,* and plays such as Shakespeare's *Hamlet* and *Macbeth.* Even Reissiger's *Die Felsenmühle zu Etaliers* has its place. These artworks are sacralized by their placement high above the heads of the public, amid the paintings of gods and goddesses. Nobody repainted the lunettes to include operas by Strauss or Puccini, Schoenberg or Britten, let alone more contemporary composers. The Semper opera house remains a shrine to the opera and theater of the past.

The operas featured in the lunettes do not, of course, represent the contemporary repertoire of the Semper opera house. *Joseph* and *Euryanthe* are gone, and the Shakespeare plays that are the subjects of such beautiful paintings are performed in another part of the city. But considering that the original decorations were created more than a century ago, there is a surprisingly large overlap between the operas in the foyer and the operas on the stage. The ossification of the repertoire, the transformation of the opera house into a museum that has been such an important theme in the scholarship of the last twenty years, finds direct expression here.

In 1989, only a few days before the mass demonstrations that were to lead to the dismantling of the East German state, the Semper Oper mounted a new production of *Fidelio*. The staging was remarkable for the way in which it reflected current events, for the entire opera takes place not in a late-eighteenth- or early-nineteenth-century prison, but in a "security installation" of the communist regime itself. A barbed-wire fence stretches across the proscenium for much of the opera, and Marzelline sings her first aria while shuffling cardboard boxes of what might be Stasi files. The chorus in the final scene appears not in costumes, but in their own street clothes. This production of *Fidelio* has been enormously popular—the performance that I attended in January of 1996 (the fifty-seventh since its premiere) was sold out. Audiences are attracted to this production, I believe, not only because of the beautiful music and excellent singing, but because it creates a sense of history, helping people to acknowledge and reflect upon their lives outside of the theater. It is to this same task—the creative reimagination of the operatic past—that my work is dedicated.

Appendix 1
Synopsis of *Das unterbrochene Opferfest*

Led by the high priest Villakumu, the people of Peru are in the middle of a religious ceremony in praise of the Sun God ("Schön glänzt die gold'ne Sonne") when they hear news of a great triumph. Murney, an Englishman in the service of the Inca, has led their troops to victory against the Spanish. Villakumu praises Murney's valor in the second number, "Wenn Siegeslieder tönen," and his sentiments appear to be shared by everyone. But in a short aside we learn that Elvira, Murney's Spanish wife, had hoped for the victory of her kinsmen and plans to take revenge for their defeat. Murney, Rocca, Mafferu, and the Inca enter ceremoniously during the third number, "O danket der mächtigen Sonne," and in the dialogue that follows the Inca names Murney as the "oberster Feldherr" of Peru, thus arousing the jealousy of Mafferu. Elvira is enraged when Myrrha, the daughter of the Inca, flirts openly with her husband. But she and Mafferu hide their true feelings during the sextet and chorus "Zieht ihr Krieger" (no. 4) and join with the others in giving thanks that the Fatherland is now free from the threat of the "bearded men."

The scene changes from the ceremonial court of the Inca to an open meadow, where Pedrillo, Murney's servant, is giving thanks for his narrow escape from the battle. Pedrillo is the "negative image" of his master—cowardly instead of courageous, and concerned (like his counterpart Papageno) almost exclusively with women and food. In his aria *alla marcia* "Man rückt in grosser Eile" (no. 5) he gives his own, far less exalted account of the victory over the Spanish. Guliru, one of Myrrha's servants and Pedrillo's primary love interest, enters in the next scene and berates him for his lack of valor. She resists his attempts to kiss her and sings an aria, "Die Mädchen, merk' es" (no. 6), in which she advises all maidens "to kiss only brave men." Pedrillo resolves to find a less particular woman to court.

The scene changes once again to a garden where Elvira sits alone. Her brother, the last scion of the house of Calvado, died in the battle, and Elvira vows once again to take revenge on her husband for his death. Murney enters in the next scene, and Elvira accuses him of loving Myrrha. Murney protests his innocence, but Elvira departs, even more enraged. In the next scene Myrrha enters and declares her love for Murney. Murney is obviously attracted to her, but explains that he must resist her love, because he is already married. (Myrrha does not see this as an impediment because in Peru, according to the libretto, it is the custom for a man to take many wives.) In their following duet (no. 7), "Wenn mir dein Auge strahlet," Myrrha dreams of a life together while Murney advises her to forget her love.

After Murney and Myrrha leave, Mafferu enters alone and gives full vent to his rage and jealousy in the bravura aria (no. 8) "Allmächt'ge Sonne, höre der Rache grössten Eid!" Mafferu hides himself as Myrrha enters. In the next number (no. 9), "Ich war, wenn ich erwachte," the soprano recalls her innocence and joy before she was smitten with love for Murney. Mafferu sees her passion as a tool to further his plans of revenge. In the dialogue and duet that follow (no. 10), "Mich machen Furcht und Hoffnung schwanken," Mafferu slowly convinces Myrrha that Murney will never love her unless his life is endangered. By accusing the Englishman of blaspheming the Sun, Mafferu continues, we can threaten him with death by burning and thereby open the way to love. Confused and distraught, Myrrha hesitantly agrees to support Mafferu's false testimony against Murney. Elvira enters shortly after Myrrha departs, and Mafferu takes advantage of her emotional turmoil. He enflames Elvira's anger by telling her that Murney plans to renounce her and marry Myrrha. By supporting his false accusations against Murney, he continues, she can be revenged both for the death of her brother and for Murney's supposed infidelity. Elvira does not require a duet to convince her to accede to Mafferu's plans, and the general leaves the stage before her virtuostic rage aria (no. 11) "Süss sind der Rache Freuden."

After Elvira exits, Pedrillo enters once more, this time chasing Balisa instead of Guliru. Balisa successfully resists Pedrillo's clumsy efforts to kiss her in the duet (no. 12) "Ich will dein Gesicht zerkrallen." The comic characters then exit, and Murney enters with Rocca, the son of the Inca. The customs of Peru, we learn, require Rocca to marry his sister Myrrha, but Rocca vows to change these laws when he becomes the Inca. The two men vow eternal friendship and depart.

For the finale of the first act (no. 13), "Du, dessen starke Macht," the scene changes to the interior of the temple. Villakumu and the other priests are preparing for a thanksgiving ceremony. The other principals (excluding the comic characters) enter during the march, and as the Inca gives praise to the Sun, Mafferu, Elvira, and Myrrha give voice to their various emotions in asides. The frightful sound of thunder interrupts the ceremony, and Villakumu asks the Oracle to explain the terrible omen. The voice of the Oracle (in actuality a priest who is in league with Mafferu) explains that the ceremony cannot take place in the presence of a blasphemer (namely, Murney), and that Murney must die. Villakumu commands the priests to seize the Englishman, but the Inca, who is grateful to Murney, refuses to believe the Oracle without further testimony. Mafferu steps forward to accuse Murney and is of course supported by Elvira and Myrrha. Amid general consternation Murney is seized and led away.

In the opening scene of the second act the male characters (excluding Pedrillo) gather in a *Gerichtsaal* where the Inca will pass judgment on Murney (quintet and chorus no. 14, "Du, der Sonnenächster Erbe"). Rocca eloquently defends his friend, but the priests are unmoved. The Inca is reluctant to condemn the man responsible for the salvation of his country and expresses his sorrow in the trio that follows (no. 15), "Mein Leben hab' ich ihm zu danken," while Mafferu and Villakumu proclaim the necessity of following divine law. The scene then changes again to the garden, where Pedrillo sits alone, ruminating on the strange customs of the Peruvians. "First they elevate a man to Generalissimo," he says, "and then they burn him." Guliru enters and asks Pedrillo if he will die nobly at the side of his master. In the duet that follows (no. 16), "Ich taug' nicht zum Verbrennen," Pedrillo expresses his reluctance, while Guliru assures him that he would "vortrefflich brennen" (burn excellently). A short aria for Syra follows (no. 17), "Was Liebe wir nennen das kennt nicht mein Herz," before all the female comic characters gather with Myrrha onstage. Myrrha is naturally disturbed, and her servants try to cheer her up by singing a comic song. In the quartet (no. 18) "Kind, willst du ruhig schlafen," Myrrha's agitated coloratura is contrasted against the simple homophony of her servants.

The next scene takes place in Murney's prison, where the hero bravely contemplates his impending death in a long aria (no. 19), "Mir graut vor dem Tode nicht." In the two short dialogues that follow this aria, Murney tells first Rocca and then Myrrha not to attempt rescue; he is happy to give his life for Peru. The Inca and Elvira enter in the following scene, where the Inca asks forgiveness for the harsh sentence he is compelled to pass. Elvira, her heart beginning to soften, asks her husband for a tender word, but Mafferu enters to tell the assembled company that the sacrificial pyre stands ready. Myrrha, Elvira, the Inca, Murney, and Mafferu give voice to their various emotions in the quintet (no. 20) "Du musst zum Tode gehen."

In an open meadow above the prison, Rocca asks Villakumu to spare

Murney's life. Villakumu agrees, provided that Rocca can find another to take Murney's place. Rocca asks Pedrillo to accept this punishment for his master, and Pedrillo of course declines. Guliru ridicules him once again for his cowardice and leaves Pedrillo alone to defend the supreme value of his own life in the comic cavatina (no. 21) "Ich bin, ich weiss am besten." Pedrillo hears Mafferu and the priest approach and hides himself in the bushes. The priest, who imitated the voice of the Oracle, is having qualms about seeing an innocent man burn. Mafferu threatens him with death unless he keeps quiet about his role in the plot.

For the finale (no. 22), "Schon deckt ein grauer Schleier," the scene changes to a courtyard. All stands ready for the sacrifice, and Villakumu urges the Inca to do his duty. Confronted by the imminent death of her husband, Elvira begins to realize that Murney was in fact true to her. Myrrha attempts to rescue Murney and is only with difficulty restrained from throwing herself on the pyre. Accompanied by Peruvian warriors, Rocca enters and tries to free Murney by force. Both Elvira and Myrrha seize this opportunity to recant their support of Mafferu's false testimony. Villakumu nevertheless continues with the ceremony until the Inca commands him to stop. The Inca and Villakumu argue about Murney's guilt until the priest at last comes forward and admits his role in Mafferu's plot. Relieved that his friend Murney is in fact innocent, the Inca commands the priests to force Mafferu to take Murney's place on the sacrificial altar. But the kind-hearted Murney forswears revenge and urges the Inca to commute Mafferu's sentence from death to banishment. The opera ends amid general rejoicing.

Appendix 2

Comparative Table:
Versions of *Das unterbrochene Opferfest*

The scenes and numbers that play a large role in the chapter discussion appear in boldface.

Neither the early printed versions, nor the various German-language librettos, nor the German-language performance materials in Dresden contain dialogue—the dialogue sections of the "Printed German" column below are based on later printed versions of the work. A printed piano-vocal score of the work came out very early (a Simrock score in the New York Public Library bears the date 1796) and was reproduced, with only very minor variations, by many publishers, including C. M. Meyer in Braunschweig and Breitkopf und Härtel in Leipzig. These scores only very occasionally contain a few cues and are in the "horizontal format" common in the early nineteenth century. A later edition (from which I have also drawn my musical examples) in "vertical format" was printed sometime in the late nineteenth or early twentieth centuries by Universal in Leipzig and Vienna.[1] "Dresden German" describes the orchestral score preserved as Sächsische Landesbibliothek Mus. 3950–F-505, "Dresden Italian" describes Sächsische Landesbibliothek Mus. 3950–F-8, and "Revised Italian" describes the orchestral parts in Sächsische Landesbibliothek Mus. 3950–F-8a.

Printed German (1796)	Dresden German (c. 1819?)	Dresden Italian (1798–1810?)
Nos. 1–4 are essentially the same in all sources, except that in the Italian score the dialogues are replaced by recitatives.		
No. 5: Aria (*Tempo di Marcia*) (Pedrillo)	Omitted	Aria (*Tempo di Marcia*) (Pedrillo)
No. 6: Aria (Gulira)	Omitted	Aria (Gulira)

Printed German (1796)	Dresden German (c. 1819?)	Dresden Italian (1798–1810?)
No. 7: *Duettto* (Myrrha, Murney)		
(not present)	(not present)	**Recitative and Aria (Mira) "Quelle pupille tenere"**
No. 8: Aria (Mafferu) "Allmächt'ger Sonne, höre"	Bound separately at the end of the *Partitur*. Same as "Printed German"	**Aria (Mafferu)**
(not present)	(not present)	*Recit* **(Mafferu alone)**
No. 9: Aria (Myrrha) "Ich war, wenn ich er-wachte"	Same as "Printed German"	(incorporated into "Quelle pupille tenere," above)
No. 10: *Duetto* (Myrrha, Mafferu)		
No. 11: Aria (Elvira) "Süss sind der Rache Freuden"	Omitted	Omitted
No. 12: *Duetto* (Pedrillo, Basila)	Omitted	*Duetto* (Pedrillo, Balisa)
No. 13: Finale		
No. 14: *Quintetto e Coro*	Shortened version	*Introduzione* (Coro)
Dialogue (Villakumu, Rocca, Mafferu, Murney, Inca, and Coro	**Dialogue**	*Recit* **(Inca solo)**
No. 15: *Terzetto*		
No. 16: *Duetto* (Pedrillo, Guliru)	Omitted	*Duetto* (Pedrillo, Guliru)
No. 17: Aria (Syra)	Omitted	Aria (Guliru)
No. 18: *Quartetto* (Myr-rha, Syra, Guliru, Balisa)	Omitted	*Canzonetta* (Mira, Guliru, Balisa)
No. 19: Aria (Murney) "Mir graut vor dem Tode nicht"	Same as "Printed German"	**Aria (Murney)** substantially revised

Printed German *(1796)*	Dresden German *(c. 1819?)*	Dresden Italian *(1798–1810?)*
(not present)	(not present)	**Aria (Mira) "Io sento già che l'alma."**
No. 20: *Quintetto*		
No. 21: Aria (Pedrillo)	Omitted	Aria (Pedrillo)
No. 22: Finale		

Appendix 3
Synopsis of Méhul's *Joseph*

The libretto for *Joseph* (by Alexander Duval) is closely based on the Bible (Genesis 37, 39–47) but tells much of the story through narrative recollection. The opera begins when Joseph is already the chief minister of the Pharaoh, and concentrates on Joseph's reunion with his father and his reconciliation with his brothers. For most of the opera, Joseph conceals his identity and is known to his father and his brothers only as "Cleophas, the chief minister of Pharaoh."

In the opening scene of the opera, Joseph is alone in his magnificent palace, brooding upon his situation. "All the honors with which Pharaoh favors me are in vain," he sings in the brief recitative ("Vainement Pharaon!"), "because my heart is tormented by the happiness that I have lost." In the first section of the aria which follows ("Champs paternels! Hébron, douce vallée"), Joseph sings of his youth, when he was surrounded by his father's love, the only time when he was truly happy. As he tells of the fraternal jealousy that destroyed that love, his lyricism is also disturbed. The tempo changes from andante to allegro, and the accompaniment becomes more agitated. Joseph imagines that his brothers are with him and begins to speak to them directly: "Were you not disturbed by our father's tears? How could you see him weep, and remain unmoved? You deserve my hatred!" "And yet," Joseph says in the final phrases of the aria, "if you were to truly repent, your tears would reconcile us."

In the dialogue which follows this aria, Joseph's faithful servant Utobal enters and asks why his master is wandering the halls of the palace so late at night, when all the inhabitants of the city are asleep. All of Memphis is preparing to honor him, Utobal reminds Joseph, for his role in saving them from the horrible famine which has swept their land. But Joseph continues to think of the past and unburdens his heart to Utobal in the following romance ("A peine au sortir de l'enfance"). Here Joseph tells the story of his brother's betrayal in three verses. He was only fourteen years old, he sings, and innocent as the lambs that he guarded in his father's fields. But his ten older brothers were jealous of the special love between Joseph and his father Jacob, and one day attacked him while he was praying. They threw him into a dark pit, and left him for dead. Three days later, some foreign merchants happened to come by and drew him up out of the pit in order to sell him as a slave.

The famine that has afflicted Egypt has no doubt affected Hebron as well, and in the dialogue that follows this romance, Joseph commands Utobal to travel to the land of the Hebrews and invite them to come to Egypt. This invitation is of course unnecessary. After Joseph exits, an officer enters and tells Utobal of the arrival of some unknown Hebrews. Utobal hurries off to tell Joseph the news, and the "unknown Hebrews," the brothers themselves, take the stage. They have come to Egypt to seek relief from the terrible famine and sense that they may meet their lost brother Joseph here. Their attitudes toward their situation are varied. Naphtali and Reuben trust in the goodness of God, but Simeon is tormented by his guilt. God has singled him out for punishment, he believes, because he was the one who incited the rest of the brothers to attack Joseph. Despite his pivotal role in the betrayal, Simeon is the most tenderhearted of the brothers and is driven almost to insanity by his remorse.

In the next number ("Non! Non! l'Éternel que j'offense"), Simeon gives voice to his agony in some of the most complex and tormented music in the entire opera. Simeon understands that his sin against Joseph was more than fraternal betrayal—it was a sin against his father, against the community, even against God himself. The other brothers also feel remorse for their misdeeds, but it is Simeon who most acutely feels their significance, thus functioning in the drama as a kind of receptacle for collective guilt. The brothers' efforts to calm and comfort him are in vain. Midway through the ensemble, some of the brothers hear someone coming. They beg Simeon to compose himself, so that their horrible crime will remain a secret. After the ensemble ends, Joseph and Utobal enter with officer and bodyguards. Joseph recognizes his brothers, but to them he appears only as a mighty minister of the Pharaoh. They present him with gifts from the land of Hebron and throw themselves on his mercy, begging for relief from the famine. Joseph maintains his "mask," but when he sees Simeon, his blood boils. His overflowing anger prompts the fourth musical number, the finale of the first act.

The finale is organized into three sections, which are clearly marked by changes in tempo, key, and texture. In the first section, Joseph expresses his anger in asides to his servant Utobal, while the brothers try to control Simeon's emotional outbursts. Joseph suppresses his anger in the second section and resolves to forgive his brothers, if they show true remorse for their misdeeds. The brothers succeed in soothing Simeon and begin the final section by praising the generosity of this "mighty lord." They are joined by a chorus of the Egyptian people, who end the act by celebrating their deliverance from the famine.

In the dialogue that opens the second act, we learn the real extent of Simeon's alienation. Joseph, his true identity still concealed from his family, wanders among the tents of the Hebrews in the hours before dawn. In front of his father's tent he comes upon Simeon, who, like him, is longing for a glimpse of his father. Simeon dares not show his face in the daylight; his crimes are too horrible for that. He and Joseph fall into conversation, a conversation that is more like Simeon's confessional to an "unknown friend." Tormented by guilt, Simeon has exiled himself from the community and can only steal a glimpse of his beloved father at night, when the old man is sleeping. He must be surreptitious, for even his very name, spoken too loudly, would defile his father's presence. In the distance, harps announce the morning prayer, and Simeon must depart.

The "Chorus of the Hebrews" ("Dieu d'Israel") was greatly admired by contemporary critics, who felt that it captured the flavor of the antique. Its simple words are repeated three times, first by the men, then by the women (who sing the same homophonic music transposed up an octave), and finally in a slightly more elaborate setting for men and women together. The primal community asks God for protection and prosperity. In the dialogue that follows this chorus, Joseph, without yet revealing his true identity, meets his young brother Benjamin. Benjamin is the only one of the sons of Jacob who remained innocent of the crime against Joseph, and his psychological and moral distance from his brothers is accentuated in Méhul's opera. Benjamin's youth is emphasized: in this dialogue Joseph refers to Benjamin as being a "baby who could hardly babble my name" when they were last together. Benjamin tells his story to the "unknown Egyptian" in the following musical number.

Benjamin's romance ("Ah! lorsque la mort trop cruelle") is very similar in style to Joseph's "A peine au sortir de l'enfance." This musical correspondence is very appropriate, for Benjamin is now approximately the same age as Joseph was at the time of his betrayal (fourteen, as we have learned from Joseph's romance). Similar to Joseph's romance, Benjamin's song is in three verses and tells a story. However, Benjamin's story is not so much about himself as it is about the people around him, particularly his father, Jacob. Benjamin tells "Cleophas" that he has taken the place of Joseph in his father's heart but can only please Jacob by constantly praising Joseph's virtue. At the end of the dialogue that follows this romance, Joseph and Benjamin hear trumpets that announce the beginning of the triumphal procession, a procession that is being held to honor Joseph. In an aside Joseph tells us that he would gladly forsake all of these honors, if only he could stay forever next to his beloved father.

In the following trio for Benjamin, Joseph, and Jacob ("Des chants lointains"), Jacob appears for the first time, awakening from his tent with a prayer for the welfare of his family. Joseph and Benjamin pray in turn for their beloved father. Joseph is so overcome with emotion that he cannot take part in the following dialogue, in which Jacob tells Benjamin of his dream. This dream—not a part of the biblical story—prefigures the reunion of Jacob with his most beloved son.

The finale to the second act is divided into four sections. In the first of these, Jacob sings of his enduring grief over the loss of his son. Only with difficulty does Joseph keep his identity a secret. Overcome with emotion, he grabs his father's hand and bathes it in tears. Utobal interrupts this emotional scene, and in the second section of the finale tells "Cleophas" that the people are waiting for him to take his place at the head of the triumphal procession. In the third section of the finale Joseph invites Benjamin and Jacob to share his place of honor in the procession. The people enter to form this procession, singing a hymn of praise and celebration.

In the first scene of the third act, Joseph, his true identity still hidden, breaks bread with his father and brothers. The men are seated at a table in the middle of the room and are flanked on either side by a chorus of the young maidens of Memphis, holding their golden harps. Simeon is missing, and Jacob is disturbed. Joseph calms his father by telling him that his soldiers are already searching for Simeon. In the meantime, Joseph continues, we will have some entertainment. Instead of asking the women to dance or sing songs of love, Joseph commands them to sing a hymn of praise to the God of Israel. They fulfill their orders admirably, with an extended chorus that was one of the most popular musical numbers of the opera. Like the two romances for Joseph and Benjamin, this chorus has three verses, sung by solo women's voices. In between each of these solo verses is a choral refrain: "Aux accents de notre harmonie," in which the women command the sons of Israel to join them in praising the Eternal One. This refrain also appears at the beginning and the end of the number, in a more elaborate and extended form.

Utobal interrupts this scene with the news that Joseph's position as chief minister to Pharaoh is threatened. There are many, he warns, who resent the preferential treatment he has given the Hebrews. Joseph puts his brothers under the protection of a bodyguard and commands Benjamin to stay in the palace with Jacob. Joseph and the rest of the brothers leave Jacob and Benjamin alone on the stage. They discuss the "mighty Egyptian" who has saved them from the famine, and Jacob notes an uncanny resemblance between "Cleophas" and his lost son Joseph. To Benjamin, it appears as if Jacob is only reopening old wounds. He tries to comfort his father in the duet that follows ("O toi, le digne appui d'un père"). Here son and father adopt the musical structure of a love duet, in alternating imitative phrases or singing together in parallel thirds. Jacob rejoices in the faithfulness of his beloved son, and Benjamin promises never to leave his father. Caring for the father and leading him in his blind old age is a sweet duty that Benjamin undertakes with pleasure.

After this duet Simeon is led into his father's presence by one of Joseph's officers. His torment has become unbearable, and so he at last reveals the truth about Joseph's disappearance. Again Simeon speaks of the emotional torments he has endured, trying, perhaps, to soften the heart of his father: "I fled my father's roof and camped alone; I tried to lose myself, wandering in the woods; I slept in caves and under cliffs, yet Joseph's name still resounded in the wastelands. God did not hear my cries; the guilt was never taken from my head, and I remain accursed."

Jacob is unrelenting. The other brothers enter and quickly see that Simeon has betrayed their secret. Benjamin falls at his father's feet and begs him for mercy, but to no avail. Jacob commands his one faithful son to distance himself from the evildoers, so that the curse of the father may not fall upon him. The brothers are being sentenced to exile, never again to look upon the father's face. This separation of the innocent from the guilty launches the next ensemble ("Quitte pour toujours").

The brothers beg for mercy, supported by Benjamin. But nothing can deter Jacob from his harsh judgment, until Joseph arrives. "If God the father can forgive sinners," Joseph sings in a lyric andante section, "cannot Jacob forgive his own sons?" Slowly, Jacob relents. Joseph's heart has been softened too, for he has seen the genuine remorse of his brothers. In the following dialogue he at last reveals his true identity, and all celebrate their reconciliation in the final chorus. In Méhul's version of the opera, this final chorus is quite brief, but when the opera was given in Germany, it was customary to substitute a more extensive final chorus by Ferdinand Fränzl. Fränzl's revision celebrates the reunification of family and nation with both a people's chorus and an extended choral section for the brothers. Joseph ends his opera center stage, in a tableau which makes visible the concentric rings of love that surround him. The community has been reconstructed.

Appendix 4

Comparative Table:
Revisions to the Final Chorus of *Joseph*

The boxes in each column indicate the individual sections of Méhul's and Fränzl's versions, placed in sequential order from top to bottom. The numbers within the boxes indicate the number of measures in each section. Heavy-lined arrows between the boxes show Fränzl's direct borrowings of Méhul's original music (sometimes Fränzl expands the music through repetition). Much of the libretto for this new finale is adapted from one of the most common German translations of the work, by Carl August Herklots, and thin lines show sections in which Fränzl used these textual borrowings.

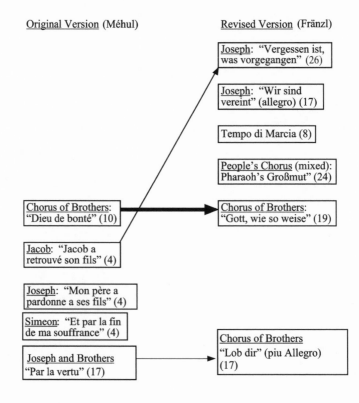

Appendix 5
Synopsis of *Euryanthe*

In contrast to *Joseph* and *Das unterbrochene Opferfest*, synopses of *Euryanthe* are readily available. Apart from the description in *The New Grove Dictionary of Opera* (the *Euryanthe* article by Clive Brown is in 2:88–90), a plot discussion may also by found in other standard reference works. The most extensive synopsis is in Michael Tusa's *"Euryanthe" and Carl Maria von Weber's Dramaturgy of German Opera*, 27–48.

The opera takes place medieval France (the title page specifies the year 1110), and all of the main characters are aristocrats. The introduction (no. 1) opens in the royal palace, with knights on one side of the hall and their ladies on the other. With ceremonial grace first the women and then the men honor the opposite gender ("Dem Frieden Heil" / "Dem Frauen Heil"), joining together to praise love and faithfulness. All join in an aristocratic dance (the *Ernster Reigen*), except for Adolar, the young duke of Nevers. In the recitative that follows the king asks Adolar why he doesn't join in the festivities. When he learns that Adolar is pining for his bride, the king invites the young duke to sing a *Minnelied* (song in praise of love) in her honor. The next number (no. 2, "Unter blüh'nden Mandelbäumen"), just like the second number in *Joseph*, is a three-verse romance for the tenor. Adolar's glorification of his beloved evokes a choral response (no. 3, "Heil Euryanth'") in which everyone commends his love. Everyone, that is, except for the villain Lysiart. In the recitative that follows this chorus Lysiart sarcastically thanks Adolar for his lovely song but claims that "a woman's breast contains no loyalty." At this point all of the women leave. Despite the king's warnings, Adolar ends up pledging all his lands on Euryanthe's faithfulness. In the next number (no. 4, scene and chorus) the die is cast. Lysiart bets all his lands that he can win Euryanthe's love. The king and the other knights try to convince him not to respond to Lysiart's goading, but Adolar has given his word. "Ich bau auf Gott und meine Euryanth'" he proclaims in the final con fuoco section of this number, singing music first heard as a principal theme in the overture.

The next scene of the opera takes place in the palace garden in Nevers, with the tomb of Adolar's sister Emma in the background. Euryanthe is alone, and in her cavatina (no. 5, "Glöcklein im Thale!") she meditates on the beauties of nature and yearns for Adolar. Eglantine's entrance for the next scene is announced by her leitmotiv. She begins the next recitative by comforting her supposed friend but ends by accusing Euryanthe of never truly trusting her. Eglantine sees Euryanthe wandering near Emma's tomb every midnight, but Euryanthe has never revealed the dark secret that draws her there. Eglantine pretends to be very upset by Euryanthe's reluctance to confide in her. "Your sympathy is not love," she sings in her aria (no. 6, "O mein Leid ist unermessen"), "you will never see me again." Earlier Adolar had sworn her to secrecy, but now Euryanthe is so deeply affected by Eglantine's feigned sorrow that she reveals the secret behind Emma's death, a secret, she tells Eglantine, that was first told to her by the ghost of Emma herself. Euryanthe quotes Emma's words above her "characteristic" chromatic accompaniment. Emma's lover, Udo, fell in battle and Emma then took poison from a ring. She must wander through the night as a restless ghost until this ring is washed by the tears of an innocent. Eglantine can barely conceal her glee, for she can use Euryanthe's betrayal of Adolar's secret, she hopes, to win the duke's love for herself. Euryanthe is immediately remorseful and gives voice to her dim sense of evil in the first section of the following duet with Eglantine (no. 7, "Unter ist mein Stern gegangen"). Eglantine reassures her of her undying devotion in the final section, and Euryanthe exits with her fears allayed, if not completely quelled. The next number is a scene and aria for Eglantine alone (no. 8, "Bethörthe! die an meine Liebe glaubt!"). Eglantine reveals not only her hatred for Euryanthe but the motive behind it: her unrequited love for Adolar. In the final allegro fiero she dedicates herself to Euryanthe's demise.

The next scene of the opera (no. 9, Finale) returns to the courtly, ceremonial world of the introduction. A chorus of peasants welcomes Lysiart and accompanying knights. As Euryanthe appears with Eglantine, the knights greet Adolar's bride as the "loveliest of the beautiful." Lysiart has been sent as a messenger of the king, and after he and Euryanthe exchange pleasantries, Lysiart invites her back to the king's palace. Euryanthe is so overjoyed that she completely ignores the villain's clumsy efforts to win her love by playing the courtier. Euryanthe leads the chorus in a joyful anticipation of her reunion with Adolar.

The second act begins with Lysiart's extensive scene and aria (no. 10, "Wo berg' ich mich?"). The aria follows the same pattern as Eglantine's aria (no. 8)—Lysiart reveals his hidden love for Euryanthe but ends the aria by vowing revenge and destruction. At the end of this number, Lysiart conceals himself as Eglantine arrives breathless from Emma's tomb. She has taken the ring from the grave and now hopes to use it in order to destroy her rival. Coming out from his hiding place, Lysiart offers himself as an instrument for Eglantine's evil plans. The two form an alliance, sealed by Lysiart's proposal of marriage. In the following duet (no. 11, "Komm denn, unser Leid zu rächen!") they call on the forces of darkness to aid them and swear revenge on the hero and heroine once more.

For the next number, the scene changes back to the royal palace. In a two-part aria (no. 12, "Wehen mir lüfte Ruh' / O Seligkeit, dich fass ich kaum") Adolar anticipates Euryanthe's arrival. The music of this aria, as well as the duet with Euryanthe that follows (no. 13, "Hin nimm die Seele mein"), figures prominently throughout the opera as an emblem for Adolar and Euryanthe's triumphant love. The happy mood of the lover's reunion is extended in the first part of the second-act Finale (no. 14). Knights and nobles fill the king's hall and sing of Euryanthe's beauty and purity. The king comes at the end of the procession and courteously greets Euryanthe. Fortissimo tutti descending octaves mark Lysiart's arrival. "The deciding hour has come" sing the knights, and Lysiart claims Adolar's lands as his own. Adolar refuses at first to believe that Euryanthe could be untrue and calls her to his breast with the music of "Ich bau auf Gott." But Lysiart shows Emma's ring as proof that he has truly won Euryanthe's heart. In what is doubtless the weakest part of the libretto, Euryanthe does not deny his accusation, but rather prays to God for deliverance. Lysiart reveals the secret of Emma's death, and Adolar asks Euryanthe if she has betrayed him. She admits that she has broken her oath, and Adolar believes all of Lysiart's claims. The chorus, who had just finished praising Euryanthe's purity, now condemns her ("Ha! die Verrätherin!"). The king reluctantly agrees that Lysiart has won the wager and accepts Lysiart's obeisance as the new duke of Nevers. Adolar calls on Euryanthe to follow him into exile. In the last section of the finale *con tutto fuoco ed energia* the entire company condemns Euryanthe once more. Euryanthe's mask of purity has been torn away, and "the cup of evil has now been filled."

The third act opens on a deserted, rocky gorge, lit only by the moon. Adolar enters in black armor, carrying his sword in his right hand, followed by Euryanthe. In the recitative of this first number (recitative and duet no.15, "Hier weilest du?, hier darf ich ruh'n?") she begs Adolar to stop and to show a bit of kindness to her. But Adolar has other plans. In a monotone voice, he tells his former bride that this is the place of her death. The duet proper begins as Adolar remembers the love he once held for Euryanthe. Euryanthe responds by begging him for mercy, but Adolar remains unmoved. Euryanthe sings that her "last breath is a blessing for you," and Adolar tells her to prepare for death. In the agitato that follows both Adolar and Euryanthe reflect on their cruel fate. Euryanthe's impending execution at the hands of her beloved is interrupted when she sees a gigantic snake threatening Adolar's life. She offers herself as a sacrifice, but Adolar pushes her aside to do battle with the monster. Euryanthe sings a short aria (scene no. 16, "Schirmende Engelschaar") in which she once again calls on divine aid. When Adolar returns victorious from his struggle with the snake, Euryanthe is ready for death. But since her warning saved his life, Adolar feels that he cannot now be her judge and decides to leave her in the barren wasteland, "in the protection of the Highest."

In the next scene (scene and cavatina no. 17, "So bin ich nun verlassen" / "Hier dicht am Quell") Euryanthe imagines her death. There will be no gravestone, but the trees, flowers, and brook will remember her. When Adolar comes again to this lonely place, she sings, they will tell him that she never betrayed him, that her love was true to the very end. Horns sound in the distance, announcing the arrival of the king and his hunting companions. The men sing of the joys of the hunt in the following chorus (*Jägerchor* no. 18, "Die Thale dampfen die Höhle glüh'n"), but are shocked to recognize Euryanthe alone in such a deserted place. In the brief duet with chorus that follows (no. 19, "Lasst mich hier in Ruh' erblassen") Euryanthe begs to be left alone, but the king refuses "in spite of her sin." Euryanthe now reveals Eglantine's duplicity (why she did not do this at the end of the second act is never explained). The king promises to bring the evildoers to justice and reconcile Euryanthe with her beloved. Euryanthe's anguish turns to joy in the following aria with chorus (no. 20, "Zu ihm!"). Overcome with her emotions, she faints, and the king and his knights carry her off to prepare for her reunion with Adolar.

The following scene with chorus (no. 21, "Der Mai bringt frische Rosen dar") opens joyfully as the peasants, led by Bertha and Rudolph, prepare for a wedding. Adolar interrupts the festivities with gloomy thoughts: all love and truth and goodness have vanished from the world. When the peasants recognize him as their former duke, they beg him to free the land from the tyranny that Lysiart has imposed. Lysiart, Bertha tells Adolar, is actually in league with Eglantine. Adolar begins to realize that he has been deceived, and in the next solo with chorus (no. 22, "Vernichte kühn das Werk der

Tücke") asks for the peasants' help. He and the peasants move to one side of the stage as the marriage procession of Lysiart and Eglantine arrives from the castle of Nevers (no. 23, "Hochzeitmarsch"). Despite all the pomp that accompanies the evil pair, the bride is deathly pale. Eglantine sees Emma's ghost before her, and the procession must stop. Adolar confronts the villains, and in the following duet with chorus (no. 24, "Trotze nicht! Vermessener!") he and Lysiart do battle. The king enters at the beginning of the Finale (no. 25) to stop the struggle. Adolar's remorse is boundless, for he believes that Euryanthe has perished in the wilderness. When Eglantine hears of her rival's demise she sings a brief victory song ("Triumph") in which she admits her theft of the poison ring. Lysiart is enraged that Eglantine has betrayed their secret and stabs her with a dagger. The king commands his death, but Adolar intervenes. "I am the murderer," he sings, and, according to the stage directions, he "sinks into despair." The king's men take Lysiart and the lifeless Eglantine offstage. A chorus of hunters arrives carrying Euryanthe, and the lovers are reunited to the music of their second-act duet ("Hin nimm' die Seele mein"). Adolar has a vision of his sister (whose music now resolves into C major), in which he finally sees her soul at peace, for the poison ring has now been washed by the tears of the innocent Euryanthe. General rejoicing ends the opera.

Notes

1. Introduction

1. Carl Maria von Weber to Hinrich Lichtenstein, 28 April 1822, *Briefe von Carl Maria von Weber an Hinrich Lichtenstein,* ed. Ernst Rudorff (Braunschweig, 1900), 111. Quoted by Michael Tusa in *"Euryanthe" and Carl Maria von Weber's Dramaturgy of German Opera* (Oxford: Clarendon Press, 1991), 57.

2. Carl Maria von Weber to Franz Danzi, 1 March 1824, quoted in Max Maria von Weber, *Carl Maria von Weber: The Life of an Artist,* trans. J. Palgrave Simpson (London: Chapman and Hall, 1869; New York: Greenwood, 1969), 2:347. The original German may be found in Hans Christoph Worbs, ed., *Carl Maria von Weber Briefe* (Frankfurt am Main: Fischer, 1982), 119–20.

3. Hunters' choruses were fairly common in German opera from the first decades of the nineteenth century. Weber's own *Preciosa* includes one, as do Conradin Kreutzer's operas *Libussa* and *Der Taucher.* Poissl's *Der Untersberg* and Marschner's *Hans Heiling* also contain hunting choruses. For a discussion of some of these works, see John Warrack, *German Opera: From the Beginnings to Wagner* (Cambridge: Cambridge University Press, 2001), 321, 322, 332–34. Alexander Ringer's dissertation, "The *Chasse:* Historical and Analytical Bibliography of a Musical Genre" (Ph.D. diss., Columbia University, 1955), includes a chapter on the *chasse* in the Romantic era (pp. 316–51) which is also of interest. Ringer's preliminary catalog of *chasse* compositions, unfortunately, is inadequate with regard to early-nineteenth-century operas.

4. The hunters' chorus from *Freischütz* includes a refrain in which a small group of four or eight singers sings in four parts while the rest of the chorus repeats a short rhythmic figure on a dominant pedal point.

5. John Warrack, *Carl Maria von Weber,* 2d ed. (Cambridge: Cambridge University Press, 1976), 281.

6. Tusa (*"Euryanthe,"* 31–33) also discusses the formal similarities between the opening scenes of *Freischütz* and *Euryanthe.*

7. Wagner's critique of *Euryanthe* (quoted in chapter 5) is perhaps the most famous example of this critical approach to the opera. See also the review of *Euryanthe* from the *Wiener Zeitschrift für Kunst, Literatur, Theater und Mode* 8 (1823), quoted by Tusa, *"Euryanthe,"* 63.

8. Aubrey Garlington, "Mega-Text, Mega-Music: A Crucial Dilemma for German Romantic Opera," in *Musical Humanism and Its Legacy: Essays in Honor of Claude V. Palisca,* ed. Nancy Kovaleff Baker and Barbara Russano Hunning, Festschrift Series no. 11 (Stuyvesant, N.Y.: Pendragon Press, 1992), 381–93. This

search, writes Garlington, "remains one of those rare moments in the western humanistic tradition when polemical theory and speculation are more significant and have a greater effect on the future than do any immediate creative realizations of the dream itself" (393).

9. Wolfgang Becker, *Die deutsche Oper in Dresden unter der Leitung von Carl Maria von Weber, 1817–1826*, vol. 22, *Theater und Drama* (Berlin and Dahlem: Colloquium Verlag, 1962), 10. The quotation comes from Johann Gottfried Herder, "Einzelne Blätter zum 'Journal der Reise 1769,'" in *Herders sämtliche Werke*, ed. Bernhard Suphan (Berlin, 1878), 4:484. Herder wrote these words attending opera performances in Paris, which he found vacuous and insipid.

10. Gottfried Günther, Albina A. Volgina, Siegfried Seifert, eds., *Herder-Bibliographie* (Berlin and Weimar: Aufbau-Verlag, 1978).

11. For a discussion of opera and criticism in the seventeenth and eighteenth centuries, see Gloria Flaherty, *Opera in the Development of German Critical Thought* (Princeton: Princeton University Press, 1978).

12. Herder, *Adrastea* (23:329–30 in *Herders sämtliche Werke*, ed. Suphan).

13. Ibid., 331.

14. Ibid., 332–33.

15. Ibid., 335.

16. A selection from Algarotti's work may be found in Wye Jamison Allanbrook, ed., *The Late Eighteenth Century: Source Readings in Music History*, ed. Oliver Strunk, vol. 5, *The Late Eighteenth Century*, Oliver Strunk, series ed., Leo Treitler, gen. ed. (New York: Norton, 1997), 175–88.

17. That Wagner's operatic theories form a subcategory of this "holistic narrative" does not need to be emphasized.

18. In the third issue of *Adrastea* Herder writes: "The course of the century will bring us to a man who, despising the cheap peddler's stock of wordless tones, saw the necessity of an intimate combination of purely human feeling, and of the plot itself, with his tones. From that dominant eminence, on which the ordinary musician arrogantly requires that poetry serve *his* art, he descended and, as far as the taste of the nation for which he wrote in tones permitted it, he caused his tones to serve the words of feeling and of the action itself. He has imitators; and perhaps there will soon be someone who will go beyond him,—will tear down the entire claptrap of operatic jingle and erect an *Odeum*, one connected lyrical structure, in which poetry, music, action, and decoration are one." Quoted by Robert T. Clark Jr. in *Herder: His Life and Thought* (Berkeley and Los Angeles: University of California Press, 1955), 429. The original German may be found in Herder, *Herders sämtliche Werke*, ed. Suphan, 23:336.

It is no accident that Gluck appeals so strongly to Herder. The composer will cast a shadow over the entire nineteenth century in Germany—not only because of his well-known adumbrations of the *Gesamtkunstwerk*, but also because of the mythology of iconoclasm that developed around him. That Gluck would be claimed as part of the German operatic heritage (rather than the Italian or French) goes without question. Early-nineteenth-century critic-reformers such as Weber, A. B. Marx, and Wagner himself would advocate a "return to Gluck" as well as a "push toward the future."

19. Herder, *Herders sämtliche Werke,* ed. Suphan, 343: "Beilage: Wirkt die Musik auf Denkart und Sitten?"

20. *Berliner allgemeine musikalische Zeitung* 4 (1827): 127 (hereafter abbreviated as *BamZ*). The quotation is taken from a "Correspondence from Dresden" and, although left unsigned, is almost certainly by Richard Otto Spazier.

21. Again, this critique is a recycling of older ideas. The attack on "superficial ornamentation" can be traced back at least to the preface to Gluck's *Alceste.*

22. Heine is being quoted by A. B. Marx, "Streit der deutschen und italienischen Oper in Dresden," *BamZ* 7 (1830): 37.

23. *Allgemeine musikalische Zeitung* 20 (1818): col. 229 (hereafter abbreviated as *AmZ*). The 24 January 1818 performance of *Elisabetta,* with which this review is concerned, marks the Dresden premiere of this piece. Surprisingly enough, it was conducted by Weber. Morlacchi was on one of his many extended trips to Italy.

24. *AmZ* 20 (1818): col. 230.

25. Ibid., col. 231-32.

26. Perhaps the wittiest attack on contemporary opera (Italian, French, *and* German) was written by Weber himself, in chapter 6 of "Ein Tonkunstler's Leben," where Italian, French, and German opera appear successively as stage characters. Italian Opera appears as "a tall, gaunt, transparent figure with a featureless face which changed little whether representing hero, swain, or barbarian, and was always marked by an extraordinary saccharine look. She wore a thin gown with a train, non-descript in colour and covered with little glittering stones, which attracted the spectator's attention. As she appeared there was a noise in the orchestra in order to silence the audience. In Italy this is called the overture. Then she began to sing." Translation by Martin Cooper, in Carl Maria von Weber, *Writings on Music,* edited and with an introduction by John Warrack (Cambridge: Cambridge University Press, 1981), 342–43.

27. Friedrich Kind, ed., *Die Muse* 1, no. 8 (August 1821): 37–76, "Ueber die Oper" (signed "A."), 46–47.

28. Theodor Mundt, "Ueber Oper, Drama, und Melodrama in ihrem Verhältniß zu einander und zum Theater," *Blätter für literarischer Unterhaltung* 152–55 (June 1831): 665 ff., 677.

29. Louis Spohr, "Aufruf an deutsche Komponisten," *Allgemeine musikalische Zeitung* 25, col. 457–64.

30. Ibid., col. 457-58.

31. Ibid., col. 463.

32. Heinrich Laube, *Zeitung für die elegante Welt* (Leipzig: Leopold Voss, 1833), 33:19. In his essay "An Attempt to Express in Tabular Form the Organization of a German Opera Company in Dresden, with Short Explanatory Notes" (Weber, *Writings*, 225–29), Weber expresses the idea that "the use of the organs of speech is directly harmful to those required for singing."

33. E. T. A. Hoffmann, *E. T. A. Hoffmann's Musical Writings: Kreisleriana, The Poet and the Composer, Music Criticism,* edited, annotated, and introduced by David Charlton, translated by Martyn Clarke (Cambridge: Cambridge University Press, 1989). Hoffmann wrote "Most so-called operas are merely inane plays with singing added, and the total lack of dramatic force, imputed now to the libretto, now to the music, is entirely attributable to the dead weight of successive scenes with no inner poetic relationship or poetic truth that might kindle the music into life" (174–75).

34. See "Poet and Composer," in Hoffmann, *Writings*, 196.

35. *AmZ* 31 (1829): col. 285–86. "Tanti palpiti" refers to the cavatina "Di tanti palpiti" from Rossini's *Tancredi.*

36. In the article "Berlin" from *The New Grove Dictionary of Opera*, 1:424–33, Thomas Baumann writes: "Admission, limited to members of the court, army officers and the higher strata of Berlin society, was free" (425). According to Baumann (s.v. "Dresden," *The New Grove Dictionary of Opera,* 1:1247) the court also distributed free tickets in early- and mid-nineteenth-century Dresden. In "Vienna," *The New Grove Dictionary of Opera,* 4:990, Bruce Alan Brown writes: "The audience for the imperial opera was restricted to members of the court, foreign ambassadors and high-ranking visitors, but from 1728 it was possible for common citizens to see operatic adaptations, billed as intermezzos, at the privately run Kärtnerthortheater (built in 1709 . . . and demolished in 1870)."

37. This distinction was abolished by a decree granting "freedom of the theaters" in January of 1791.

38. For a discussion of the five principal Viennese theaters and the relative status, as well as a map showing their geographical location, see Alice Marie Hanson, *Musical Life in Biedermeyer Vienna* (Cambridge: Cambridge University Press, 1985), 61–64.

39. The architecture and decor of the theaters themselves also embodied this genre hierarchy. In the book *München* from the series Musikstädte der Welt, ed. Silke Leopold (Laaber: Laaber Verlag, 1992), Christoph Henzel writes: "The seating area of the Cuvilliés Theater reflected the social hierarchy of the Munich court. The predominant center was the ducal loge. The parterre loges, with their simply ornamented breastworks and supports, were designated for the city nobles. The upper nobility, on the other hand, could be found in the richly decorated first row of the balcony, with its red draperies, displaying the same Atlases, Carytids, and rich cartouches as the decorations of the ducal

loge. The second balcony, already decorated with much simpler taste, housed the lesser nobility, and in the third balcony the court officials."

40. The repertoire differences between the Morettische Haus and the Linkesche Bad can readily be seen in the *Tagebuch des Königl. Sächs. Hoftheaters* by Carl August Kornmann. A convenient reproduction of the repertoire list for the year 1817, as well as an interesting discussion of the institutional structure of the Dresden Hoftheater, may be found in Hans John, "Carl Maria von Webers erstes Dresdner Amtsjahr," in *Die Dresdner Oper im 19. Jahrhundert,* Schriften-reihe der Hochschule für Musik "Carl Maria von Weber" Dresden, vol. 1, ed. Michael Heinemann, Hanns-Werner Heister, Matthias Herrmann, and Hans John (Laaber: Laaber Verlag, 1995), 73–84.

41. This urban geography forms an interesting contrast with late-twentieth-century and early-twenty-first-century America, in which the inner city is often a region of poverty and despair, and wealth is concentrated in the suburbs.

42. Günther Jäckel, "Aspekte der Dresdner Kulturgeschichte zwischen 1763 und 1832," in *Die italienische Oper in Dresden von Johann Adolf Hasse bis Francesco Morlacchi, 3 Wissenschaftliche Konferenz zum Thema "Dresdner Operntradi-tionen,"* ed. Günther Stephan and Hans John, Dresden, Musik in Dresden, Schriftenreihe der Hochschule für Musik "Carl Maria von Weber," Dresden (Dresden: n.p., 1982), 11:417. The "Altstadt" lies on the south bank of the Elbe and contains the Zwinger, the Kreuzkirche, the Frauenkirche, the Schloß, and the Opera House. The "Neustadt" lies on the north side of the river and was built in the eighteenth century.

43. Bruce Alan Brown, s.v. "Vienna," *The New Grove Dictionary of Opera,* 4:993–94:

> Characteristically taking quick and drastic action, in 1776 Emperor Joseph II suspended the agreement with the bankrupt Kohary's trustee [an impresario], dismissed the Italian singers and their orchestra and installed the German actors in the Burgtheater, henceforth called a "Nationaltheater." At the same time, he declared a "Schauspielfreiheit" (an end to the court's monopoly on spectacles), allowing other compa-nies to use the Kärntnerthortheater known as the Kaiserlich-königliches Hofoperntheater nächst dem Kärntnerthor from 1776—and (on free evenings) the Burgtheater, as well as other venues . . . Joseph ended the experiment in 1783 and engaged an [Italian] opera buffa company. . . . The opera buffa ensemble did not enjoy the undivided support of Vien-nese high society, or even of the emperor. In 1785 Joseph installed a "Deutsche Opéra Comique" in the Kärntnerthor theater as healthy compe-tition for the Italians.

This "Deutsche Opéra Comique" lasted only until 1787.

44. Some scholars have rejected the term *Bildungsbürgertum* because of its connotations of economic class. In *The Civilizing Process* Norbert Elias uses the term *Intelligenz* to describe the German-speaking educated classes, who in

this period began to define themselves against the French-speaking aristocracy. For an interesting discussion of these terms, see Wolfgang Wagner, *Carl Maria von Weber und die deutsche Nationaloper,* Weber-Studien, vol. 2, ed. Gerhard Allrogen and Joachim Veit (Mainz: Schott, 1994), 18–19.

45. The tremendous blossoming of music criticism in late-eighteenth- and early-nineteenth-century Germany has been frequently noted, most accessibly perhaps in Max Graf's *Composer and Critic: Two Hundred Years of Musical Criticism* (New York: Norton, 1946). Graf speaks about this new criticism as part of a "new bourgeois musical society." "These many musical magazines," he writes, "the greater number of which were published in Germany, demonstrate how greatly the interest had increased in the age of the classics. The new critical language shows that music had become the art of a much broader segment of the public." The newly expanded role of music in bourgeois life, Graf continues, was manifested in the many amateur performing societies that were established in late-eighteenth- and early-nineteenth-century Germany, societies such as the Liebhaberkonzert (1770), the Konzert für Kenner und Liebhaber (1787), the Berliner Singakademie (1790), and Zelter's Liedertafel (1809).

These societies became popular throughout Germany, and later in the century some of them formed a kind of national federation, which printed its own newspaper, the *Zeitschrift für Deutschlands Musik-Vereine und Dilettanten* (ed. Ferdinand Simon Gassner, Stuttgart, 1841–43). The contents are very eclectic, including correspondence, advertisements, music catalogs, and some music criticism. We can get some idea of the social composition of the *Singverein* from a "Verzeichniss [*sic*] der Mitwerkenden bei den Mozart Production [1842 uncovering of the Mozart-monument]." The participants are listed not only according to name but also by profession. Many of them were professional or at least semiprofessional musicians, but if they were not, they were almost always listed as teachers, students, professors, and occasionally jurists or a doctors, the same class of people that Hodgskin refers to as the "learned men" of Dresden, the same type of people who sat in the failed Frankfurt Parliament: in short, the *Bildungsbürgertum.*

46. For a comprehensive list of nineteenth-century periodical literature on music, see Imogen Fellinger, *Verzeichnis der Musikzeitschriften des 19. Jahrhunderts* (Regensburg: Gustav Bosse, 1968).

47. In his biography of Wagner, *Richard Wagner* (Munich: R. Piper and Co. Verlag, 1980), Martin Gregor-Dellin makes a similar point about the connection between the struggle for bourgeois emancipation and German nationalism in the early nineteenth century point by quoting the historian Heinrich August Winkler: "From the *Vormärz* into the *Reichsgründungszeit* nationalist discourse was in the first place an expression of bourgeois efforts for emancipation. . . . The demand for national unity placed itself in opposition to the landowning nobility, which was seen as the carrier of fractured particularism. The bourgeoisie, on the other hand, conceived itself as the incarnation of German unity" (202–203).

48. Krug is quoted in James J. Sheehan, *German History, 1770–1866* (New York: Oxford University Press, 1989), 448. Sheehan points out that the terms "liberal" and "liberalism" were borrowed from contemporary Spain.

49. See Frank Eyck, *The Frankfurt Parliament, 1848–1849* (London and Melbourne: Macmillan; New York: St. Martin's Press, 1968). The association between liberal politics and a particular social class may be seen in the composition of the 1848 German Parliament in Frankfurt that was supposed to create a newly united, liberal Germany. The parliamentary representatives were predominantly from the educated upper bourgeoisie, the *Bildungsbürgertum*. In his analysis of the professions of the Frankfurt Parliament members (95 ff.), Frank Eyck shows that most of the parliamentary members were administrators, professors, teachers, lawyers, and judicial officials.

50. James J. Sheehan, *German Liberalism in the Nineteenth Century* (Chicago: University of Chicago Press, 1978), 26.

51. Throughout Germany the *Bildungsbürgertum* grouped itself into *Vereine* that were often centered around some cultural activity. One of these groups was the famous *Liederkreis* in Dresden, to which Weber (as well as Friedrich Kind and Wilhelmine von Chezy) belonged. The most important book on the *Liederkreis* is still H. A. Krüger's *Pseudoromantik: Friedrich Kind und der Dresdener Liederkreis* (Leipzig: H. Haeffel Verlag, 1904). For more information on *Vereine* in general, see Thomas Nipperdey, "Verein als soziale Struktur in Deutschland im späten 18. und frühen 19. Jahrhundert," in *Geschichtswissenschaft und Vereinwesen im 19. Jahrhundert,* ed. H. Boockmann et al. (Göttingen: Vandenhoeck and Ruprecht, 1972), 1–44.

   The political and social advancement of the liberal bourgeoisie and their efforts to redefine German identity were closely connected to what historians and sociologists have called the emergence of the "public sphere" in German life. Although national identity was certainly a topic in eighteenth-century discourse, the power of this discourse to effect changes through broad strata of society was severely limited by physical circumstances. Communication between different parts of Germany was extremely slow during the eighteenth century—most people lived their entire lives within a few miles of their home. The lack of a capital city such as London or Paris also hampered the development of a national identity. Book production and distribution remained on a very small scale. The classic work on the development of the public sphere is Jürgen Habermas's *Strukturwandel der Öffentlichkeit: Untersuchungen zu einer Kategorie der bürgerlichen Gesellschaft* (Neuwied am Rhein, Germany, and Berlin: Luchterhand, 1968). For estimates of the size of the German reading public during this period, see Sheehan, *German History,* 157 ff.

52. Klaus Theweleit, *Male Fantasies,* trans. Stephen Conway (Minneapolis: University of Minnesota Press, 1987), 1:350–51. Becker (*Die deutsche Oper,* 8) makes a similar point about the antiaristocratic nature of German bourgeois culture, focusing in particular on Hiller's *Löttchen am Hofe,* in which a virtu-

ous bourgeois girl is seduced by an evil aristocrat. The same plot trope, of course, occurs in the Mozart-DaPonte *Nozze di Figaro* and *Don Giovanni*.

53.   *Tagebuch der deutschen Bühnen,* ed. Karl Theodor Winkler (1816–35).

54.   Quoted in Becker, *Die deutsche Oper,* 54, from Weber's letter to Georg Friedrich Treitschke, 29 January 1820. "Rossini-fever" came to Vienna with the 1822 season of Barbaja. The 1826 and 1827 seasons were commonly regarded as the high-water mark of Rossini's popularity in Berlin.

55.   Richard Otto Spazier, *Scherz und Ernst über Ernst Scherzlieb's Dresden wie es durch eine Goldbrille ist; nebst Bemerkungen über Nationalität in der dramatischen Musik* (Leipzig, 1830), 53.

56.   Spazier, *Scherz und Ernst,* 56.

57.   Spohr seems to have regarded *Freischütz* as somewhat vulgar, an example of Weber's "peculiar gift and capacity for writing for the masses." For a fuller discussion of Spohr's attitude toward Weber, as well as his aesthetic principles generally, see Clive Brown, *Louis Spohr: A Critical Biography* (Cambridge: Cambridge University Press, 1984). Brown's biography is the most comprehensive and informative English-language account of Spohr's life and works.

58.   Clive Brown's description of *Jessonda* may be found on pp. 157–63 of *Louis Spohr.*

59.   Warrack, *Weber,* 183.

60.   Saxony was the most important theater of battle in the 1813 War of Liberation, and Dresden itself was the site of a major battle in August of that year. E. T. A. Hoffmann left a vivid description of the battle scene in his book *Die Vision auf dem Schlachtfelde bei Dresden* (Bamberg, 1814; Paderborn: Belser Verlag, 1987).

61.   E. T. A. Hoffmann to Friedrich Speyer, 13 July 1813, *Selected Letters of E. T. A. Hoffmann,* trans. Johanna C. Sahlin, with an introduction by Leonard J. Kent and Johanna C. Sahlin (Chicago and London: University of Chicago Press, 1977), 193.

62.   Ibid., 194.

63.   The decree authorizing this reorganization is partially reprinted in Robert Prölss, *Geschichte des Hoftheaters zu Dresden: Von seinen Anfängen bis zum Jahre 1862* (Dresden, 1878), 366 n. 1. The decree also designated Tuesdays and Fridays as performance days for the Italian opera and set aside Sundays, Mondays, Wednesdays, and Thursdays for German-language performances.

64.   Quoted by Becker in *Die deutsche Oper,* 24–25. The original document, the contract of 29 January 1817, may be found in the Sächsische Hauptstaatsarchiv, Loc 15146 Bd. 20, Bl. 129. Warrack also discusses Vitzthum's plans in *Weber,* 177, and points out that the Dresden German opera was established at the same time that the reinstatement of Italian opera was decreed in Munich.

65.   Quoted by Becker in *Die deutsche Oper,* 24 (Sächsische Hauptstaatsarchiv, Loc 15147, Bl. 253).

66. The announcement of the new company can be found in the *AmZ* 19 (1817): "So eben erfahren wir die sehr angenehme Nachricht, das der ausgezeichnete Componist, Virtuos und Director, Hr. Carl Maria von Weber, von Sr. Majestät unserm Könige, zu einem Seiner Kapellmeister, mit ehrenvollen Bedingungen ernannt sey, vornähmlich auch, um bey einer zu errichtenden, neuen deutschen Oper, neben der fortbestehenden italienischen, mitzuwirken" (col. 31).

67. Carl August Kornmann, *Tagebuch des Königl. Sächs. Hoftheaters.*

68. Marschner's activities in Dresden are discussed in the standard biography of the composer by A. Dean Palmer, *Heinrich August Marschner, 1795–1861: His Life and Stage Works,* Studies in Musicology 24, ed. George Buelow (Ann Arbor: UMI Research Press, 1978), 25 ff. Palmer's work incorporates some material from an older biography of Marschner, Georg Fischer's *Marschner Erinnerungen* (Hanover and Leipzig: Hahnsche Buchhandlung, 1918).

69. "There were six performances days in the Dresden theatre week," writes Warrack (*Weber,* 178), "By tradition Friday was free, with Wednesday and Saturday reserved for the Italians and the remainder shared between German plays and opera."

    Weber was by no means an inveterate opponent of Morlacchi's music, and a very favorable review of Morlacchi's oratorio *Isacco* may provide an example of the amicable tone that he occasionally adopted: "Generally speaking, Italians and Germans find each other's music alien and unsatisfying. A closer familiarity and wider musical education will bring greater understanding and the ability to distinguish what is outstanding in either field." Translated by Cooper in Weber, *Writings,* 216.

70. Warrack, *Weber,* 177.

71. The term "exclusiv-höfisch" comes from Eberhard Kremtz, "Das 'Deutsche Departement' des Dresdner Hoftheaters," in *Die Dresdner Oper im 19. Jahrhundert,* 107–12. For a fuller discussion of Kremtz's ideas, see chapter 5, below.

72. See the review of the 25 September 1817 performance of Catel's *Die vornehmen Wirthe, AmZ* 19 (1817): col. 754 ff.

73. *AmZ* 18 (1816): col. 388.

2. The Native and the Foreign

1. *AmZ* 2 (1799–1800): col. 838; *AmZ* 4 (1801–1802): cols. 439–41.

2. According to Alfred Loewenberg, *Annals of Opera, 1597–1940,* 3d ed. (Totowa, N.J.: Rowman and Littlefield, 1978), cols. 600–601, French-language performances of *Joseph* took place in Hamburg and Bern in 1809.

3. The extent of French influence in the parts of Germany directly occupied by Napoleonic armies can also be seen in the many French-German editions of German operas and songs printed in west German firms, such as Simrock. There were also French touring companies that gave French-language performances of vaudevilles in Dresden during the 1820s and 1830s. Despite these

isolated examples, however, French performances in Germany remained exceptional for all of the late eighteenth and early nineteenth centuries. For a more extensive discussion of French opera in Germany, see chapter 9 of John Warrack's *German Opera: From the Beginnings to Wagner* (Cambridge: Cambridge University Press, 2001), 191–213.

4. The German-language examples in the article on the recitative in Johann George Sulzer's *Allgemeine Theorie der schönen Künste* (Leipzig, 1787), 4:4–19, for example, are almost all from sacred works. The operatic examples are in Italian.

5. *AmZ* 25 (1823): col. 283. It must be said that many German works, particularly those by well-known composers, were identified primarily by composer and only secondarily by librettist.

6. German critics often approached this topic by expanding or commenting upon the work of foreign musicians. Algarotti, Arteaga, and Castil-Blaze were well-known in Germany, and the work of Niccola Tacchinardi seems to have had at least some circulation. Algarotti's "Saggio sopra l'opera" was translated into German by Raspe in 1768 and forms the starting point of Wieland's *Versuch über das deutsche Singspiel und einige dahin einschlagende Gegenstände* (1775). Arteaga's "Le rivoluzione del teatro musicale italiano" was translated by Forkel in 1789.

7. A more extensive discussion of the dramatic material of turn-of-the-century *Singpiel* may be found in *The Age of Beethoven, 1790–1830,* ed. Gerald Abraham, Oxford History of Music, vol. 8 (London: Oxford University Press, 1982), chap. 10, "German Opera," by Winton Dean, 452–522, particularly 455–58.

8. *AmZ* 2 (1799–1800): col. 530.

9. *BamZ* 5 (1828): 195–97; 203–206.

10. Ibid., 195: "Die Musik kann im Drama überhaupt eine zweifache Bedeutung haben. Sie kann entweder als Gesang den handelnden Personen statt der Sprache dienen, gleich der Rede in der Wirklichkeit und den Versen im versifizierten Drama. Oder sie kann sich als wirkliche Lebenserscheinung, wie im Leben selbst geltend machen, im Form von Tanz, Marsch, Lied und so fort."

11. Ibid., 197: "Oper / Schauspiel mit Gelegenheitsmusik / Aelteres Melodrama / Schauspiel mit Chören / Schauspiel mit Chören und Gelegenheitsmusik / Neueres Melodrama." Marx does not think very highly of these works (and unfortunately he gives no examples). The public, he writes, has been spoiled by new melodramas that rely on special lighting and machinery, on thunder, battles, and sea storms for their effects, "und die innere Zerstreutheit des Werkes durch möglichste Zersteuung des Publikums zu verbergen oder auszugleichen."

12. Marx also includes an interesting description of opera in Italy, France, and Germany. Discussion of opera in Germany is complicated by the fact that German opera composers have borrowed so much from Italy and France. Some

names are only translations of French or Italian terms, and some have independent meaning.

13. In *Die deutsche Oper in Dresden unter der Letiung von Carl Maria von Weber, 1817–1826*, Wolfgang Becker, although he does not quote Marx directly, also addresses the concept of genre in the early nineteenth century. He places the various operatic genre terms along a continuum, stretching from "high" to "low" art, which may serve as a useful guide to the confusing nomenclature of the period: "Große Oper—heroische Oper—Oper—romantische Oper—Komische Oper—Singspiel—Vaudeville—Liederposse—Ballett—Melodrama—Schauspiel mit Gesang—Schauspiel mit Musik" (vol. 22, *Theater und Drama* [Berlin and Dahlem: Colloquium Verlag, 1962], 91).

14. Anno Mungen discusses genre diversity of late-eighteenth- and early-nineteenth-century German composers in "Morlacchi, Weber und die Dresdner Oper," in *Die Dresdner Oper im 19. Jahrhundert*: "Winter, on the other hand, is the perfect example of a composer who grew great in Germany, who served various genres around the turn of the century and had composed Italian *opere serie*, French *Tragédies lyriques*, and German *Singspiele*" (Michael Heinemann and Hans John, eds., Musik in Dresden, Schriftenreihe der Hochschule für Musik "Carl Maria von Weber," Dresden, vol. 1, ed. Michael Heinemann, Hanns-Werner Heister, Matthias Herrmann, and Hans John [Laaber: Laaber Verlag, 1995], 94).

15. The opera did not prove to be a success and was withdrawn after only three performances. But when Reissiger was applying for the positions of *Musikdirektor* and *Kapellmeister* after Weber's death (see chapter 5), the head of the *Hoftheater* frequently mentioned this opera as proof of Reissiger's compositional skill.

16. Dresden audiences of the 1820s and early 1830s could see *Don Juan* in German as a dialogue opera, or they could hear the original version performed with recitatives at the Italian opera. German-language performances of the work appear to have been more popular. See David Charlton's commentary in *E. T. A. Hoffmann's Musical Writings: Kreisleriana, The Poet and the Composer, Music Criticism*, edited, annotated, and introduced by David Charlton, trans. Martyn Clarke (Cambridge: Cambridge University Press, 1989), 397. According to Charlton, German words were not fitted to the recitatives until 1845.

17. This type of modification was of course not limited to the late eighteenth or early nineteenth century—the best-known example of "genre transformation" in the later nineteenth century is probably *Carmen*.

18. The appelation "*heroisch-komische*" was used to describe many German operas during this period (including *Das unterbrochene Opferfest*) that incorporated both tragic and comic elements. For a fuller explanation of the term, see Helen Geyer-Kiefl, *Die heroisch-komische Oper, ca. 1770–1820*, 2 vols., Würzburger Musikhistorische Beiträge, vol. 9 (Tutzing: Schneider, 1987).

19. Peter von Winter (1754–1828) was *Kapellmeister* in Munich from 1798 until his death and was one of the most successful German opera composers in the

period between Mozart and Weber. He wrote operas in Italian, French, and German, including a sequel to *Die Zauberflöte* (also with a libretto by Schikaneder) entitled *Das Labyrinth, oder Der Kampf mit den Elementen* (1798). The information on the performance history of *Das unterbrochene Opferfest* is drawn from Loewenberg, *Annals,* col. 526, where the author describes the opera as "Winter's most famous work and about the most successful German opera between *Zauberflöte* (1791) and *Freischütz* (1821)." Geyer-Kiefl, *Die heroisch-komische Oper,* 146, gives 1795 as the date of the first performance.

20.   According to Geyer-Kiefl, ibid., 146 n. 102, Winter's opera was also given as *Il sacrifizio interotto* in Prague. The Italian version of the opera even traveled to Italy itself—a libretto from an 1818 performance in Florence is preserved in the Syracuse University Bird Memorial Library (ML 48.I79 1976). Although this libretto is clearly based on the Italian version of the opera described below, it differs from the Dresden version in many important respects.

21.   Like many other operas that Weber was to perform in his Dresden years, *Das unterbrochene Opferfest* was an important part of Weber's repertoire in Prague when he was *Kapellmeister* there, 1813–1816. Weber's Prague repertoire is extensively chronicled in his *Notizen-buch,* the essentials of which are reproduced and analyzed by Jaroslav Buzga, "Carl Maria von Webers Prager 'Notizen-Buch' (1813–1816) Kommentar und Erstveröffentlichung des Originals," *Oper Heute* 8 (1985): 7–44. According to Buzga, *Das unterbrochene Opferfest* (German version) was given in Prague for the first time on 14 September 1814.

22.   M. [Jean François] Marmontel, *The Incas, or The Destruction of the Empire of Peru,* 2 vols. (London: J. Nourse, P. Elmsly, E. Lyde, and G. Kearsly, 1777).

23.   For a fuller account of the influence of *Les Incas* on German opera and drama, see Lawrence Marsden Price, "The Vogue of Marmontel on the German Stage," in *University of California Publications in Modern Philology,* ed. Rudolph Altrocchi et al., vol. 27 (Berkeley and Los Angeles: University of California Press, 1947), 87–95.

24.   This same basic plot found its way onto the English stage via Kotzebue's play, most notably in Sheridan's *Pizarro,* but also in Anne Plumptre's *The Spaniards in Peru,* Thomas Dutton's *Pizarro in Peru,* and Matthew Lewis's *Rolla.* For a description of Sheridan's play (which contains a great deal of music), see Paul Ranger, *'Terror and Pity reign in every Breast': Gothic Drama in the London Patent Theatres, 1750–1820* (London: Society for Theatre Research, 1991): 126 ff.

25.   Huber also wrote the text for Beethoven's *Christus am Oelberge* (1803).

26.   Another brief synopsis of the opera may be found in Geyer-Kiefl, *Die heroisch-komische Oper,* 146–47.

27.   These terms are taken from a translation and summary of Niccola Tacchinardi's "Dell'opera in musica sul teatro italiano, e de' suoi diffetti." (2d ed., Florence, 1833) that appears in the *AmZ* 39 (1837): cols. 787–92; 804–806. Alongside the familiar genre divisions of *opera seria, opera semiseria,* and

opera buffa is a classification of "singing schools" that Tacchinardi divides in the following way: "Three singing schools belong to opera: the *kraftvolle* (or *di forza*), the *zärtliche* (*affetuoso*) or legato, and the brilliant or *läufige* (*di agilità*) styles; there is also a speaking or syllabic (*parlante o sillabico*) type of song, that however has no school of its own" (col. 778). The different styles of singing and the schools through which they are developed, Tacchinardi continues, correspond to specific types of characters or even to specific voice types: e.g., the *kraftvolle* style belongs most commonly to the tenor or soprano.

28. Dean, "German Opera," in *The Age of Beethoven*, 459.

29. In *"Euryanthe,"* Tusa writes: "It is the very heterogeneity of genre and style that in fact identifies . . . German opera, since to a greater or lesser extent *all* German operas of the later eighteenth and early nineteenth century were characterized by their appropriation of genres, styles and techniques of French and Italian opera" (55). Dean (*The Age of Beethoven*, 452 ff.) also discusses this heterogeneity of musical styles.

30. Translation by Martin Cook from Carl Maria von Weber, *Writings on Music*, ed. John Warrack (Cambridge: Cambridge University Press, 1981), 226.

31. The Sächsische Landesbibliothek houses *Das unterbrochene Opferfest* performance materials that come from the very early years of the nineteenth century. The Italian score of the opera *Il sacrifizio interroto* comes from the period before 1810 and may have been used in the 1798 Dresden premiere of the work.

    A score in the Leipzig Stadtbibliothek contains an Italian version of the introduzione (no. 1) with Italian words added above the original German. An annotation in the score indicates that the Italian version was performed at the trade fair in November 1799. The Italian words are the same as those of in the Dresden score.

32. "When the songs of victory sound / and the victor is crowned with palms / then Murney is named / and counted among our heroes."

33. "In the triumphal hymns / of the rejoicing people / one will hear the name of your husband / being celebrated."

34. The German and Italian versions do use slightly different rhyme schemes: *aabc* versus *abbc*.

35. The Italian translator of the work is unknown.

36. Writers on music from the eighteenth and nineteenth centuries often spoke about the differences between German and Italian vocal technique. In a section entitled "Vom Gesang" from his *Ideen zu einer Ästhetik der Tonkunst*, ed. Ludwig Schubart (Vienna, 1806), for instance, C. F. D. Schubart (335 ff.) speaks about "Der Kehlenton" as the "pure tone from the full throat," and claims it as "the [special] property of the Germans."

37. Some sources, including the article on *Orazi e i Curiazi* by Gordana Lazarevich in *The New Grove Dictionary of Opera* (3:717–18), give the title of this opera as *Gli orazi ed i Curiazi*. A printed orchestral score of the opera (Paris:

Imbault, 1802) has been reprinted as *Monumenti musicali Italiani*, vol. 9, no. 2 (Milan: Edizioni Suvini Zerboni, 1985). According to the *Annals of Opera*, *Gli Orazi e i Curiazi* was first performed in Dresden in May of 1805. Its Vienna premiere, however, took place in 1797, only a year after the premiere of *Das unterbrochene Opferfest* in that city and a year before the first Dresden performance of *Il sacrificio interotto*. It could be that Winter (who was active in Vienna at the time) or some other composer directly associated with the Dresden court first heard Cimarosa's opera in the Austrian capital, and later came upon the idea of incorporating some of its music into *Il sacrificio interotto*. Just as with Murney's aria, the changes to Myrrha's part could have been largely motivated by the vocal resources of a particular performer. "Quelle pupille tenere" seems to have enjoyed particular popularity, and it may have come to Dresden in the baggage of the soprano cast as Myrrha in the Dresden premiere of *Il sacrificio interotto*. The Italian composer-arranger of *Il sacrificio interotto* may have also thought of using an aria from *Gli Orazi e i Curiazi*, because both operas employ priests and mysterious oracles as plot devices. Further similarities between the two stories, however, are rather remote.

38. Staatsbibliothek zu Berlin (Haus 2), Signaturen Tw 596/1–12. The librettos are all entitled *Arien und Gesänge aus der Oper "Das unterbrochene Opferfest"* and unfortunately contain none of the dialogue.

39. This additional aria appears in many of the librettos from this period but is not present in the early Dresden performing version. It seems likely that his inserted aria is the "mad scene" to which Weber refers in his review of the 1811 Munich performance of *Das unterbrochene Opferfest*, reprinted in Weber, *Writings*, 94–95.

40. The performance that Weber is reviewing took place in Munich on 31 October 1811 and first appeared in the 6 November issue of the *Gesellschaftsblatt für gebildete Stände*. It is reprinted in Carl Maria von Weber, *Sämtliche Schriften* (Berlin and Leipzig: Schuster and Loeffler, 1908), 119. Annotated librettos from Königsberg also show that a similar version of the opera, purged of comic characters, was also in use there during the 1830s. In addition to describing the form of the opera, this quotation also hints at Weber's somewhat ambivalent attitude toward Winter. In a review of Weigl's *Das Waisenhaus* from 1817, Weber refers to both Weigl and Winter as composers whose reputations depend on a single work. Although he doesn't specifically identify *Das unterbrochene Opferfest* as this work, in Winter's case, it could be no other opera. For further comment, see Warrack, *German Opera*, 229.

41. Quoted by Geyer-Kiefl, *Die heroisch-komische Oper*, 148 n. 103, from Hoffmann's *Gesammelten Schriften über Musik*, 12:290.

42. The date may be found in a *Solostimme* part book for Mafferu, Sächsische Landesbibliothek, Mus. 3850–F-15, which corresponds to other German-language performing materials collected under the Signatur Mus. 3850–F-505. The appellation "*heroisch-tragische*" appears in many librettos of the opera from the mid-nineteenth century.

43. Pedrillo's arias "Ich bin ich weiss am besten" and "Mann rükt in größter Eile" (*sic*), for instance, appear in the *Auswahl der vorzüglichsten Compositionen für das Piano-Forte oder Clavier von den berühmtesten Componisten/Von einem Musik-Freunde gesammelt* (Hamburg, n.d.). Myrrha's "Ich war, wenn ich erwachte" was also very popular.

44. The parts for the first and second violin are preserved in the Sächsische Landesbibliothek under the Signatur Mus. 3950-F-8a. In appendix 2 I list these under "Revised Italian." Unfortunately no continuo part survives, so it is impossible to know how the recitatives were treated.

45. In the index to the new productions at the Königliches Sächsisches Hoftheater between 1 October 1816 and 1 January 1862 (*Geschichte des Hoftheaters zu Dresden: Von seinen Anfängen bis zum Jahre 1862* [Dresden, 1878]), Robert Prölss mentions a performance of *Il sacrifizio interotto* on 11 December 1816. According to Prölss, the Italian version of the opera was only performed three more times after this date.

46. Arndt was not the only writer during this period to sound this type of call. Joseph Görres's *Der Rheinische Merkur* (1814–15) preached a remarkably similar blend of nationalism and yearning for the Middle Ages. Johann Gottlieb Fichte's *Reden an die deutsche Nation* (1808) is perhaps the most famous example of this "literature of national renewal."

47. The *Kurzer Katechismus für deutsche Soldaten* may be found on pp. 127–46 of Ernst Moritz Arndt, *Ausgewählte Gedichte und Schriften,* ed. Gustav Erdmann (Berlin: Union Verlag, 1969). For a short discussion of Arndt's contribution to early-nineteenth-century culture, see James J. Sheehan, *German History, 1770–1866* (New York: Oxford University Press, 1989), 380–83. A fuller account may be found in Alfred G. Pundt, *Arndt and the Nationalist Awakening in Germany* (New York: Columbia University Press, 1935; New York: AMS Press, 1968).

48. Eric L. Hobsbawm, *Age of Revolution, 1789–1848,* writes: "Retrospective patriotism has created a German 'war of liberation' in 1813–14, but it can safely be said that, in so far as this is supposed to have been based on popular resistance to the French, it is a pious fiction" ([New York: World, 1962], 108).

49. Arndt, *Katechismus,* in *Ausgewählte Gedichte und Schriften,* 137. Arndt was a preacher before he became a pamphleteer, and his words remind one of the Gospel of Matthew: "Truly I say to you, unless you turn and become like children, you can never enter the kingdom of heaven" (Revised Standard Version, Matthew 18:3). Only in this case Germany has taken the place of God's kingdom.

50. See also Heinrich Gotthard von Trietschke, *History of Germany in the Nineteenth Century,* selections from "Deutsche Geschichte im neunzehnten Jahrhundert," trans. Eden Paul and Cedar Paul, edited and with an introduction by Gordon A. Craig (Chicago: University of Chicago Press, 1975).

51. Writing in 1813, Arndt must try to understand why so many of the German states (such as Saxony and Bavaria) remained allied to Napoleon even as the War of Liberation was beginning.

52. Arndt, *Katechismus,* in *Ausgewählte Gedichte und Schriften,* 127.

53. Quoted by Pundt in *Arndt and the Nationalist Awakening,* 49–50.

54. Arndt, *Katechismus,* in *Ausgewählte Gedichte und Schriften,* 135. Just as in the quotation above, Arndt's language resonates powerfully with the Bible.

55. Friedrich Rühs, *Historische Entwickelung des Einflusses Frankreichs und der Franzosen auf Deutschland und die Deutschen* (Berlin: Nicolaische Buchhandlung, 1815), *Vorrede* (beginning).

56. Scharnhorst's essay is entitled "Entwicklung der allgemeinen Ursachen des Glücks der Franzosen in dem Revolutionskriege und insbesondere in dem Feldzuge von 1794" and is described by Sheehan, *German History,* 230.

57. Sheehan (*German History,* 294) quotes the Prussian diplomat Johann Streunsee: "The creative revolution was made in France from below [he told the French *chargé d'affaires* in 1799]; in Prussia it will be made more slowly and from above. The king is a democrat in his own way—he is working untiringly to restrict the privileges of the nobility. . . . In a few years there will be no privileged class in Prussia."

58. Wolfgang M. Wagner, *Carl Maria von Weber und die deutsche Nationaloper,* 101.

59. For a discussion of *couleur locale,* see Heinz Becker, "Die 'Couleur locale' als Stilkategorie der Oper," in *Die Couleur locale in der Oper des 19. Jahrhunderts,* ed. Heinz Becker, Studien zur Musikgeschichte des 19. Jahrhunderts, vol. 42 (Regensburg: Gustav Bosse, 1976), 23–46.

60. Weber clearly had a great deal of trouble with his company in the early years. The best discussion of the personnel of the German opera during this period may be found in Becker, *Die deutsche Oper,* 95 ff. Weber was so strapped for female singers, Becker writes, that for the first performance of *Joseph* he was forced to use a boy's choir for the chorus of the young maidens of Memphis, artfully concealed behind a few female dancers in the front row.

61. Jaroslav Buzga has studied Weber's Prague years extensively. Of particular interest are his articles "Die deutschen Opern in Webers Prager Repertoire, 1813–1816," in *Carl Maria von Weber und der Gedanke der Nationaloper,* vol. 1, Schriftenreihe der Hochschule fur Musik Carl Maria von Weber, Dresden, proceedings of the 2d scholarly conference on Dresden opera traditions, held in conjunction with the Dresdner Musikfestspiele 1986 under the auspices of the Hochschule für Musik Carl Maria von Weber, Dresden, ed. Hans John and Günther Stephan, vol. 10 Sonderheft (Dresden, n.p., 1987), 270–76, and "Carl Maria von Webers Prager 'Notizen-Buch' (1813–1816): Kommentar und Erstveröffentlichung des Originals," *Oper heute* 8 (1985), 7–44. See also John Warrack, "Französische Elemente in Webers Opern," in *Carl Maria von Weber und der Gedanke der Nationaloper,* 277–79 (reprinted without musical examples in *Die Dresdner Oper im 19. Jahrhundert*).

62. Warrack's analysis of Weber's repertoire as director of the Prague opera (Warrack, *Weber,* 149) confirms this idea of evolution: "Not until a full year had

elapsed did Weber really begin introducing a substantial number of German operas; and he never produced one of his own. Weber was in fact almost literally setting the scene for the appearance of German Romantic opera; and to this end it was necessary to go to French opera." In *The New Grove Early Romantic Masters 2* Warrack writes, "The repertory which Weber . . . introduced in Prague and Dresden was chosen to set the stage for the appearance of German Romantic Opera. . . . It was chiefly in French opera that he discerned the foundation of Romantic opera; and his repertories show a practical understanding of what the French had to offer German audiences and German musicians" (38).

63. Quoted by Robert Tallant Laudon, *Sources of the Wagnerian Synthesis: A Study of the Franco-German Tradition in Nineteenth-Century Opera* (Munich and Salzburg: Musikverlag Emil Katsbichler, 1979), 8. Cerubini's opera *Les deux journées* was known in Germany as *Der Wasserträger*. According to John Deathridge, *Wagner's "Rienzi": A Reappraisal Based on a Study of the Sketches and Drafts* (Oxford: Clarendon Press, 1977), 37, Wagner singled out this work (*Joseph*) as the high point of his activities in Riga several times in his *Collected Writings*.

64. Edward J. Dent, *The Rise of Romantic Opera,* ed. Winton Dean (Cambridge: Cambridge University Press, 1976).

65. Winton Dean, "French Opera," in *The Age of Beethoven,* 1790–1830, ed. Gerald Abraham, Oxford History of Music, vol. 8. (London: Oxford University Press, 1982), 26–119.

66. Warrack, "Französische Elemente in Webers Opern," in *Carl Maria von Weber.* Warrack uses Weber's review of *Léhéman* (1811) to show a connection between Dalayrac's use of a "characteristic motive" and Eglantine's use of a "deception motive" in *Euryanthe.*

67. For a succinct description of the composition and first performances of *Joseph,* see Elizabeth Bartlet's article "*Joseph,*" *The New Grove Dictionary of Opera,* 2:920–21. A more detailed account may be found in Bartlet's dissertation "Etienne Nicholas Méhul and Opera during the French Revolution, Consulate, and Empire: A Source, Archival, and Stylistic Study" (Ph.D. diss., University of Chicago, 1982). As Anke Schmitt points out in *Der Exotismus in der deutschen Oper zwischen Mozart und Spohr* (Hamburg: Verlag der Musikalienhandlung Karl Dieter Wagner, 1988), 95 ff., *Joseph* was only the most popular of a group of biblical operas from the early nineteenth century, which included the melodrama *Omasis* by Bösinger (Vienna, 1811) on the same subject.

68. Weber reviewed the opera in Munich in July of 1811. His highly favorable words first appeared in the Munich *Gesellschaftsblatt für gebildete Stände* 54 (10 July 1811) and may be found both in Weber, *Schriften,* 110–12 and Weber, *Writings,* 79–81.

69. The Hassourek translation, "Joseph und seine Brüder: Ein historisches Drama mit Musik in drey Aufzügen," is preserved in the Berlin Staatsbibliothek

(Haus 1), Signatur Tm 566/11. The libretto is quite different from the Herklots translation, which seems to have been more current in northern and eastern Germany.

70. That these set pieces should contain the most extensive revisions is not surprising. Just as in modern performances of frequently translated works (*The Merry Widow*, for instance), performers or conductors become familiar with a particular set of words and use the version they think will be the most effective.

71. In this respect *Joseph* is somewhat of an anomaly, typical neither of Méhul's scores nor of the *opéra comique* in general.

72. Weber, *Writings*, 209. The original German appears in Weber, *Schriften*, 280. Weber's concept of the opera was very much in line with more broadly held critical views that singled out the simplest musical numbers for particular praise. Joseph's first-act romance, the "Morning Prayer of the Hebrews," and the "Chorus of the Young Maidens of Memphis" were special favorites.

73. Johann George Sulzer, *Allgemeine Theorie der schönen Künste* (Leipzig, 1787), 4: 101–102. See also Thomas Baumann's comments on the romance in late-eighteenth-century German opera in *North German Opera in the Age of Goethe* (Cambridge: Cambridge University Press, 1985), 34.

74. James Parakilas makes the point that the distinction between the male chorus and the larger mixed chorus was often extremely important in nineteenth-century opera. See James Parakilas, "Political Representation and the Chorus in Nineteenth-Century Opera," *19th-Century Music* 16, no. 2 (Fall 1992): 181–202.

75. Berlin SB (Haus 1), Signatur Mus Km 141/1: *Joseph und seine Brüder / Oper in 3 Aufzügen / Musik von / Méhul. . . . / Wien, / bei Ant. Diabelli und Comp.* This score also uses a different translation than the one that seems to have been used in Dresden.

76. In some early sources, such as the piano-vocal score printed by C. M. Meyer in Braunschweig (Berlin SB, Km 141/6), Fränzl's finale is attributed to Joseph Weigl. Fränzl (1770–1833) was appointed *Kapellmeister* in Munich in 1806. His opera *Carlo Fioras* dates from 1810.

77. Berlin SB (Haus 2), Signatur Mus Tm 566/4: *Jacob und seine Söhne in Egypten/Ein musikalisches Drama in Drei Aufzügen. . . . /München, 1808/bei Franz Seraph Hübschmann.*

78. "Joseph steht in Jacobs Armen, Benjamin zu seiner linken die Hand reichend, Simeon kniet vor Joseph und küßt sein Gewand. Jacob legte seine rechte Hand verzeihend auf Simeons Haupt. Die Brüder stehen in Gruppen rechts und links und richten befriedigt ihre Blicke auf Joseph. Die Großwürdenträger und Ägypter füllen den Mittelgrund. Die Sklaven mit den Geschenken steher hinter ihnen. Die Leibwache im Hintergrund."

79. The lives and works of the Nazarene artists are chronicled in Keith Andrews, *The Nazarenes: A Brotherhood of German Painters in Rome* (Oxford: Claren-

don, 1964). *Die Geschichte Josephs* is now in the National Gallery in Berlin, and a small study for the fresco is housed in the Galerie der Romantik, also in Berlin.

80.   Andrews, *The Nazarenes,* 33–34.

81.   Ibid., 34, quoted from E. Förster, *Peter von Cornelius* (Berlin, 1874) 1:155. It is interesting here that Cornelius invokes painters of the Italian Renaissance rather than Dürer or any other German artists. The parallel with Weber's early repertoire at the German opera in Dresden is striking—in each case plans for national artistic regeneration are mediated by foreign art.

82.   Terry Eagleton, *The Ideology of the Aesthetic* (Oxford: Basil Blackwell, 1990), 24.

83.   Weber, *Writings,* 209–10. The original German may be found in Weber, *Schriften,* 280–81.

84.   This score, included under the Signatur Mus. 4105-I-508 in the Sächsische Landesbibliothek, contains only three lines: a bass line, the vocal line, and then an additional orchestral staff that shows a melody along with some indication of the instrumentation. Other materials, such as orchestra parts, are also included under this Signatur. Some of these correspond to the numbering in the prompter's score; others seem to belong to a performance that also included Joseph's aria (no. 1).

85.   In 1907 Max Zenger created a new version of *Joseph,* with a new translation and recitatives to replace the dialogue. In a *Geleitsbrief* to the score he claims (using passages from Pougin's biography of Méhul to support his argument) that Duval originally conceived of his libretto as a *grand opéra* and not as an *opéra comique.* A prompter's score of this Zenger version in the Berlin Staatsbibliothek (Haus 2, Signatur 4° N. Mus. 2383) shows many annotations, including dates of performances stretching from 1909 to 1919. For the final chorus, interestingly enough, Zenger returns to Méhul's original version.

That the story of Joseph continued to have resonance in Germany well into the twentieth century is perhaps best shown by Thomas Mann's four-volume *Joseph und seine Brüder,* published in the 1930s.

86.   Weber conducted *Preciosa* in Dresden in June of 1822, and *Abu Hassan* was premiered early the following year.

3. *Der Freischütz* and the Character of the Nation

1.   Daniel Sanders, *Wörterbuch der Deutschen Sprache,* s.v. "Charakter" (Leipzig: Otto Wigand, 1860), 252.

2.   Heinrich Christoph Koch, *Musikalisches Lexikon,* s.v. "Charakter" (Frankfurt, 1802; Hildesheim: Georg Olms, 1964), col. 313–14.

3.   Ignaz Franz von Mosel (1772–1844) was a critic and composer who from 1820 to 1829 was the vice director of the two court theaters in Vienna. He was also the author of an important biography of Salieri, *Über das Leben und die Werke des Antonio Salieri* (Vienna, 1827). A brief article on Mosel by C. F.

Pohl and Bruce Carr may be found in *The New Grove Dictionary of Opera*, 12:609.

That Weber was aware of Mosel's compositions is clear from an article in the Dresden *Abend-Zeitung* (16 March 1820) in which he speaks highly of two Mosel operas, *Salem* and *Cyrus* (quoted by Michael Tusa, *"Euryanthe," and Carl Maria von Weber's Dramaturgy of German Opera* [Oxford: Clarendon Press, 1991], 51). Weber visited Mosel during his trip to Vienna in 1822 and consulted with him about the libretto of *Euryanthe*.

4. Heinrich Christoph Koch, *Versuch einer Anleitung zur Composition* (1782–93), Johann Mattheson, *Der vollkommene Capellmeister* (1739), Joseph Riepel, *Anfangsgrunde zur musikalischen Setzkunst* (1752–68), Johann George Sulzer, *Allgemeine Theorie der schönen Künste* (1771–74).

5. Ignaz Franz von Mosel, *Versuch einer Aesthetik des dramatischen Tonsatzes* (Vienna, 1813), 42.

6. Ibid., 43.

7. Ibid., 44.

8. Carl Dahlhaus, "Die Kategorie des Charakteristischen in der Ästhetik des 19. Jahrhunderts," in *Die Couleur locale in der Oper des 19. Jahrhunderts*, ed. Heinz Becker, Studien zur Musikgeschichte des 19. Jahrhunderts, vol. 42 (Regensburg: Gustav Bosse, 1976), 9–10. Edward Lippmann also discusses Körner's essay in *A History of Western Musical Aesthetics* (Lincoln: University of Nebraska Press, 1992), 134–36.

9. Quoted by James J. Sheehan, *German History, 1770–1866* (New York: Oxford University Press, 1989), 364. Humboldt, *Werke*, 2:342, 356.

10. Franz Danzi (1763–1827), *Kapellmeister* in Stuttgart, wrote a through-composed opera, *Iphegenia in Aulis*, in 1807, and although the work had little popular success, it had an important influence on later composers. E. T. A. Hoffmann's *Undine*, composed in 1813–14 and first performed in Berlin, 3 August 1816, also features long sections of through-composed writing, even though it also includes some dialogues. But despite favorable reviews such as Weber's, and the apparent popularity of the opera in Berlin, *Undine's* influence on the repertoire was effectively terminated when its stage decorations and costumes were destroyed in a disastrous fire on 27 July 1817.

11. Carl Maria von Weber, *Writings on Music*, translated by Martin Cooper, edited and with an introduction by John Warrack (Cambridge: Cambridge University Press, 1981), 201–202. The original review, written in early January 1817, may be found in Carl Maria von Weber, *Sämtliche Schriften* (Berlin and Leipzig: Schuster and Loeffler, 1908), 127–35.

12. In the putative interview between the composer and Johann Christian Lobe, "Gespräche mit Carl Maria von Weber," in *Fliegende Blätter für Musik* (Leipzig, 1855), 1:27–34, 1:110–22, Weber also speaks favorably of *Joseph* (p. 29). An abbreviated version of Lobe's account is reprinted in *Consonanzen und Disso-*

nanzen: Gesammelte Schriften aus älterer und neuerer Zeit (Leipzig, 1869), 122–46. One frequently encounters ideas or direct quotations from these "Gespräche" in the secondary literature on *Freischütz*, for example, in Hermann Abert's "Carl Maria von Weber und sein *Freischütz*," in *Jahrbuch der Musikbibliothek Peters,* vol. 33 (Leipzig: C. F. Peters, 1926), 9–29.

13.   For an overview of the "authenticity problems" concerning these conversations, see Tusa, *"Euryanthe,"* 31 n. 6. Oftentimes, Lobe puts words into Weber's mouth that sound as if they come from a common pool of early-nineteenth-century rhetoric about musical aesthetics. Weber's discussion of "character," for instance, reads almost like a paraphrase of Koch: "Do not overlook the fact that a character doesn't consist of only one feature, but rather emerges from a combination of features that may even be quite different from each other. These features are free to step in and out of the foreground as the situation demands. Those features which occur most frequently and prominently form the essence of the character" ("Gespräche mit Weber," in *Fliegende Blätter für Musik,* 30–31).

14.   Ibid., 29.

15.   Ibid., 31.

16.   In his article "Weber und sein *Freischütz*," in *Jahrbuch der Musikbibliothek Peters,* for instance, Abert uses the "grundlegenden Stimmungsunterschiede" (fundamental mood differences) between the demonic powers and the hunting life as the point of departure for his discussion of the key areas of *Freischütz* (25). Theo Cornelissen, in his *"Der Freischütz" von C. M. von Weber,* in *Die Oper: Schriftenreihe zum Musikunterricht in der mittleren und höheren Schule,* 3d ed. (Berlin: Robert Lienau, 1959), uses the Lobe quotation to begin his section "Weber über die Komposition des *Freischütz*" (26).

17.   Wilhelm Jähns gives a detailed chronology of Weber's composition in *Carl Maria von Weber in seinen Werken: Chronologisch-thematisches Verzeichniss seiner sämmtlichen Compositionen nebst Angabe unvollständigen, verloren gegangenen, zweifelhaften und untergeschobenen* (Leipzig, 1873; Berlin-Lichterfelde: Lienau, 1967), 297–326.

18.   From his work on the compositional drafts of *Euryanthe,* Michael Tusa has uncovered some evidence that seems to suggest that Weber followed this type of method for his later work. See Tusa *"Euryanthe,"* 207.

19.   In *North German Opera in the Age of Goethe,* Thomas Baumann discusses *Das wütende Heer* and includes a musical excerpt of the section that seems to have influenced Weber ([Cambridge: Cambridge University Press, 1985], 189–91). Abert also describes some compositional influences on Weber ("Weber und sein *Freischütz*," in *Jahrbuch der Musikbibliothek Peters*).

20.   Baumann, *North German Opera,* 40.

21.   Bernd Göpfert, *Stimmtypen und Rollencharaktere in der deutschen Oper von 1815–1848* (Wiesbaden: Breitkopf and Härtel, 1977), 77–79.

22. John Warrack discusses the tradition of D-minor "rage" arias on pp. 180–82 of *German Opera: From the Beginnings to Wagner* (Cambridge: Cambridge University Press, 2001).

23. For a discussion of the relationship between the instrumental rondo and vocal *rondò*, and for a more detailed description of the *rondò* aria, see Helga Lühning, "Die Rondo-Arie im späten 18. Jahrhundert: Dramatischer Gestalt und musikalischer Bau," *Hamburger Jahrbuch für Musikwissenschaft* 5 (1981): 219–46.

24. Quoted by Daniel Heartz in "Mozart and His Italian Contemporaries," in *Mozart's Operas*, ed. Daniel Heartz (Berkeley and Los Angeles: University of California Press, 1990), 306. The slow to fast progression of tempos in the *rondò* aria, Heartz points out, make the form an important precursor of the cantabile-cabaletta arias that were so important in nineteenth-century Italian opera.

25. The term is borrowed from James Webster, "The Analysis of Mozart's Arias," in *Mozart Studies*, ed. Cliff Eisen (Oxford: Clarendon, 1991), 101–200.

26. According to Lobe, this aria (or more specifically, the text associated with the allegro) had special significance for Weber: "The principal properties of *Freischütz* do not lie there [in the depiction of the hunting life]. The most important place for me was the words of Max: 'mich umgarnen finstere Mächte,' for these words showed me which principal character to give to the entire opera. Through sound and melody I needed to remind the audience of these 'dark powers' as often as possible" ("Gespräche mit Weber," in *Fliegende Blätter für Musik*, 32).

27. I am using "tableau" here in the sense of "stage set."

28. Max Maria von Weber, *Carl Maria von Weber: The Life of an Artist*, trans. J. Palgrave Simpson (London: Chapman and Hall, 1865; New York: Greenwood, 1969), 2:227.

29. The entire review is reprinted in Hans Schnoor, *Weber auf dem Welttheater: Ein Freischützbuch*, 4th ed. (Hamburg: Deutscher Verlag, 1963), 141–48.

30. Ibid., 143.

31. Franz Grillparzer, *Sämtliche Werke*, ed. Peter Frank and Karl Pörnbacher (Munich: Carl Hanser, 1964), 3:888.

32. Richard Wagner, *Richard Wagner's Prose Works*, trans. William Ashton Ellis (London: Kegan Paul, Trench, Trübner and Co., 1895–1912; St. Clair Shores, Mich.: Scholarly Press, 1972), 5:55.

33. Carl Dahlhaus, "Weber's *Freischütz* und die Idee der deutschen Oper," *Österreichische Musikzeitschrift* 38, nos. 7–8 (July–August 1983): 381–88.

34. Translations from *Der Freischütz*, piano-vocal score, edited and translated by Natalia MacFarren and Th. Baker (New York and London: Schirmer, 1904).

35. Quoted by Wolfgang Wagner in *Carl Maria von Weber und die deutsche Nationaloper* (Mainz: Schott, 1994), 123.

57. Carl Dahlhaus, *Nineteenth-Century Music,* trans. J. Bradford Robinson (Berkeley and Los Angeles: University of California Press, 1989), 39.

58. Wagner, *Weber und die deutsche Nationaloper,* 11–12.

59. Jean-Jacques Nattiez, *Music and Discourse: Toward a Semiology of Music,* trans. Carolyn Abbate (Princeton: Princeton University Press: 1990), ix.

4. Euryanthe

1. Michael Tusa, *"Euryanthe" and Carl Maria von Weber's Dramaturgy of German Opera* (Oxford: Clarendon Press, 1991), 50.

2. Hermann Dechant, *E. T. A. Hoffmann's Oper "Aurora,"* Regensburger Beiträge zur Musikwissenschaft, vol. 2 (Regensburg: G. Bosse, 1975). In 1808, Hoffmann had used the term *Romantische Oper* to describe his *Der Trank der Unsterblichkeit,* and Spohr also called his *Alruna* a *romantische Oper.* Weber himself used the title for his *Silvana.* See John Warrack, *German Opera: From the Beginnings to Wagner* (Cambridge: Cambridge University Press, 2001), 246, 250, 252–53. See also David Charlton, "Introduction to *The Poet and the Composer:* Hoffmann and Opera," in *E. T. A. Hoffmann's Musical Writings: Kreisleriana, The Poet and the Composer, Music Criticism,* ed. David Charlton, trans. Martyn Clarke (Cambridge: Cambridge University Press, 1989), 169–87. Charlton discusses the idea of *romantische Oper* on pp. 183–85.

3. Carl Maria von Weber, *Writings on Music,* translated by Martin Cooper, edited and with an introduction by John Warrack (Cambridge: Cambridge University Press, 1981), 233–34.

4. For information about the Dresden *Liederkreis* (which also counted Friedrich Kind, the librettist of *Der Freischütz,* among its members) see Hermann Anders Krüger, *Pseudoromantik: Friedrich Kind und der Dredener Liederkreis* (Leipzig: H. Haeffel Verlag, 1904).

5. In *"Euryanthe,"* Tusa emphasizes the extent to which Weber himself was responsible for the libretto and must share the blame for its weaknesses.

6. "The order of the earliest pieces," writes Tusa in *"Euryanthe,"* "those composed up through the summer of 1822, suggests that at the outset of composition Weber was concerned with establishing the primary musical colors for characterizing the opera's four principal spheres: the love-filled world of the youthful, *sensible* troubadour Adolar (No. 12); the demonic realm of the villains (No. 11); the ceremonial domain of medieval chivalry (the Introduzione Nos. 1–4); and Emma's ethereal spirit world (*Vision*)" (207).

7. In *"Euryanthe"* (117) Tusa discusses these plans. He speculates that "Weber came to view the visible representations of Emma as superfluous because the kind of music eventually associated with the ghost provided a much more subtle symbol for her ineffable, ethereal presence in the realm of spirits; in the final version of the opera Emma's purely spiritual presence is communi-

cated only by her music, a quintessentially Romantic treatment of music as the 'natural' medium for the supernatural" (117).

8. The *Charakteristik der Töne* may be found on pp. 377–82 of C. F. D. Schubart's *Ideen zu einer Ästhetik der Tonkunst,* ed. Ludwig Schubart (Vienna, 1806). In *"Euryanthe"* (171–74) Tusa discusses Weber's selection of B major for this duet (as well as many other aspects of tonal planning in *Euryanthe*).

9. See Simon Schama's chapter "Der Holzweg," in *Landscape and Memory* (New York: Knopf, 1995), 75–134.

10. Tusa (in *"Euryanthe"*) also describes an early manuscript of this aria, proofed by Weber and Chezy, in which a storm brewing in the background is specified.

11. This quotation (Weber, *Writings on Music,* trans. Martin Cooper, ed. John Warrack [Cambridge: Cambridge University Press, 1981], 304–305) is from the "Metronomische Bezeichnungen zur Oper *Euryanthe* nebst einigen allgemeinen Bemerkungen über die Behandlung der Zeitmaße" that Weber wrote at the request of the Leipzig *Kapellmeister* Aloys Präger in March of 1824. These "Metronome markings and recommendations for *Euryanthe*" appear in Weber, *Writings,* 302–306, and in Carl Maria von Weber, *Sämtliche Schriften* (Berlin and Leipzig: Schuster and Loeffler, 1908), 220–25.

12. In addition to the correspondence between the arias of Eglantine and Elvira, Tusa (*"Euryanthe,"* 173 n. 18) calls attention to "other bravura soprano arias at the end of the eighteenth and beginning of the nineteenth century: Fiordiligi's Act 2 Rondò in *Così fan tutte;* Leonore's 'Komm Hoffnung' in *Fidelio;* Amenäide's Act 2 *Scena ed aria* in Rossini's *Tancredi;* and of course Agathe's 'Leise, leise' from the second act of *Freischütz.*"

13. *BamZ* 2 (1825): 86.

14. An extensive discussion of Mozart's aria forms may be found in James Webster, "The Analysis of Mozart's Arias," in *Mozart Studies,* ed. Cliff Eisen (Oxford: Clarendon, 1991), 101–200.

15. Tusa (*"Euryanthe,"* 37) makes this point and compares the aria to Rossini models.

16. Gustav Schilling, *Versuch einer Philosophie des Schönen in der Musik* (Mainz, 1838), 337–38.

17. Schubart, *Characteristik der Töne,* 378. Schubart's description of C minor was quoted almost verbatim by Schilling in his *Versuch* (457).

18. In her versification of the libretto, Tusa reports (*"Euryanthe,"* 92), Chezy claimed to have been "guided by Weber's instructions to make the verse as interesting and difficult as possible."

19. The construction of Lysiart's and Eglantine's character bears a certain resemblance to the "nested" narrative strategy of writers such as Hoffmann, Eichendorff, and Tieck, as well as much early-nineteenth-century criticism. See for example Tieck's *Musical Joys and Sorrows,* Eichendorff *Magic in Autumn,* and of course Hoffmann's magnificent *Don Juan.* These works tell the bulk of

their narrative as a story within a story, and the denouement comes when the different narrative layers are shown to bear an inner relation to each other.

20. Bernd Göpfert's stimulating book *Stimmtypen und Rollencharaktere in der deutschen Oper von 1815–1848* (Wiesbaden: Breitkopf and Härtel, 1977) classifies Lysiart as a "character baritone," a category that also includes Telramund from *Lohengrin* and Bois-Guilbert from *Der Templer und die Jüdin* (74–77). "The plot motivation of this nihilistic character," notes Göpfert, "is most often unrequited love (a parallel to the dramatic mezzo)" (76). Like many other scholars, Göpfert mentions Lysiart and Eglantine as models for Telramund and Ortrud in *Lohengrin*. Göpfert's discussion of *Euryanthe* is unfortunately marred by the fact that he classifies Eglantine as a "dramatic mezzo" rather than as a soprano (81).

The parallels between *Euryanthe* and Wagner's operas (specifically *Die Hochzeit, Tannhäuser*, and *Lohegrin*) are extensively explored by Michael Tusa in "Richard Wagner and Weber's *Euryanthe*," *19th-Century Music 9*, no. 3 (1985–86): 206–21.

21. John Warrack (*Carl Maria von Weber*, 2d ed. [Cambridge: Cambridge University Press, 1976], 286) also draws attention to "the superior forcefulness of the evil pair."

22. *Wiener Zeitschrift für Kunst, Literatur, Theater und Mode* (1823), 1111.

23. Winton Dean, "German Opera," in *The Age of Beethoven, 1790–1830*, ed. Gerald Abraham, Oxford History of Music, vol. 8 (London: Oxford University Press, 1982), 497.

24. Marschner also follows this strategy in *Der Vampyr* and *Hans Heiling*.

25. That the two sections of Adolar's aria are in the same character and are separated by only a brief transition is typical of Rossini's double arias.

26. Tusa ("*Euryanthe*," 32) also makes this point: "The placement of the Romanza as the second piece in the opera reflects another convention that became commonplace in French and German opera in the first half of the nineteenth century, that is, the opening gambit of an introductory chorus followed by a strophic song."

27. These kinds of scenes, of course, are not restricted to Weber's works, but are a more general feature of early-nineteenth-century opera. In his article "Preghiera" in *The New Grove Dictionary of Opera* (3:1090), Julian Budden gives numerous examples of *preghiere* from early-nineteenth-century Italian opera, such as "Deh calma, o ciel, nel sonno" (*Otello*, Rossini, 1816) and "Deh! tu di un umile preghiera" (*Maria Stuarda*, Donizetti, 1835). German examples include "Allmächt'ger Vater, blick herab" (*Rienzi*, Wagner, 1842) and "Allmächt'ge Jungfrau, hör mein Flehen" (*Tannhäuser*, 1845). The tenor Huon sings a *preghiera* in Weber's *Oberon*.

28. Carl von Rotteck und Theodor Welcker, eds., *Staats-Lexicon, oder Encyclopädie der Staatswissenschaften* (Altona, 1834–43). Welcker's article "Geschlechts-verhältnisse: Frauen, ihre rechtliche und politische Stellung in der Gesell-

schaft; Rechtswohlthaten und Geschlechtsbeistände der Frauen; Frauenvereine und Vergehen in Beziehung auf die Geschlechtsverhältnisse" appears in 6:629–65.

29. Welcker, "Geschlechtsverhältnisse," in *Staats-lexicon,* 6:629–30.

30. Quoted and translated by Dagmar Herzog, "Liberalism, Religious Dissent, and Women's Rights: Louise Dittmar's Writings from the 1840's," in *In Search of a Liberal Germany: Studies in the History of German Liberalism from 1789 to the Present,* ed. Konrad H. Jarausch and Larry Eugene Jones (Providence, R.I.: Berg Publishers, 1990), 55–85. The original German may be found on p. 647.

31. Welcker, "Geschlechtsverhältnisse," in *Staats-lexicon,* 6:637. Welcker's words echo Hegel's in *Philosophy of Right* (quoted by Sheehan, *History,* 539): "man has his actual substantive life in the state, in learning, and so forth, as well as in labour and struggle with the external world and with himself so that it is only out of his diremption that he fights his way to self-subsistent unity with himself. In the family he has a tranquil intuition of this unity, and there he lives a subjective ethical life, on the plane of true feeling. Woman, on the other hand, has her substantive destiny in the family, and to be imbued with family piety is her ethical frame of mind."

32. "Du hast mir mein Geheimnis abgelauscht? / Zur Sühne beut dir Forest seine Hand, / die Fesseln wandl'ich in ein Rosenband. / Beherrschen sollst du diese reichen Gauen."

33. Welcker, "Geschlächtsverhältnisse," in *Staats-lexicon,* 6:636.

34. Tusa (*"Euryanthe,"* 190) discusses the orchestration of this section.

35. *Euryanthe,* of course, is not the only opera in which masculine and feminine worlds are sharply opposed to one another. Wagner frequently uses the same types of orchestral colors to articulate the genders (i.e., woodwind = feminine, brass and percussion = masculine), most notably perhaps in *Der fliegende Holländer.*

36. Schubart's description of B major reads: "Foretelling strongly colored, wild passions; depicted in the most glaring colors. Wrath, rage, envy, frenzy, despair, and every burden of the heart lie in its region." C major, according to Schubart, "is completely pure. Its character is innocence, simplicity, naïveté, and the language of children."

37. Adolf Bernhard Marx, *Die Musik des neunzehnten Jahrhunderts und ihre Pflege,* 2d ed. (Leipzig: Breitkopf and Härtel, 1873), 73–74. Translated by August Heinrich Wehrman as *The Music of the Nineteenth Century and Its Culture* (London: Robert Cocks, 1855), 60.

38. In his *Carl Maria von Weber in seinen Werken: Chronologisch-thematisches Verzeichniss seiner sämmtlichen Compositionen nebst Angabe unvollständigen, verloren gegangenen, zweifelhaften und untergeschobenen* (Leipzig, 1873; Berlin-Lichterfelde: Lienau, 1967), Friedrich Wilhelm Jähns quotes a letter that Weber later wrote to his wife in which the composer complains that "[i]n an organically connected whole such as a *grosse Oper,* it is really most

difficult to cut anything out" (364). Jähns's book is still the most extensive and detailed discussion of the *Euryanthe* cuts.

Tusa (*"Euryanthe,"* 25) also describes Weber's cuts: "The early performance history of *Euryanthe* also entailed a number of revisions that deserve mention. Weber shortened a number of passages in the opera between the first performance and his death in 1826, perhaps a tacit admission that the opera in fact suffered from certain intrinsic problems. Immediately after the first performance in Vienna Weber abbreviated the recitative between Euryanthe and Eglantine in the first act and eliminated part of the G-minor section of Euryanthe's Act III *Scena e cavatina* no. 17. On 20 November 1823, shortly after his return to Dresden, Weber composed a shorter version of Euryanthe's *Vision* narrative in the first act, compressing the twenty-two measures of the original version into fifteen measures."

39. Jähns, *Chronologisch-thematisches Verzeichniss,* 365.

40. Tusa (*"Euryanthe,"* 57–58) also discusses the reception of the opera. See also Warrack, *Weber,* 262 ff.

41. Franz Grillparzer, *Tagebücher und literarische Skizzenhefte: Zweiter Teil: 1822 bis Mitte 1830,* ed. August Sauer, in *Sämtlicher Werke,* part 2, vol. 8 (Vienna, 1916), 128–29.

42. Julius Cornet, *Die Oper in Deutschland und das Theater der Neuzeit aus dem Standpuncte practische Erfahrung* (Hamburg, 1849), 45. Cruel anecdotes about Chezy abound, as, for instance, in Henry F. Chorley's *Modern German Music* (London, 1854), 299 ff.

43. Helmina von Chezy, "Carl Maria von Weber's *Euryanthe*: Ein Beitrag zur Geschichte der deutschen Oper," *Neue Zeitschrift für Musik* 13 (1840): 1–3, 5–6, 9–11,13–14, 17–19, 21–22, 33–35, 37–39, 41–42.

44. See Tusa, *"Euryanthe,"* 57 ff.

45. Richard Wagner, *Richard Wagner's Prose Works,* trans. William Ashton Ellis (London: Kegan Paul, Trench, Trübner and Co., 1893; St. Clair Shores, Mich.: Scholarly Press, 1972), 8:56.

46. Chorley, *Modern German Music,* 303–304.

47. According to Robert Prölss, *Geschichte des Hoftheaters zu Dresden: Von seinen Anfängen bis zum Jahre 1862* (Dresden, 1878), *Euryanthe* received eighty performances during the period 1816–1861, making it the eleventh most popular opera in Dresden during this period, between Mozart's *Don Giovanni* and Boieldieu's *La dame blanche.*

48. Weber, *Lichtenstein Briefe,* 133–34, quoted by Tusa (*"Euryanthe,"* 25).

49. *Euryanthe* was given for the fiftieth time on 21 October 1844, and for the sixty-sixth time 21 January 1849.

50. *Dresden Anzeiger,* 31 March 1849. For a fuller discussion of *Euryanthe* as the archetypal German opera, see Wolfgang Becker, *Die deutsche Oper in Dresden*

unter der Letiung von Carl Maria von Weber, 1817–1826, vol. 22, *Theater und Drama* (Berlin and Dahlem: Colloquium Verlag, 1962), 66–67. For another example of this "archetypal" use of *Euryanthe* in modern scholarship, see Aubrey Garlington's "Mega-Text, Mega-Music: A Crucial Dilemma for German Romantic Opera," in *Musical Humanism and Its Legacy: Essays in Honor of Claude V. Palisca*, ed. Nancy Kovaleff Baker and Barbara Russano Hunning, Festschrift Series no. 11 (Stuyvesant, N.Y.: Pendragon Press, 1992), 381–93.

51.   The theater was ceremonially opened on 12 April 1841 with a performance of Weber's *Jubelouverture* and Goethe's *Torquato Tasso.*

52.   Marx, *Pflege*, 77.

53.   See for example Günther Jäckel, "Aspekte der Dresdner Kulturgeschichte zwischen 1763 und 1832," in *Die italienische Oper in Dresden von Johann Adolf Hasse bis Francesco* Morlacchi, 3 Wissenschaftliche Konferenz zum Thema "Dresdner Operntraditionen," ed. Günther Stephan and Hans John, Dresden, Musik in Dresden, Schriftenreihe der Hochschule für Musik "Carl Maria von Weber," Dresden (Dresden: n.p., 1982), 11:417–38.

54.   Eric L. Hobsbawm, *The Age of Revolution, 1789–1848* (New York: World, 1962), writes of an "epidemic of history writing" during this period (335 ff.). In his *German History* (543–45) Sheehan also describes the new popularity of history in the 1830s and 1840s.

5. Epilogue

1.   *BamZ* 2 (1825): 83 ("Correspondence from Dresden").

2.   Philip Gossett, introduction to *Tebaldo e Isolina*, Italian Opera, 1810–1840, vol. 24 (Dresden, 1825; New York: Garland, 1989). Gossett documents the development of this myth with quotations from Max Weber and John Warrack.

      The musicological reaction to the "metaphor of battle" can also be seen in Wolfgang Becker, *Die deutsche Oper in Dresden unter der Letiung von Carl Maria von Weber, 1817–1826*, vol. 22, *Theater und Drama* (Berlin and Dahlem: Colloquium Verlag, 1962). A useful discussion of the demonization of the foreign may also be found in Anno Mungen, "Morlacchi, Weber, und die Dresdner Oper," in *Die Dresdner Oper im 19. Jahrhundert*, ed. Michael Heinemann and Hans John, Musik in Dresden, Schriftenreihe der Hochschule für Musik "Carl Maria von Weber," Dresden, vol. 1, ed. Michael Heinemann, Hanns-Werner Heister, Matthias Herrmann, and Hans John (Laaber: Laaber Verlag, 1995), 85–89.

3.   Eberhard Kremtz, "Das 'Deutsche Departement' des Dresdner Hoftheaters," in *Die Dresdner Oper im 19. Jahrhundert*, 107–12.

4.   *Henriette, oder Die schöne Sängerin: Eine Geschichte unserer Tage* (Leipzig, 1826). Rellstab used the pseudonym "Freimund Zuschauer" for this novella. Rellstab depicts the partisans of Italian opera as boorish, pretentious, and ignorant.

5.   *BamZ* 4 (1827): 321.

6.   *BamZ* 7 (1830): 33 ff.

7.   Ibid. Although the bulk of German music criticism during this period was anti-Italian, there are many counter-examples, perhaps the most notable of which is Wagner's 1834 article *Die deutsche Oper*. Marx himself, although his sympathies clearly lay with the "new German school," was even-handed enough to print Heine's witty defense of Rossini: "Rossini, divino Maestro, Helios of Italy, thou spreadest thy resounding rays through the entire world. Forgive my poor compatriots, who attack you on writing and blotting paper. For myself, I rejoice in your golden tones, your melodic light, your sparkling butterfly dreams that flutter around me so delightfully, and kiss my heart like the lips of the graces. Divino Maestro, forgive my poor compatriots, who do not see your depth because you cover them with roses, who do not think you serious and substantial, because you flutter so lightly, with god-given wings" (*BamZ* 7 [1830]: 37). In his criticism of Rossini, Schumann also adopts the metaphor of the butterfly, but here the butterfly is a negative image of superficiality rather than lightness. See *Neue Zeitschrift für Musik* 1 (11 August 1834): 150.

8.   *BamZ* 7 (1830): 358–59.

9.   Becker, *Die deutsche Oper*, 70.

10.   The principal English-language biography of Marschner is A. B. Palmer, *Heinrich August Marschner, 1795–1861: His Life and Stage Works*, Studies in Musicology 24, George Buelow, series ed. (Ann Arbor, Mich.: UMI Research Press, 1978). On p. 44 Palmer writes: "Marschner, in desperate need of money to support himself, his pregnant wife, and his mother, was taking advantage of every opportunity to make a profit with his music, no matter how hastily it had been dashed off, and he began to look less and less like the comrade-in-arms against Italian music that Weber had originally envisioned him to be."

11.   The most extensive account of these negotiations may be found in Jörg Heyne, "Die Ära Reißiger am Hoftheater in Dresden," in *Die Dresdner Oper im 19. Jahrhundert*, 143–78. Although it comes from the early part of this century, Kurt Kreiser's *Carl Gottlieb Reissiger: Sein Leben nebst einigen Beiträgen zur Geschichte des Konzertwesens in Dresden* (Dresden: Johannes Päßler, 1918) is still the most extensive biography of the composer.

12.   During his last years at the German opera, by comparison, Weber earned eighteen hundred thalers per year. No conductor could match the salaries of the highest paid singers during this period. During the 1830s the prima donna Wilhelmine Schröeder-Devrient earned four thousand thalers per year at the Dresden opera.

13.   Both Heyne, "Die Ära Reißiger," in *Die Dresdner Oper im 19. Jahrhundert*, and Kreiser, *Carl Gottlieb Reissiger* (59 ff.), reprint the terms of this contract in full.

14.   Kreiser, *Carl Gottlieb Reissiger*, 58.

15. Reissiger's most famous opera, *Die Felsenmühle zu Etaliers,* also had its first performance in Dresden in 1831.

16. Sächsisches Hauptstaatsarchiv, Loc. 15147, *Das Kgl. Theater,* vol. 7, p. 7a, quoted by Heyne, "Die Ära Reißiger," in *Die Dresdner Oper im 19. Jahrhundert,* 154.

17. *AmZ* 31 (1829): col. 725–77.

18. The *Männerchor* movement was surprisingly large, particularly in Dresden. The first all-German *Männerchorfest* took place in Dresden in 1842. In the second *Männerchorfest* in Dresden, held early in 1843, the *NZfM* 16 (1843) reports that nearly one thousand singers and instrumentalists sang in a performance of Cherubini's *Requiem,* directed by Reissiger (23).

19. Kreiser, *Carl Gottlieb Reissiger,* 68.

20. Arthur Brooke Faulkner, *Visit to Germany and the Low Countries in the Years 1829, 30, and 31* (London: Richard Bentley, 1833), 1:305–306.

21. Ibid., 2:74.

22. Ibid., 2:75.

23. *Charaktergemälde von Dresden, grau in grau; für Alle, welche die Elbresidenz bewohnen oder kennen zu lernen wünschen* (Pößneck: Ernst Voglen, 1833), 230–31.

24. Aubrey Garlington, "Mega-Text, Mega-Music: A Crucial Dilemma for German Romantic Opera," in *Musical Humanism and Its Legacy: Essays in Honor of Claude V. Palisca,* ed. Nancy Kovaleff Baker and Barbara Russano Hunning, Festschrift Series no. 11 (Stuyvesant, N.Y.: Pendragon Press, 1992), 381.

25. Carl Dahlhaus, "Wagner's Place in the History of Music," in *Wagner Handbook,* ed. Ulrich Müller and Peter Wapnewski, trans. John Deathridge (Cambridge and London: Harvard University Press, 1992), 97–114.

26. Spohr's career evidences a similar development. Like *Jessonda,* his *Der Berggeist* (1824) is a through-composed opera, but with *Pietro von Albano* (1827) and *Der Alchymist* (1830) Spohr began again to use spoken dialogue. As Clive Brown notes, "the wave of enthusiasm on the crest of which these works [*Der Freischütz* and *Jessonda*] had ridden was losing its impetus during the 1820s as the bulk of the public increasingly returned their allegiance to the less demanding products of the French and Italian schools" (*Louis Spohr: A Critical Biography* [Cambridge: Cambridge University Press, 1984], 206).

27. The Viennese court composer Paul Wranitzky (1756–1808) had already written a popular opera on the Oberon story (*Oberon,* 1789).

28. Becker, *Die deutsche Oper,* provides a detailed description of the Morettische Haus as well as the Linkesche Bad theaters on pp. 29 ff.

29. For a description of the first Semper opera house, complete with plans and contemporary drawing and lithographs, see Wolfgang Hänsch, *Die Semper Oper: Geschichte und Wiederaufbau der Dresdner Staatsoper,* 3d ed. (Berlin: Verlag für Bauwesen, 1986), 33–36. Semper himself published many of his

plans, as well as an extensive commentary, in his *Das Königliche Hoftheater zu Dresden* (Braunschweig, 1849). Robert Prölss includes some interesting information on the mechanical capabilities of the new theater in his *Geschichte des Hoftheaters zu Dresden: Von seinen Anfängen bis zum Jahre 1862* (Dresden, 1878).

30. Julius Benedict, *Carl Maria von Weber* (London: S. Low, Searle, and Rivington, 1885). See also Michael Tusa, "Richard Wagner and Weber's *Euryanthe*," *19th-Century Music* 9, no. 3 (1985–86): 206–21.

31. In his book *Music and the Middle Class: The Social Structure of Concert Life in Paris, London and Vienna* (New York: Holmes and Meier, 1975), William Weber traces this ossification of the repertoire to the period 1830–1870.

Appendix 2

1. The Staatsbibliothek in Berlin (Signaturen O. 26378/6 and /7) contains a copy of this later printed edition: Das unterbrochene Opferfest / Heroisch-komische Oper in zwei Acten / Text von . . . / Musik von . . . / Klavierausgabe mit Text und vollständiger Dialog / Nach dem Partitur berichtigt und neu bearbeitet / von / Richard Kleinmichel / Universal Edition Aktiengesellschaft / Wien-Leipzig.

Bibliography

A. "Ueber die Oper." *Die Muse* 1, no. 8 (August 1821): 37–76.

Abert, A. A. "Weber *Euryanthe* und Spohrs *Jessonda* als grosse Opern." In *Festschrift für Walter Wiora*, edited by Ludwig Finscher and Christoph-Helmut Mahling, 435–41. Kassel, Basel, Paris, London, and New York: Bärenreiter, 1967.

Abert, Hermann. "Carl Maria von Weber und sein *Freischütz*." In *Jahrbuch der Musikbibliothek Peters*, 9–29. Vol. 33. Leipzig: C. F. Peters, 1926.

Abraham, G. "Weber as Novelist and Critic." *Musical Quarterly* 20 (1934): 27–38.

Allanbrook, Wye Jamison, ed. *The Late Eighteenth Century: Source Readings in Music History*. Vol. 5, *The Late Eighteenth Century*. Oliver Strunk, series ed., Leo Treitler, gen. ed. New York: Norton, 1997.

Andrews, Keith. *The Nazarenes: A Brotherhood of German Painters in Rome*. Oxford: Clarendon, 1964.

Applegate, Celia. "What Is German Music? Reflections on the Role of Art in the Creation of a Nation." *German Studies Review* 15 (Winter 1992): 21–32.

Arndt, Ernst Moritz. *Ausgewählte Gedichte und Schriften*. Edited by Gustav Erdmann. Berlin: Union Verlag, 1969.

Bailey, Robert. "Visual and Musical Symbolism in German Romantic Opera." In *International Musicological Society, Report of the Twelfth Congress, Berkeley 1977*, edited by Daniel Heartz and Bonnie Wade, 440–43. Kassel: Bärenreiter; Philadelphia: American Musicological Society, 1981.

Balthazar, Scott. "Evolving Conventions in Italian Serious Opera: Scene Structure in the Works of Rossini, Bellini, Donizetti and Verdi, 1810–1850." Ph.D. diss., University of Pennsylvania, 1985.

———. "Mayr, Rossini, and the Development of the Early Concertato Finale." *Journal of the Royal Musical Association* 116 (1991): 236–66.

Bartlet, Elizabeth C. "Etienne Nicolas Méhul and Opera during the French Revolution, Consulate, and Empire: A Source, Archival, and Stylistic Study." Ph.D. diss., University of Chicago, 1982.

Bartlitz, Eveline, comp. *Carl Maria von Weber: Autographenverzeichnis*. Vol. 9, *Deutsche Staatsbibliothek Handschrifteninventare*. Berlin: Werkstätten der deutschen Staatsbibliothek, 1986.

Baumann, Thomas. *North German Opera in the Age of Goethe*. Cambridge: Cambridge University Press, 1985.

Becker, Heinz. "Die 'Couleur locale' als Stilkategorie der Oper." In *Die Couleur locale in der Oper des 19. Jahrhunderts*, edited by Heinz Becker, 23–46. Studien zur Musikgeschichte des 19. Jahrhunderts, vol. 42. Regensburg: Gustav Bosse, 1976.

Becker, Wolfgang. *Die deutsche Oper in Dresden unter der Letiung von Carl Maria von*

Weber, 1817–1826. Vol. 22, *Theater und Drama*. Berlin and Dahlem: Colloquium Verlag, 1962.

Benedict, Julius. *Carl Maria von Weber*. 2d ed. London: S. Low, Searle, and Rivington,
1885.

Blackbourn, David, and Geoff Eley. *The Peculiarities of German History: Bourgeois
Society and Politics in Nineteenth-Century Germany*. Oxford and New York:
Oxford University Press, 1984.

Blühm, Andreas, ed. *Philipp Otto Runge, Caspar David Friedrich: The Passage of Time*.
Essays by Hanna Hohl and Werner Busch, translated by Rachel Esnen. Zwolle:
Waanders Publishers, n.d.

Boehn, Max von. *Biedermeier*. Berlin: B. Cassirer, 1911.

Borchardt, Georg Hermann, ed. *Das Biedermeier im Spiegel seiner Zeit*. Oldenburg:
G. Stalling, 1965.

Börsch-Supan, Helmut. *Caspar David Friedrich*. Munich: Prestel Verlag, 1973.

Boyd, Malcolm, ed. *Music and the French Revolution*. Cambridge: Cambridge University Press, 1992.

Brendel, Franz. *Geschichte der Musik in Italien, Deutschland und Frankreich*. Leipzig,
1852.

Brescius, Hans von. *Die Königl. Sächs. musikalische Kapelle von Reissiger bis Schuch
(1826–1898): Festschrift zur Feier des 350 jährigen Kapelljubiläums (22 September
1898)*. Dresden, 1898.

Brown, Clive. *Lous Spohr: A Critical Biography*. Cambridge: Cambridge University
Press, 1984.

Brühl, Heinrich Graf von. *Neueste Kostüme auf beiden königlichen Theatern in Berlin*.
Berlin, 1822.

Buzga, Jaroslav. "Carl Maria von Webers Prager 'Notizen-Buch' (1813–1816) Kommentar
und Erstveröffentlichung des Originals." *Oper Heute* 8 (1985): 7–44.

———. "Die deutschen Opern in Webers Prager Repertoire, 1813–1816." In *Carl Maria
von Weber und der Gedanke der Nationaloper*. 2, 270–76. Schriftenreihe der
Hochschule fur Musik Carl Maria von Weber, Dresden, proceedings of the 2d
scholarly conference on Dresden opera traditions, held in conjunction with
the Dresdner Musikfestspiele 1986 under the auspices of the Hochschule für
Musik Carl Maria von Weber, Dresden, ed. Hans John and Günther Stephan,
vol. 10, Sonderheft. Dresden, n.p., 1987. Reprinted without musical examples
in *Die Dresdner Oper im 19. Jahrhundert*, edited by Michael Heinemann and
Hans John. Musik in Dresden, Schriftenreihe der Hochschule für Musik "Carl
Maria von Weber" Dresden, vol. 1, edited by Michael Heinemann, Hanns-
Werner Heister, Matthias Herrmann, and Hans John. Laaber: Laaber Verlag,
1995. Charaktergemälde von Dresden, grau in grau; für Alle welche die Elbresidenz bewohnen oder kennen zu *lernen wünschen*. Pößneck: Ernst Voglen, 1833.

Charlton, David. "Introduction to *The Poet and the Composer*: Hoffmann and Opera."
In *E. T. A. Hoffmann's Musical Writings: Kreisleriana, The Poet and the Com-
poser, Music Criticism*, edited by David Charlton, translated by Martyn
Clarke, 169–87. Cambridge: Cambridge University Press, 1989.

Chezy, Helmina. "Auch ein Wort über die *Euryanthe* von der Dichterinn." *Wiener allgemeine Theaterzeitung und Unterhaltungsblatt für Freunde der Kunst, Literatur und des geselligen Lebens* 16, no. 134 (8 November 1823): 536.

——. "Carl Maria von Webers *Euryanthe:* Ein Beitrag zur Geschichte der deutschen Oper." *Neue Zeitschrift für Musik* 13 (1840): 1–3, 5–6, 9–11, 13–14, 17–19, 21–22, 33–35, 37–39, 41–42.

——. *Erinnerungen aus meinen Leben.* Schaffhausen, 1863–64.

Chiesa, Mary Tibaldi. *Cimarosa e il suo tempo.* 3d ed. Milan: Garzanti, 1949.

Chorley, Henry F. *Modern German Music.* London, 1854.

——. *Musical and Manners in France and Germany.* 3 vols. London, 1841–44; New York: DaCapo Press, 1987.

——. *Thirty Years' Musical Recollections.* Edited and with an introduction by Ernest Newman. London, 1862. New York, London: A. A. Knopf, 1926.

Clark, Robert T., Jr. *Herder: His Life and Thought.* Berkeley and Los Angeles: University of California Press, 1955.

Cornelissen, Theo. *"Der Freischütz" von C. M. von Weber.* In *Die Oper: Schriftenreihe zum Musik unterricht in der mittleren und höheren Schule.* 3d ed. Berlin: Robert Lienau, 1959.

Cornet, Julius. *Die Oper in Deutschland und das Theater der Neuzeit aus dem Standpuncte practische Erfahrung.* Hamburg, 1849.

Dahlhaus, Carl. "Die Kategorie des Charakteristischen in der Ästhetik des 19. Jahrhunderts." In *Die Couleur locale in der Oper des 19. Jahrhunderts,* edited by Heinz Becker, 9–21. Studien zur Musikgeschichte des 19. Jahrhunderts, vol. 42. Regensburg: Gustav Bosse, 1976.

——. *Nineteenth-Century Music.* Translated by J. Bradford Robinson. Berkeley and Los Angeles: University of California Press, 1989.

——. "Wagner's Place in the History of Music." In *Wagner Handbook,* edited by Ulrich Müller and Peter Wapnewski, translated by John Deathridge, 97–114. Cambridge and London: Harvard University Press, 1992.

——. "Weber's *Freischütz* und die Idee der deutschen Oper." *Österreichische Musikzeitschrift* 38, nos. 7–8 (July–August 1983): 381–88.

Daverio, John. *Nineteenth Century Music and the German Romantic Ideology.* Toronto: Maxwell MacMillan Canada, 1993.

Dean, Winton. "French Opera." In *The Age of Beethoven, 1790–1830,* edited by Gerald Abraham, 26–119. Oxford History of Music, vol. 8. London: Oxford University Press, 1982.

——. "German Opera." In *The Age of Beethoven, 1790–1830,* edited by Gerald Abraham, 452–522. Oxford History of Music, vol. 8. London: Oxford University Press, 1982.

Deathridge, John. *Wagner's "Rienzi": A Reappraisal Based on a Study of the Sketches and Drafts.* Oxford: Clarendon Press, 1977.

Dechant, Hermann. *E. T. A. Hoffmann's Oper "Aurora."* Regensburger Beiträge zur Musikwissenschaft, vol. 2. Regensburg: G. Bosse, 1975.

Dent, Edward J. *The Rise of Romantic Opera.* Edited by Winton Dean. Cambridge: Cambridge University Press, 1976.

Eagleton, Terry. *The Ideology of the Aesthetic.* Oxford: Basil Blackwell, 1990.

Ehrenhaus, M. *Die Operndichtung der deutschen Romantik. Breslauer Beiträge zur Literaturgeschichte.* Vol. 29. Breslau, 1911.

Elias, Norbert. *The Civilizing Process.* Translated by Edward Jephcott. New York: Urizen, 1978.

Engländer, Richard. "The Struggle between German and Italian Opera at the Time of Weber." *The Musical Quarterly* 32 (1946): 333–43.

Estermann, Alfred. *Die deutschen Literatur-Zeitschriften (1815–1850).* Munich, London, New York, and Paris: K. G. Saur, 1991.

Eyck, Frank. *The Frankfurt Parliament, 1848–1849.* London and Melbourne: Macmillan; New York: St. Martin's Press, 1968.

Fambach, Oscar. *Das Repertorium des Hof-und National Theater in Mannheim, 1804–1832.* Mitteilungen zur Theatergeschichte der Goethezeit, vol. 1. Edited by Norbert Oellers and Karl Konrad Polheim, with assistance from Joachim Krause. Bonn: Bouvier Verlag Herbert Grundmann, 1980.

———. *Das Repertorium des Königlichen Theaters und der Italienischen Oper zu Dresden, 1814–32.* Mitteilungen zur Theatergeschichte der Goethezeit, vol. 8. Edited by Norbert Oellers and Karl Konrad Polheim, with assistance from Joachim Krause. Bonn: Bouvier Verlag Herbert Grundmann, 1985.

———. *Das Repertorium des Stadttheaters zu Leipzig, 1817–1828.* Mitteilungen zur Theatergeschichte der Goethezeit, vol. 2. Edited by Norbert Oellers and Karl Konrad Polheim unter Mitwirkung von Joachim Krause. Bonn: Bouvier Verlag Herbert Grundmann, 1980.

Faulkner, Arthur Brooke. *Visit to Germany and the Low Countries in the Years 1829, 30, and 31.* London: Richard Bentley, 1833.

Fellinger, Imogen. *Verzeichnis der Musikzeitschriften des 19. Jahrhunderts.* Regensburg: Gustav Bosse, 1968.

Fink, Gottfried Wilhelm. *Wesen und Geschichte der Oper: Eine Handbuch für alle Freunde der Tonkunst.* Leipzig, 1838; Kassel: Bärenreiter, 1982.

Fischer, Georg. *Marschner Erinnerung.* Hannover and Leipzig: Hahnsche Buchhandlung, 1918.

Flaherty, Gloria. *Opera in the Development of German Critical Thought.* Princeton: Princeton University Press, 1978.

Förster, E. *Peter von Cornelius.* 2 vols. Berlin, 1874.

Frensdorf, Viktor Egon. "Peter Winter als Opernkomponist." Ph.D. diss., University of Munich, 1907.

Friedrich, Caspar David. *Was die fühlende Seele sucht: Briefe und Bekenntnisse.* Edited by Sigfrid Hinz. Berlin: Henschel Verlag, 1968.

Gaartz, Hans. *Die Opern Heinrich Marschners.* Leipzig: Breitkopf und Härtel, 1912.

Garlington, Aubrey. "August von Schlegel and the German Romantic Opera." *Journal of the American Musicological Society* 30 (1977): 500–506.

———. "Mega-Text, Mega-Music: A Crucial Dilemma for German Romantic Opera." In *Musical Humanism and Its Legacy: Essays in Honor of Claude V. Palisca,* edited by Nancy Kovaleff Baker and Barbara Russano Hunning, 381–93. Festschrift Series no. 11. Stuyvesant, N.Y.: Pendragon Press, 1992.

———. *Sources for the Study of Nineteenth Century Italian Opera in the Syracuse Uni-*

versity Libraries: An Annotated Libretto List. Syracuse: Syracuse University Libraries, 1976.

Gassner, Ferdinand Simon, ed. *Zeitschrift für Deutschlands Musik-Vereine und Dilettanten.* Stuttgart, 1841–43.

Genast, Eduard. *Aus dem Tagebuche eines alten Schauspielers.* Leipzig, 1862–66.

Geyer-Kiefl, Helen. *Die heroisch-komische Oper, ca. 1770–1820.* 2 vols. Würzburger Musikhistorische Beiträge, vol. 9. Tutzing: Schneider, 1987.

Göpfert, Bernd. *Stimmtypen und Rollencharaktere in der deutschen Oper von 1815–1848.* Wiesbaden: Breitkopf and Härtel, 1977.

Goslich, Siegfried. *Die deutsche romantische Oper.* Tutzing: Hans Schneider, 1975.

Gossett, Philip. Introduction to *Tebaldo e Isolina.* Italian Opera, 1810–1840, vol. 24. Dresden, 1825; New York: Garland, 1989.

Graf, Max. *Composer and Critic: Two Hundred Years of Musical Criticism.* New York: Norton, 1946.

Gregor-Dellin, Martin. *Richard Wagner.* Munich: R. Piper and Co. Verlag, 1980.

Grillparzer, Franz. *Sämtliche Werke.* Edited by Peter Frank and Karl Pörnbacher. 4 vols. Munich: Carl Hanser, 1964.

Günther, Gottfried, Albina A. Volgina, Siegfried Seifert, eds. *Herder-Bibliographie.* Berlin and Weimar: Aufbau-Verlag, 1978.

Habermas, Jürgen. *Strukturwandel der Öffentlichkeit: Untersuchungen zu einer Kategorie der bürgerlichen Gesellschaft.* Neuwied am Rhein and Berlin: Luchterhand, 1968.

Hagemann, C. *Wilhelmine Schröder-Devrient.* Wiesbaden: Walther Gericke, 1947.

Hänsch, Wolfgang. *Die Semper Oper: Geschichte und Wiederbau.* 3d ed. Berlin: Verlag für Bauwesen, 1986.

Hanson, Alice Marie. *Musical Life in Biedermeyer Vienna.* Cambridge: Cambridge University Press, 1985.

——. "The Social and Economic Context of Music in Vienna from 1815–1830." Ph.D. diss., University of Illinios, 1980.

Heartz, Daniel. *Mozart's Operas.* Edited by Daniel Heartz. Berkeley and Los Angeles: University of California Press, 1990.

Hempel, Siegfried. *Dresdener Oper.* Leipzig: Offizin Andersen Nexö, 1987.

Henderson, Donald G. "The Magic Flute of Peter Winter." *Music and Letters* 64 (1983): 193–205.

Henderson, Donald G., and Alice H. Henderson. *Carl Maria von Weber: A Guide to Research.* Garland Composer Resource Manuals, vol. 24. New York: Garland, 1990.

Henzel, Christoph. *München.* Musikstädte der Welt. Silke Leopold, ser. ed. Munich: Laaber Verlag, 1992.

Herder, Johann Gottfried. "Einzelne Blätter zum 'Journal der Reise 1769.'" In *Herders sämtliche Werke,* edited by Bernhard Suphan. Berlin, 1878.

——. *Herders sämtlicht Werke.* Edited by Bernhard Suphan. Berlin, 1878.

Hertz, Frederick. *The German Public Mind in the Nineteenth Century: A Social History of German Political Sentiments, Aspirations, and Ideas.* Edited by Franck Eyck, translated by Eric Northcott. Totowa, N.J.: Rowman and Littlefield, 1975.

Herzog, Dagmar. "Liberalism, Religious Dissent, and Women's Rights: Louise Ditt-
    mar's Writings from the 1840's." In *In Search of a Liberal Germany: Studies in
    the History of German Liberalism from 1789 to the Present,* edited by Konrad H.
    Jarausch and Larry Eugene Jones, 55–85. Providence, R.I.: Berg Publishers,
    1990.
Heyne, Jörg. "Die Ära Reißiger am Hoftheater in Dresden." In *Die Dresdner Oper
    im 19. Jahrhundert,* edited by Michael Heinemann and Hans John, 143–78.
    Musik in Dresden, Schriftenreihe der Hochschule für Musik "Carl Maria
    von Weber," Dresden, vol. 1, edited by Michael Heinemann, Hanns-Werner
    Heister, Matthias Herrmann, and Hans John. Laaber: Laaber Verlag, 1995.
Hobsbawm, Eric L. *The Age of Revolution, 1789–1848.* New York: World, 1962.
Hodgskin, Thomas. *Travels in the North of Germany (Describing the Present State of the
    Social and Political Institutions, the Agriculture, Manufactures, Commerce, Edu-
    cation, Arts and Manners in That Country, Particularly in the Kingdom of Han-
    nover).* Edinburgh, 1820.
Hoffmann, E. T. A. *E. T. A. Hoffmann's Musical Writings: Kreisleriana, The Poet and
    the Composer, Music Criticism.* Edited, annotated, and introduced by David
    Charlton, translated by Martyn Clarke. Cambridge: Cambridge University
    Press, 1989.
———. *Selected Letters of E. T. A. Hoffmann.* Translated by Johanna C. Sahlin, with an
    introduction by Leonard J. Kent and Johanna C. Sahlin. Chicago and London:
    University of Chicago Press, 1977.
———. *Die Vision auf dem Schlachtfelde bei Dresden.* Bamberg, 1814; Paderborn: Belser
    Verlag, 1987.
Hoffmann, Werner, ed. *Caspar David Friedrich, 1774–1840.* Exhibition catalog, Ham-
    burger Kunsthalle 14 September–3 November 1974. Munich: Prestel Verlag,
    1974.
Hogarth, G. *Memoirs of the Opera.* London, 1851.
———. *Musical History, Biography, and Criticism.* London, 1848; New York: Da Capo
    Press, 1969.
Holmes, Edward. *A Ramble among the Musicians of Germany.* London, 1828; New York:
    Da Capo Press, 1969.
Hürlimann, Martin, ed. *Carl Maria von Weber in seinen Schriften und in zeitgenössischen
    Dokumenten.* Zürich: Manesse Verlag, 1973.
Jäckel, Günther. "Aspekte der Dresdner Kulturgeschichte zwischen 1763 und 1832."
    In *Die italienische Oper in Dresden von Johann Adolf Hasse bis Francesco Mor-
    lacchi. 3 Wissenschaftliche Konferenz zum Thema "Dresdner Operntraditionen,"*
    edited by Günther Stephan and Hans John, 417–38. Dresden, Musik in Dres-
    den, Schriftenreihe der Hochschule für Musik "Carl Maria von Weber," Dres-
    den, vol. 11. Dresden: n.p., 1988.
———, ed. *Dresden Zwischen Wiener Kongress un Maiaufstand: Die Elbestadt von 1815
    bis 1850.* Berlin: Verlag der Nation, 1989.
Jacobi, Ernst. *Begegnungen eines deutschen Tenors, 1820–1866: Aus den Tagebüchern des
    Hofopernsänger Carl Adam Bader.* Frankfurt am Main: Haag und Herchen,
    1991.

Jähns, Friedrich Wilhelm. *Carl Maria von Weber: Eine Lebensskizze nach authentischen Quellen.* Leipzig, 1873.

————. *Carl Maria von Weber in seinen Werken: Chronologisch-thematisches Verzeichniss seiner sämmtlichen Compositionen nebst Angabe unvollständigen, verloren gegangenen, zweifelhaften und untergeschobenen.* Berlin: Schlesinger'schen Buch-und Musikhandlung 1871; Berlin-Lichterfelde: Lienau, 1967.

Jarausch, Konrad H., and Larry Eugene Jones, eds. *In Search of a Liberal Germany: Studies in the History of German Liberalism from 1789 to the Present.* Providence, R.I.: Berg Publishers, 1990.

John, Hans. "Carl Maria von Webers erstes Dresdner Amtsjahr." In *Die Dresdner Oper im 19. Jahrhundert,* edited by Michael Heinemann and Hans John, 73–84. Musik in Dresden, Schriftenreihe der Hochschule für Musik "Carl Maria von Weber," Dresden, vol. 1, edited by Michael Heinemann, Hanns-Werner Heister, Matthias Herrmann, and Hans John. Laaber: Laaber Verlag, 1995.

John, Hans, and Günther Stephan, eds. *Die italienische Oper in Dresden von Johann Adolph Hasse bis Francesco Morlacchi. 3 Wissenschaftliche Konferenz zum Thema "Dresdner Operntraditionen,"* edited by Günther Stephan and Hans John. Musik in Dresden, Schriftenreihe der Hochschule für Musik "Carl Maria von Weber," Dresden, vol. 11. Dresden: n.p., 1988.

————. *Giacamo Meyerbeer (1791–1864) Große Oper—Deutsche Oper.* Musik in Dresden, Schriftenreihe der Hochschule für Musik "Carl Maria von Weber," Dresden, vol. 24. Dresden: n.p., 1992.

Kapp, J. "Die Uraufführung des *Freischütz.*" In *Blätter der Staatsoper,* 9. Berlin, 1921.

Kindermann, Heinz. *Romantik.* Vol. 6, *Theatergeschichte Europas.* Salzburg: Otto Müller Verlag, 1964.

Kirby, F. E. "Herder and Opera." *Journal of the American Musicological Society* 15 (1962): 316–26.

Kirchmeyer, Helmut. *Wagner in Dresden.* Vol. 1, *Situationsgeschicht der Musikkritik und des musikalischen Pressewesens in Deutschland: Das zeitgenössische Wagner-Bild.* Vol. 7, *Studien zur Musikgeschichte des 19. Jahrhunderts.* Regensburg: Gustav Bosse Verlag, 1972.

Knüpfer, Volker. "Presse und Liberalismus in Sachsen vom Anfang des 19. Jahrhunderts bis 1833." In *Neues Arhiv für sächsische Geschichte* 65, edited by Karlheinz Blaschke. Weimar: Verlag Herman Böhlaus Nachfolger, 1995.

Koch, Heinrich Christoph. *Musikalisches Lexicon.* Frankfurt, 1802; Hildesheim: Georg Olms, 1964.

Kornmann, Carl August. *Tagebuch des Königl. Sächs. Hoftheaters.* Dresden, 1818.

Kreiser, Kurt. *Carl Gottlieb Reissiger: Sein Leben nebst einigen Beiträgen zur Geschichte des Konzertwesens in Dresden.* Dresden: Johannes Päßler, 1918.

Kremtz, Eberhard. "Das 'deutsche Departement' des Dresdner Hoftheaters." In *Die Dresdner Oper im 19. Jahrhundert,* edited by Michael Heinemann and Hans John, 107–12. Musik in Dresden, Schriftenreihe der Hochschule für Musik "Carl Maria von Weber," Dresden, vol. 1, edited by Michael Heinemann, Hanns-Werner Heister, Matthias Herrmann, and Hans John. Laaber: Laaber Verlag, 1995.

———. "Weber—Hoffmann—Spontini: Deutsche Oper—Französische Oper." In *Die Dresdner Oper im 19. Jahrhundert*, edited by Michael Heinemann and Hans John, 113–18. Musik in Dresden, Schriftenreihe der Hochschule für Musik "Carl Maria von Weber," Dresden, vol. 1, edited by Michael Heinemann, Hanns-Werner Heister, Matthias Herrmann, and Hans John. Laaber: Laaber Verlag, 1995.

Kretzschmar, Hermann. *Geschichte der Oper*. Leipzig, Breitkopf und Härtel, 1919; Wiesbaden: JVD, 1970.

Krieger, Peter. "Caspar David Friedrich." In *Galerieder Romantik: Katalog der ausgestellten Werke*, edited by Dieter Honisch, 32. Berlin: Staatliche Museen Preußischer Kutturbesitz, 1986.

Kroll, Erwin. "E. T. A. Hoffman und Weber." *Neue Musik-Zeitung* 42 (1921): 336.

Krüger, Hermann Anders. *Pseudoromantik: Friedrich Kind und der Dredener Liederkreis*. Leipzig: H. Haeffel Verlag, 1904.

Kuckuk, Ludwig. "Peter von Winter als deutscher Opernkomponist: Ein Beitrag zur Entwicklungsgeschichte der zweiten Opernbewegung." Ph.D. diss., Heidelberg Universität, 1924.

Küstner, Karl Theodor von. *Album des königlichen Schauspiels und der königlichen Oper zu Berlin*. Berlin, 1858.

Landmann, Ortrun. "Die italienische Oper in Dresden nach Johann Adolf Hasse: Entwicklungszüge, 1765–1832." In *Die italienische Oper in Dresden von Johann Adolf Hasse bis Francesco Morlacchi. 3 Wissenschaftliche Konferenz zum Thema "Dresdner Operntraditionen*," edited by Günther Stephan and Hans John, 393–417. Musik in Dresden, Schriftenreihe der Hochschule für Musik "Carl Maria von Weber," Dresden, vol. 11. Dresden: n.p., 1982.

Laube, Heinrich. *Zeitung für die elegante Welt*. Leipzig: Leopold Voss, 1833.

Laudon, Robert Tallant. *Sources of the Wagnerian Synthesis: A Study of the Franco-German Tradition in Nineteenth-Century Opera*. Munich and Salzburg: Musikverlag Emil Katsbichler, 1979.

Laux, Karl. *Carl Maria von Weber*. Leipzig: Deutsche Verlag für Musik, VEB, 1978.

Lippman, Edward. *A History of Western Musical Aesthetics*. Lincoln and London: University of Nebraska Press, 1992.

Lippmann, Friedrich. "Über Cimarosas Opere serie." In *Analecta Musicologica 21: Colloquium: Die Stilistische Entwicklung der italienischen Musik zwischen 1770 und 1830 und ihre Beziehungen zum Norden (Rom, 1978)*, edited by Friedrich Lippmann, 21–60. Munich: Laaber Verlag, 1982.

Lobe, Johann Christian. *Consonanzen und Dissonanzen: Gesammelte Schriften aus älterer und neuerer Zeit*. Leipzig, 1869.

———. *Fliegende Blätter für Musik*. Leipzig, 1855.

———. *Musikalische Briefe: Wahrheit über Tonkunst und Tonkunstler von einem Wohlbekannten*. Leipzig, 1858.

Loewenberg, Alfred. *Annals of Opera, 1597–1940*. 3d ed. Totowa, N.J.: Rowman and Littlefield, 1978.

Lühning, Helga. "Die Rondo-Arie im späten 18. Jahrhundert: Dramatischer Gestalt und musikalischer Bau." *Hamburger Jahrbuch für Musikwissenschaft* 5 (1981): 219–46.

Lyser, Johann Peter. *Giacomo Meyerbeer: Sein Streben, sein Wirken, u. seine Gegner.* Dresden, 1838.

Magee, Bryan. *Aspects of Wagner.* 2d ed. Oxford: Oxford University Press, 1988.

Marmontel, M. [Jean François]. *The Incas, or The Destruction of Peru.* 2 vols. London: J. Nourse, P. Elmsly, E. Lyde, and G. Kearsly, 1777.

Marx, Adolf Bernhard. *Die Kunst des Gesanges.* Berlin, 1826.

——. *Die Musik des neunzehnten Jahrhunderts und ihre Pflege.* 2d ed. Leipzig: Breitkopf and Härtel, 1873.

Mentsell, Dolores. "E. T. A. Hoffmann and Carl Maria von Weber as Critics of Music." Ph.D. diss., University of Southern California, 1962.

Morelli, Giovanni, and Elvidio Surian. Preface to *Domenico Cimarosa Gli Orazi e i Curiazi: Tragedia per musica in tre atti di Antonia Simeone Sografi. II. Facsimile dell'edizione Imbault, Parigi 1802.* Edited by Giovanni Morelli and Elvidio Surian. Monumenti Musicali Italiani, vol. 9, no. 2. Milan: Edizioni Suvini Zerboni, 1985.

Morrow, Mary Sue. "Of Unity and Passion: The Aesthetics of Concert Criticism in Early Nineteenth Century Vienna." *19th Century Music* 13, no. 3 (Spring 1990): 193–206.

Mosel, Ignaz Franz von. *Versuch einer Aesthetik des dramatischen Tonsatzes.* Vienna, 1813.

Mundt, Theodor. *Aesthetik: Die Idee der Schönheit und des Kunstwerks im Lichte unserer Zeit.* Berlin, 1845; Göttingen: Vandenhoek and Ruprecht, 1966.

——. "Ueber Oper, Drama, und Melodrama in ihrem Verhältniß zu einander und zum Theater." *Blätter für literarische Unterhaltung,* 152–55 (June 1831): 665–79.

Mungen, Anno. "Morlacchi, Weber und die Dresdner Oper." In *Die Dresdner Oper im 19. Jahrhundert,* edited by Michael Heinemann and Hans John, 85–106. Musik in Dresden, Schriftenreihe der Hochschule für Musik "Carl Maria von Weber," Dresden, vol. 1, edited by Michael Heinemann, Hanns-Werner Heister, Matthias Herrmann, and Hans John. Laaber: Laaber Verlag, 1995.

Nattiez, Jean-Jacques. *Music and Discourse: Toward a Semiology of Music.* Translated by Carolyn Abbate. Princeton: Princeton University Press, 1990.

Nipperdey, Thomas. "Verein als soziale Struktur in Deutschland im späten 18. und frühen 19. Jahrhundert." In *Geschichtswissenschaft und Vereinwesen im 19. Jahrhundert,* edited by Hartmut Boockmann, 1–44. Göttingen: Vandenhoeck and Ruprecht, 1972.

Palmer, A. Dean. *Heinrich August Marschner, 1795–1861: His Life and Stage Works.* Studies in Musicology, vol. 24, George Buelow, ser. ed. Ann Arbor: UMI Research Press, 1978.

Parakilas, James. "Political Representation and the Chorus in Nineteenth-Century Opera." *19th-Century Music* 16, no. 2 (Fall 1992): 181–202.

Pfitzner, Hans. "Was ist uns Weber? Zum 100. Todestag Carl Maria von Webers." In *Gesammelte Schriften.* Vol. 1. Augsburg, 1926.

Price, Lawrence Marsden. "The Vogue of Marmontel on the German Stage." In *University of California Publications in Modern Philology,* edited by Rudolph Altrocchi, 27–123. Vol. 27. Berkeley and Los Angeles: University of California Press, 1947.

Prölss, Robert. *Geschichte des Hoftheaters zu Dresden: Von seinen Anfängen bis zum Jahre 1862*. Dresden, 1878.

Pundt, Alfred G. *Arndt and the Nationalist Awakening in Germany*. New York: Columbia University Press, 1935; New York: AMS Press, 1968.

Raab, F. Ch. *Frauenspiegel, oder kurze Lebensbeschreibungen berühmter Frauen aus ältern und neuern Zeit*. Leipzig, 1845.

Ranger, Paul. *'Terror and Pity reign in every Breast': Gothic Drama in the London Patent Theatres, 1750–1820*. London: Society for Theatre Research, 1991.

Reiber, Joachim. *Bewahrung und Bewährung: Das Libretto zu Carl Maria von Webers "Freischütz" im literararischen Horizont seiner Zeit*. Munich: W. Ludwig Verlag, 1990.

Ringer, Alexander. "The *Chasse*: Historical and Analytical Bibliography of a Musical Genre." Ph.D. diss., Columbia University, 1955.

Rosengard, Rose. "Popularity and Art in Lortzing's Operas: The Effects of Social Change on a National Operatic Genre." Ph.D. diss., Columbia University, 1973.

Rühs, Friedrich. *Historische Entwickelung des Einflusses Frankreichs und der Franzosen auf Deutschland und die Deutschen*. Berlin: Nicolaische Buchandlung, 1815.

Sanders, Daniel. *Wörterbuch der Deutschen Sprache*, s.v. "Charakter." Leipzig: Otto Wigand, 1860.

Schafer, R. Murray. *E. T. A. Hoffmann and Music*. Toronto and Buffalo: University of Toronto Press, 1975.

Schama, Simon. *Landscape and Memory*. New York: Knopf, 1995.

Schilling, Gustav. *Versuch einer Philosophie des Schönen in der Musik*. Mainz, 1838.

Schmitt, Anke. *Der Exotismus in der deutschen Oper zwischen Mozart und Spohr*. Hamburg: Verlag der Musikalienhandlung Karl Dieter Wagner, 1988.

Schnoor, Hans. *Weber auf dem Welttheater: Ein Freischützbuch*. 4th ed. Hamburg: Deutscher Verlag, 1963.

———. *Weber: Gestalt und Schöpfung*. Dresden: VEB Verlag der Kunst, 1953.

Schubart, C. F. D. *Ideen zu einer Ästhetik der Tonkunst*. Edited by Ludwig Schubart. Vienna, 1806.

Schumann, Robert. *Gesammelte Schriften über Musik und Musiker*. 5th ed. Leipzig: Breitkopf and Härtel, 1914.

———. *On Music and Musicians*. Edited by Konrad Wolff, translated by Paul Rosenfeld. Berkeley and Los Angeles: University of California Press, 1946.

———. *Schumann on Music: A Selection from the Writings*. Translated, edited, and annotated by Henry Pleasants. New York: Dover, 1965.

Schütze, St. "Ueber den text der Oper Euryanthe." *Caecilia* 2 (1825): 42–65.

Seeger, Horst, and Matthias Rank, eds. *Oper in Dresden*. Berlin, 1985.

Segarra, Eda. *Tradition and Revolution: German Literature and Society, 1830–1890*. New York: Basic Books, 1971.

Semper, Gottfried. *Das Königliche Hoftheater zu Dresden*. Braunschweig, 1849.

Semrau, Arno. *Studien zur Typologie und zur Poetik der Oper in der ersten Hälfte des 19. Jahrhunderts*. Kölner Beiträge zur Musikforschung, vol. 178, edited by Klaus Wolfgang Niemöller. Regensburg: Gustav Bosse, 1993.

Sheehan, James J. *German History, 1770–1866*. New York: Oxford University Press, 1989.

————. *German Liberalism in the Nineteenth Century.* Chicago: University of Chicago Press, 1978.

Siegel, Linda, ed. *Music in German Romantic Literature: A Collection of Essays, Reviews, and Stories.* Translated by Linda Siegel. Novato, Calif.: Elra Publications, 1983.

Sincerus, Al [pseud.]. *Das Dresdner Hoftheater und seine gegenwärtigen Mitglieder.* Zerbst, 1852.

Spazier, Richard Otto. *Scherz und Ernst über Ernst Scherzlieb's Dresden wie es durch eine Goldbrille ist; nebst Bemerkungen über Nationalität in der dramatischen Musik.* Leipzig, 1830.

Spohr, Louis. *Autobiography.* Translator unknown. London: Longman, Green, Longman, Roberts and Green, 1865; New York: Da Capo Press, 1969.

Steblin, Rita. *A History of Key Characteristics in the Eighteenth and Early Nineteenth Centuries.* Rochester: University of Rochester Press, 1996.

Sulzer, Johann George. *Allgemeine Theorie der schönen Künste.* 4 vols. Leipzig, 1787.

Tagesell, David August. *Tagebuch eines Dresdner Bürgers.* Dresden, 1854.

Theweleit, Klaus. *Male Fantasies.* Vol. 1. Translated by Stephen Conway. Minneapolis: University of Minnesota Press, 1987.

Thomas, W. "Carl Maria von Weber als Musikpolitiker." *Neue Zeitschrift für Musik* 103 (1936): 1443.

Trietschke, Heinrich Gotthard von. *History of Germany in the Nineteenth Century.* Selections from *Deutsche Geschichte im neunzehnten Jahrhundert.* Translated by Eden and Cedar Paul, edited and with an introduction by Gordon A. Craig. Chicago: University of Chicago Press, 1975.

Tusa, Michael. "Carl Maria von Weber's *Euryanthe:* A Study of Its Historical Context, Genesis, and Reception." Ph.D. diss., Princeton University, 1983.

————. *"Euryanthe" and Carl Maria von Weber's Dramaturgy of German Opera.* Oxford: Clarendon Press, 1991.

————. "Richard Wagner and Weber's *Euryanthe.*" *19th-Century Music* 9, no. 3 (1985–86): 206–21.

————. "Weber's *Große Oper:* A Note on the Origins of *Euryanthe.*" *19th-Century Music* 8, no. 2 (Autumn 1984): 119–24.

Voss, J. von, and A. von Schaden. *Lebensgemälde üppiger gekrönte Frauen der alten und neuen Zeit, nebst morlaischen Betrachtungen über den Rechtshandel der Königin von England.* Berlin, 1821.

Wagner, Richard. *Gesammelte Schriften und Dichtungen.* 2d ed. Hildesheim: Oms, 1976.

————. *Richard Wagner's Prose Works.* Translated by William Ashton Ellis. London: Kegan Paul, Trench, Trübner and Co., 1895–1912; St. Clair Shores, Mich.: Scholarly Press, 1972.

Wagner, Wolfgang. *Carl Maria von Weber und die deutsche Nationaloper.* Weber-Studien, vol. 2, edited by Gerhard Allrogen and Joachim Veit. Mainz: Schott, 1994.

Warrack, John. *Carl Maria von Weber.* 2d ed. Cambridge: Cambridge University Press, 1976.

————. "Carl Maria von Weber." In *New Grove Early Romantic Masters* 2, 1–84. New York and London: Norton, 1985.

———. "Carl Maria von Weber in His Diaries." In *Slavonic and Western Music: Essays for Gerald Abraham*, edited by Malcolm Hamrick Brown and Roland John Wiley, 131–38. Ann Arbor and Oxford: University of Michigan Press, 1985.

———. "Französische Elemente in Webers Opern." In *Carl Maria von Weber und der Gedanke der Nationaloper*, 277–90. Schriftenreihe der Hochschule fur Musik Carl Maria von Weber, Dresden, proceedings of the 2d scholarly conference on Dresden opera traditions, held in conjunction with the Dresdner Musik-festspiele 1986 under the auspices of the Hochschule für Musik Carl Maria von Weber, Dresden, ed. Hans John and Günther Stephan, vol. 10, Sonderheft. Dresden, n.p., 1987. Reprinted without musical examples in *Die Dresdner Oper im 19. Jahrhundert*, edited by Michael Heinemann and Hans John. Musik in Dresden, Schriftenreihe der Hochschule für Musik "Carl Maria von Weber" Dresden, vol. 1, edited by Michael Heinemann, Hanns-Werner Heister, Matthias Herrmann, and Hans John. Laaber: Laaber Verlag, 1995.

———. *German Opera: From the Beginnings to Wagner.* Cambridge: Cambridge University Press, 2001.

Weber, Carl Maria von. *Briefe von Carl Maria von Weber an Hinrich Lichtenstein.* Edited by Ernst Rudorff. Braunschweig, 1900.

———. *Carl Maria von Weber Briefe.* Edited by Hans Christoph Worbs. Frankfurt am Main: Fischer, 1982.

———. *Carl Maria von Weber: Briefe an den Grafen Karl von Brühl.* Edited by Georg Kaiser. Leipzig, 1911.

———. "Carl Maria von Webers Briefe an Gottfried Weber." In *Jahrbuch des Staatlichen Instituts für Musikforschung Preußischer Kulturbesitz 1972*, edited by Werner Bollert and Arno Limke, 7–103. Berlin, 1973.

———. *Der Freischütz.* Piano-vocal score. Edited and translated by Natalia MacFarren and Th. Baker. New York and London: G. Schirmer, 1904.

———. *Reisebriefe von Carl Maria von Weber an seine Gattin Caroline.* Edited by Carl von Weber. Leipzig, 1886.

———. *Sämtliche Schriften.* Critical edition by Georg Kaiser. Berlin and Leipzig: Schuster and Loeffler, 1908.

———. *Writings on Music.* Translated by Martin Cooper, edited and with an introduction by John Warrack. Cambridge: Cambridge University Press, 1981.

Weber, Max Maria von. *Carl Maria von Weber: The Life of an Artist.* 2 vols. Translated by J. Palgrave Simpson. London: Chapman and Hall, 1865; New York: Greenwood, 1969.

Weber, William. *Music and the Middle Class: The Social Structure of Concert Life in London, Paris, and Vienna.* New York: Holmes and Meier, 1975.

Webster, James. "The Analysis of Mozart's Arias." In *Mozart Studies,* edited by Cliff Eisen, 101–200. Oxford: Clarendon, 1991.

Wehnert, Martin. "Carl Maria von Weber und Caspar David Friedrich: Doppelgänger im Geist?" In *Weber-Studien 1,* edited by Gerhard Allrogen and Joachim Veit, 237–74. Mainz: Schott, 1993.

Welcker, Theodor. "Geschlechtsverhältnisse: Frauen, ihre rechtliche und politische Stellung in der Gesellschaft; Rechtswohlthaten und Geschlechtsbeistände der Frauen; Frauenvereine und Vergehen in Beziehung auf die Geschlechtsverhält-

nisse." In *Staats-Lexicon, oder Encyclopädie der Staatswissenschaften*, 14 vols.,
ed. Carl von Rotteck and Theodor Welcker, 6:629–65. Altona, 1834–43.

Winkler, K. T. (Karl Gottfried Theodor), ed. *Tagebuch der deutschen Bühnen*. Dresden:
Beim Herausgeber, 1816–35.

Wirth, Irmgard. *Berlin Malerei im 19. Jahrhundert: Von der Zeit Friedrich des Großen
bis zum Ersten Weltkrieg*. Berlin: Siedler Verlag, 1990.

Worbs, Hans Christoph. "Zur deutschen und österreichischen Rossini-Rezeption im
Vormärz." In *Festschrift Heinz Becker*, edited by Jürgen Schläder and Reinhold
Quant, 106–15. Munich: Laaber-Verlag, 1982.

Youens, Susan. *Schubert, Müller, and "Die Schöne Müllerin."* Cambridge and New
York: Cambridge University Press, 1997.

Zielske, Harald. *Deutsche Theaterbauen bis zum zweiten Weltkrieg: Typologisch-
historische Dokumentation einer Baugattung*. Schriften der Gesellschaft für
Theatergeschichte, vol. 65. Berlin: Selbstverlag der Gesellschaft für Theatergeschichte, 1971.

Zimmermann, Reiner. *Giacomo Meyerbeer: Eine Biographie nach Dokumenten*. Berlin:
Henschel Verlag, 1991.

———. "Glücklose Synthese: Beim Lesen des Euryanthe Autographs. Weber und der
Gedanke der Nationaloper." In *Die Dresdner Oper im 19. Jahrhundert*, edited
by Michael Heinemann and Hans John, 317–26. Musik in Dresden, Schriftenreihe der Hochschule für Musik "Carl Maria von Weber," Dresden, vol. 1,
edited by Michael Heinemann, Hanns-Werner Heister, Matthias Herrmann,
and Hans John. Laaber: Laaber Verlag, 1995.

Zuschauer, Freimund [Ludwig Rellstab]. *Henriette, oder Die schöne Sängerin: Eine
Geschichte unserer Tage*. Leipzig, 1826.

Index

of the Night in, 46, 85; compared to *Das un-terbrochene Opferfest* (Winter), 36, 38, 46, 48; compared to *Oberon* (Weber), 169–70; as "elevated *Singspiel*," 26, 33; sequel to, 207–208n19

Difesa della musica moderna (Manfredini), 88, 91

Don Giovanni (Mozart), 49, 82, 88, 90–91, 203–204n52; alterations to, 33–34; performances of, 22, 75, 167, 207n16, 225n47

Donizetti, Gaetano, 159, 167; *Maria Stuarda*, 223n27

Dresden

——conflict between German and Italian opera companies in, 24–25,158–59, 161–62, 172
——decline of Italian opera company in, 164–68
——1830 revolution in, 165–66
——geography of, 13–14, 201n42
——German opera company in, 21–23, 162–65, 167–68
——operatic performances in, 158–59, 201n40, 205n69; performance of *Der Frei-schütz* in, 112; performance of French operas in, 29, 57, 205–206n3; performances of *Das unterbrochene Opferfest* in, 35, 46, 47, 49–51; performances of *Joseph* in, 56, 60, 73–75; premiere of *Euryanthe* in, 8, 154–55
——social environment of, 21–22, 172
——theaters in, 13, 22, 25, 171–72, 174–75, 201n40

Dresden Abend-Zeitung (periodical), 15, 165
Dresden Anzeiger (periodical), 155
Dutton, Thomas, *Pizarro in Peru*, 208n24
Duval, Alexander, 58, 62, 69, 184

Eagleton, Terry, 72
Einsiedel, Count Detlev, 165
Elias, Norbert, 201–202n44
Euryanthe (Weber)
——character of Adolar in, 3, 58, 118, 146–47, 149–50; aria "Wehen mir Lüfte Ruh," 141–42; duets with Euryanthe, 149; Romanze "Unter blüh'nden Mandelbäumen," 137–38, 142
——character of Eglantine in, 118, 139, 148–49; aria "Bethörthe, die an meine Liebe glaubt," 128–29, 131–34, 136, 141; aria "O mein Leid ist untermessen," 123, 138
——character of Euryanthe in, 3, 118, 120, 146–47, 150; cavatina "Glöcklein im Thale!"

142; scene and cavatina "So bin ich nun verlassen/Hier dicht am Quell," 128, 143–46
——character of Lysiart in, 118, 138, 148–49; aria "Wo berg ich mich," 129, 132, 134–36, 138, 139, 140, 141, 142; chivalric facade of, 129–31; duet with Eglantine, 149
——*Charakter* in, 119–22, 137
——chivalric world in, 125–27, 129–30, 142, 149, 221n6
——compared to *Der Freischütz*, 2–4, 116, 117, 119–22, 125–28, 138, 139, 144–45, 145–46, 222n12
——compared to Spohr's *Jessonda*, 20–21
——criticism of, 8, 115, 150, 153–54, 156, 158, 172
——cuts administered to, 151–53, 224–25n38
——depiction in the architecture of the Semper Oper, 174
——"Der Mai bringt frische Rose dar," 125–27
——hunters' chorus in, 1–3, 125–26, 197n3
——introduction to ("Dem Frieden Heil!"), 125, 149
——key relationships in, 123–24, 149
——libretto of, 118, 126,136–37, 150–51, 153–54, 156, 221n5, 222n18
——music for Emma's ghost in, 118, 122–25, 126, 221n6
——performances of, 162, 164; in Dresden, 8, 154–55; in Vienna, 130–31, 152–53
——plot structure of, 116–19
——reception of, 151–55, 173, 175
——synopsis of, 191–95
——villains in, 128–40, 141–42, 148–49, 152, 223n20
Eyck, Frank, 203n49

Faulkner, Sir Arthur Brooke, 166–67
Faust (Spohr), 20
Fichte, Johann Gottlieb, *Reden an die deutsche Nation*, 211n46
Fidelio (Beethoven), 51, 58, 95, 222n12; Dresden performances of, 161–62, 175; as national opera, 112; Pizarro's aria in, 87; prison scene in, 38, 95, 96
Fink, Gottfried Wilhelm, 12, 111
Fioravanti, Valentino, *Le cantatrici villane*, 13
Florence, performance of *Das unterbrochene Opferfest* in, 35, 208n20
The Flying Dutchman. See Der fliegende Holländer
Forkel, Johann Nikolaus, 206n6

STEPHEN C. MEYER is Assistant Professor in the Department of Fine Arts, Syracuse University. His articles have appeared in the *Journal of the American Musicological Society*, the *Opera Journal*, the *Opera Quarterly*, and the *Cambridge Opera Journal*. In addition to his scholarly work, he maintains an active career as a performer.